PRAISE FOR *MY CULINARY COMPULSION*

Alona's stories are so endearingly honest and familiar, that even in the confluence of her vast cultural and ethnic influence—Israeli, Latino, American—they call to mind the reader's own personal comforts and indulgences. Her recipes, though unique to her multicultural life, entice and relate to us all."

—Tara Mataraza Desmond, author of *Full Belly: Good Eats for a Healthy Pregnancy, Choosing Sides: From Holidays to Every Day, 130 Delicious Recipes to Make the Meal*, and co-author of *Almost Meatless: Recipes That Are Better for Your Health and the Planet.*

In *My Culinary Compulsion* Alona has accomplished what so many food writers dream of doing. She has collected a set of recipes, yes; but lovingly glided them with stories and vignettes from a life well-lived. Reading them, then putting them aside, you find yourself longing to have a glass of wine or cup of coffee with your amigo; the one that makes you shriek with laughter at the naughty stories, or swoon at the sweet ones. *My Culinary Compulsion* is more than a collection of recipes, it's a beautiful homage to the people and the food she loves.

—Jacqueline Church, Culinary Consultant/Instructor

Witty and delectable, this culinary memoire enchants and delights! You'll want to make every recipe.

—Sandra A. Gutierrez, *author of Latin American Street Food*

Alona, Thanks for sharing your book with me. This is a charming collection of exuberant food stories and recipes that invite you into the kitchen like a neighbor. It's warm, personal, and the dishes look completely mouth-watering.

> —Dave Joachim. David Joachim has authored, edited, or collaborated on more than 40 cookbooks, including the IACP Award-winning reference books, *The Food Substitutions Bible and The Science of Good Food,* which also won a World Gourmand Award for Best Food Literature Book and a Cordon d'Or Award for Best Culinary Reference Book.

Alona packed this cookbook and memoir full of funny, sensuous, and rebellious stories and recipes. You'll see that she has the ravenous, restless mind of a stay-at-home mom who might be a little bored. The recipes show how she loves to tinker and experiment with all kinds of food.

The product of an Israeli father and an American mother, Alona grew up in Venezuela and settled in Miami to raise a family. So you get this heady mix of Latin food, mommy dishes, Middle Eastern food, French dishes inspired by restaurant meals, and travel-inspired dishes from around the world. You'll also find a few Jewish holiday dishes in a chapter named Extra Holiday Pounds, which includes a recipe for Venezuelan Ham Bread. If you haven't figured this out by now, *My Culinary Compulsion* is a delightful read.

> —Dianne Jacob, author, *Will Write for Food*

My Culinary

COMPULSION

My Culinary Compulsion

SERVING UP SIZZLE

ALONA ABBADY MARTINEZ

My Culinary Compulsion: *serving up sizzle*

Copyright ©2017 Alona Abbady Martinez

ISBN: 978-1-940769-81-3

Publisher: Mercury HeartLink, www.heartlink.com

Printed in the United States of America

Cover art and interior drawings: Jason D. LeViere

All rights reserved. This book, or sections of this book, may not be reproduced or transmitted without permission from the author.

Contact: *alonamartinez@live.com*

Mercury HeartLink
www.heartlink.com

Contents

Acknowledgements	xv
Introduction	xix
Ingredient Notes	xxiii

CHAPTER ONE
Growing Up Global

Marilyn's *Moussaka*	6
Mom's Pineapple Upside Down Cake	11
3-Step Asparagus Soup	14
Oaxacan Cream and Raspberry Jam Toast	20
Piña Colada Ice Pops	24
Soft-Boiled Egg	26
Bone Marrow Beef Soup	30
Mom's Sour Cream Apple Pie	35
Pasticcio	39
Beef Okra Stew	43
Yoli's Signature Flan	48
Pork Sausage Gravy & Biscuits	54

CHAPTER TWO
Ravenous Relationships

Banana Pudding Pie	66
Raging Bull Cocktail	72
Roasted Beets	76
Ile Flottante (Floating Island)	82
Clementine *Clafoutis*	86
Coconut Cake	91
Blondies	100
Carrot Spice Mini Muffins	106

CHAPTER THREE
Everyday Insights

Quick Steak *Au Poivre* with Watercress	113
Tortilla Española	120
Yoli's Chicken with Potatoes	124
Abuela Margarita's *Bajo Las Circunstancias* Spaghetti *Tortilla*	128
Aloo Gobi (Cauliflower and Potato Curry)	133
Sam's Favorite Waffles	137
Classic Orange Cake	142

Heart and Soul Challah	*148*
Do-It-Yourself Pizza	*154*
Roasted Zucchini Soup	*159*
Herb Omelet	*166*

CHAPTER FOUR
Motherhood Crazy

Vivian's Sinfully Rich Chocolate Pie	*174*
Coffeecake with Blackberry Swirl	*180*
Sour Cherry-Berry Pie	*182*
Ginger Kugel	*186*
Salmon *en Papillote*	*192*
Husband's **Dulce De Mango**	*198*
Labneh Chicken Salad	*201*
Deal-Breaking Chocolate Cake	*206*
Quick Chocolate Frosting	*207*
Marilyn's Brownies	*211*
Potato Chip Frittatas	*214*
Thyme Roasted Chicken	*219*
Babaganoush	*224*
Purist Mac and Cheese	*228*
Mirjana's Apricot Marmalade	*233*
Raspberry Vanilla Cake with Whipped Cream	*239*

Chapter Five
Tasting the World

Linguine Alla Vongole (Linguine in Clam Sauce)	248
Cachapa Con Queso / *Cachapa* with Cheese	252
Dolphin with Bajan Seasoning	256
Slow-Cooked Brisket	263
Shakshouka	267
Homemade Harissa	268
Mario's *Paella*	274
Tropical Scallops with *Chile* and Mango	281
Chilled Cream of Avocado Soup	285
Mary de Pedro Cookies	289
Agua de Jamaica: Dried Hibiscus Punch	293
Crunchy Coconut Shrimp	297
Chilaquiles en Salsa Verde	302
Chicken Mole	308
Mint Tea	315
Orange Roughy with Citrus Herbs	320

CHAPTER SIX
Extra Holiday Pounds

Venezuelan Ham Bread	*327*
Light Lime Cheesecake	*336*
Easy Goy Toffee	*339*
Uncle Joe's Fabulous Latkes	*343*
Sephardic Meatballs	*346*
Tropical Passover Sangria	*349*
Drunk Matzo Chocolate Cake	*350*

CHAPTER SEVEN
Delicious Addictions and Secrets

Huevitos de Codorniz con Salsa Rosada	
(Cornish Hen Eggs in Pink Sauce)	*357*
Tipsy French Toast	*360*
Butterscotch Sauce	*364*
Potato-Leek Soup	*368*
Chili Con Carne con Cubito	*372*
Epilogue	*377*
About the Author	*381*

ACKNOWLEDGEMENTS

This book would not have been possible without the guidance and insight of my editor, Judyth Hill. Thanks, J, for always having my back. To Stewart Warren at Mercury HeartLink, who magically and perfectly transformed my manuscript into the beautiful book it is today, and to the fabulous Jason D. LeViere for knowing exactly what images belonged with my words. I'm so glad I stumbled upon your mural in Coral Gables!

To the countless friends and fellow writers who volunteered their time to take a peek, edit, question, or simply laugh out loud as My Culinary Compulsion came to life. I am forever indebted to you all. To Beth, for doing all that and *still* finding Oxford commas that had gone AWOL – you are definitely my best friend for that and so much more. I'd like to thank my family for allowing me to share them with the world through my culinary lens and send a special thanks to Yeshua for being my number one cheerleader, my love.

xviii   Alona Abbady Martinez

INTRODUCTION

Eggplants, offered whole over the open gas flame, popped rhythmically under the fire every Wednesday at four o'clock in my childhood house. I'd come home exhausted from a long school bus ride and be greeted, not by my mother, or even by my nanny Yolanda, but rather, by that undeniably Middle Eastern scent of charred eggplant. It was the promise of something exquisite to come, both in food and in company: the aroma announced my father was home early and was making his buttery, smoked *Babaganoush*.

Memories are capricious things: so much time compressed in a moment: the sound of a rusty swing, the paper thin skin of aged arms felt during a grandmother's embrace, the heated breath of a lover's kiss. Seconds really, nothing more. My kaleidoscope of seconds turns with food: the fine dance between burnt and fire-roasted eggplants, the brightness a squeeze of fresh lime juice gives garlic-infused hummus, the sweet cloud of rum slowly heating in my mother's custard that would wrap itself around my face like a lustful temptress. With such daily seductions, it was inevitable that food would be my destiny.

The daughter of an Israeli father and an American mother, I was born and raised in Caracas, Venezuela, in a home that obsessed over food. Every event warranted a culinary extravaganza: sister-got-braces-tightened called for *Moussaka*, soft to the bite, and, for sustentative comfort, followed by the Dalai Lama of smoothness:

Yoli's Signature Flan, always generous with the rum. There were plenty of others. Alona-just-barely-made-a-B-in-math was always feted with a showstopper: Mom's Sour Cream Apple Pie, after having devoured the infallible favorite, Rosemary-crusted Roasted Leg of Lamb, *au jus*, just as Julia Child specifies.

My mother would make microscopic incisions all over the lamb; tuck even smaller slivers of fragrant garlic in them; coat the meat with extra virgin olive oil, fresh rosemary, and coarse sea salt and add a final splash of soy sauce for that awe-inspiring golden color.

Of course, we celebrated all the traditional festivities as well: birthday parties, anniversaries, guests from abroad, but it was these smaller occurrences; our moments of success, our stumblings: miniscule occasions that in other families went unnoticed, never did in my household: they were always crowned with a rich and savory stock, or a humble Pineapple Upside-Down Cake.

When my mother wasn't at the helm of the kitchen, Yolanda was. Yolanda, our petite and feisty Colombian nanny, filled our kitchen with a string of characters: Mercedes and Tilsa and Sra. Isabela and Elizabeth: small, tall, thin, plump, all shapes and sizes of women pecking around the dented metal table at the far end of the kitchen they'd *yak, yak, yak* about which cousin was dumped by which man for what other woman and all because she used *culantro* instead of *cilantro* in the *Mondongo* and don't you know that the secret to that sauce is to braise the meat first, of course, that fool, she deserved to be left alone if she never properly braised the meat. You can't serve pale and tasteless food to a man and expect him to stay.

I never knew who these women were exactly, relatives or friends or friends of friends, but it didn't matter. I followed their soap opera stories amidst the steam of soup and the chopping of tomatoes all the while attached to Yola's hip, spoon in hand, an oversized apron tied around my bony waist, learning, chopping, and laughing.

My passion for cooking followed me when I came to the U.S. to go to college. I graduated from Barnard College and ended up moving to South Florida for a job in corporate America, drawn by the allure of power suits and spread-sheets. But the highlight of my time there turned out to be exchanging delectable brought-in meals with my colleague and, now, long-time friend, Ana Paula, in the dank lunchroom. Sales stats and P&L's weren't in my blood, food was. I left the corner cubicle when the adventure of motherhood called, raising two kids, and writing my blog on escapades with food and family, *www.culinarycompulsion.com*.

This book presents life and food in all its sticky, sloppy, luscious reality; I invite you to dive in and get cooking. Like the Slow-Cooked Brisket whose thick, rich sauce demands to be scooped up by a crusty baguette or the Purist Mac and Cheese that satiates hungry teens, I hope these simple, homey recipes will keep you licking your fingers as these tales of life's everyday trials and jubilations will keep you turning the pages.

xxii   Alona Abbady Martinez

INGREDIENT NOTES

WHAT'S THE DEAL WITH ALL THE DIFFERENT FLOURS?

You're an observant reader, I just know it. And so, you are going to notice that I am a bit of a player when it comes to flours. Sometimes I'm into bread flour, other times it's all about all-purpose flour, and just when you think you've got this infatuation figured out, I hone in on cake flour! Before you get frustrated, I'm gonna set the score straight on the different flours and when to use what. The secret to getting your flour to really work for you is protein level (yes, all flour has protein).

Bread Flour:

Bread flour has more protein than all-purpose flour. More protein means it will have better gluten development. Better gluten development makes for a more elastic dough, something you want for yeasted breads.

Cake Flour:

Cake flour has less protein than all-purpose flour, which renders an overall lighter cake with a very tender crumb. If you are fresh out, you can also make cake flour at home: just take 1 cup of all-purpose flour, remove 2 tablespoons and replace with 2 tablespoons of cornstarch. Now you have a cup of cake flour!

All-Purpose Flour:

All-purpose flour is the middle-of-the-road of flour: sturdy enough to hold its structure in yeasted bread and light enough to produce a decent crumb in a cake, which begs the question: do you *have* to make space in your pantry for *three* different flours if all-purpose flour will serve for both cake and bread? No. You *can* use all-purpose flour for all of the recipes. The sky won't fall down. The recipes will still be delightful. But…will your cakes be a bit lighter, your bread rise better, if you use cake and bread flours? Yes! I am a big fan of King Arthur flours. And no one (but experience) has paid me to say that. Using the precise flour for the precise recipe will score you the hardest-earned praise: a nod of approval from your toughest critic (whomever that may be!), a "this-is-better-than-my-Grandma's" from your husband (*yowzaaaaaaaa!!!!*) and an actual hug from your teenage son, even when friends are watching. (*Okay, maybe not when friends are watching, but you'll get that half-smile from him as all his friends, who will be readily inhaling everything you bake, will tell you how awesome this is and you will know you've entered the Cool Mom Zone and entering such a place of joy is worth the effort of finding space in your pantry for several bags of flour*).

WELCOME TO THE NUT HOUSE!
(A word on toasted nuts)

Toasting nuts deepens their nutty flavor while giving them an extra crunch, making them an even more memorable addition to recipes. It's best to toast them in advance so they have time to cool completely before being added to the recipe. If you are as much a nutaholic as I am, make sure you toast with your noshing requirement in mind, otherwise they'll all be gone before they make it into the recipe.

Toasted Nuts (good for any shelled nut):

Line the baking sheet of your toaster oven with aluminum foil. Sprinkle on the amount of nuts the recipe (and your appetite) call for. Toast the nuts on the dark setting of the toaster oven, keeping an eye on them (let the nuts get dark, but not too dark, as they can turn bitter if they over-toast!) Allow to fully cool before using.

Note: You can do a large quantity and save the remaining cooled nuts in a plastic bag in the refrigerator.

Oven-roasted nuts:

You can also toast nuts in the oven:

Preheat the oven to 350°F. Spread the nuts in an even layer on a baking sheet. Roast for 5 minutes.

WHIPPED INTO SHAPE!
Real, homemade whipped cream!

Homemade whipped cream is easy to make and will have you passing by the canned stuff at the grocery market with a chuckle.

1 cup heavy whipping cream

2 tablespoons confectioner's sugar

With a handheld mixer, beat the cream until it starts to thicken. Add the confectioner's sugar and whip until it forms stiff peaks.

Uh…yup, that's it! You can jazz it up from here if you'd like: a sprinkle of ground cinnamon, a bit of vanilla extract or scraped bean, cocoa or ground ginger is always nice (use ¼ teaspoon).

Store in an air-tight container for up to 24 hours.

SPICE IT UP! (Exploring chile powders)

Polvo de *Chile*, aka, *Chile* Powder:

In Mexico, there is a *chile* powder for every second of every minute of every hour of every day. Food markets dedicate major square footage to huge sacks brimming with all types of smoked, spicy, and tangy powdered *chiles*, ranging in color from amber to gunpowder black. *Chile* powder is made by drying and then pulverizing one or more varieties of *chile* pepper, sometimes with the addition of other spices. It is used on EVERYTHING in Mexico, from fresh fruit to succulent, rich sauces. Some of the popular *chile* powders are more readily available now in the United States- these are the ones I've used in my recipes.

Ancho *Chile* Powder:

You guessed it, this is ground ancho *chile* (aka, *poblano*). It has a deep, smoky flavor with a mild to moderate heat factor and is popular in tamales and mole sauces.

Chipotle *Chile* Powder:

The chipotle *chile* powder is your familiar jalapeño pepper, smoked and dried. It has an almost sweet, fruity flavor with mild to moderate heat.

Jalapeño *Chile* Powder:

Harder to find than chipotle *chile* powder, this powder comes from jalapeños that are not smoked and tends to have a fresh, almost grassy-like flavor with medium heat.

New Mexico *Chile* Powder:

This *chile* powder can be found in the green and red variety, but I prefer the latter, with its rich, garnet color, earthy undertones and a slightly acidic flavor, almost like dried cherries. It's true this is sounding like a wine review, but once you begin exploring all the dried *chile* options out there, you'll become enthralled, like a good sommelier, with all the varieties and subtleties in fragrance and flavor. Just don't sniff too much or your eyes will be tearing for a good long while! New Mexico *chile* powder has a wide range of heat: from roaring, killer hot (Chimayo) to a mild heat (Hatch) that lingers.

Plain 'Ole Chili Powder:

Chili powder is not one specific dried *chile*, but rather, dried *chile* combined with other spices, such as garlic powder, oregano, and salt. It also has cumin in it, which has a distinct and rather potent taste: slightly nutty, earthy, with a hint of lemon. Cumin's bold flavor leaves a strong mark in whatever dish it is used in.

Contrary to popular opinion, Mexicans do not use chili powder in their cooking. They prefer pure dried *chile* powders, like the ones mentioned above, that are not mixed with any other spices. Chili powder, however, is very popular in Tex-Mex cooking and is used in Tex-Mex dishes like *chili con carne* and *chimichangas*.

YOU HAD ME AT CHOCOLATE!

I could dedicate an entire book to this topic. I probably should. But, for purposes of finishing this book first, let me keep it simple. Chocolate. Just say the word out loud (or in your head) and you are happy, right?

I splurge on the chocolate I use in my cooking and recommend that you do too. I mean, I won't use chocolate bars specked with gold flakes in my cooking (ok, I wouldn't even be able to buy that stuff to munch on either!), but I do find that using a better quality chocolate renders a richer, more extraordinary dessert. What's a better chocolate, you ask? Good question! My general rule of thumb is: go for something you'd enjoy nibbling on without a baking premise. Unless your recipe calls for unsweetened chocolate: if so, you don't want to nibble at all! But choosing a chocolate bar (or cocoa powder) from a reputable source, even if it is more of a strain on your budget than the run-of-the-mill or store brand, will pay off in the flavor and the accolades you'll receive in the end.

THE BEST OF THE BASICS:
Mildred's Famous Pie Crust

This pie crust recipe belongs to my grandmother, Mildred. I never met my father's mother, a native from Canada who moved to Palestine after WWI when she was just nineteen. I have a feeling we would have gotten along, particularly in the kitchen.

2 egg yolks

2 cups all-purpose flour

¾ cup and 3 tablespoons butter

3 tablespoons sour cream

3 tablespoons ice water

Combine the flour and butter with a pastry blender or your fingers until coarse.

Add the egg yolks and sour cream and blend, working quickly.

Add water and mix until the dough forms ball.

Cut the dough in half.

Roll out one half of the dough on a lightly floured surface until it is 1/4 –inch thick and place in pie dish. Make sure there is excess dough folded over the pie plate so you can crimp the edges (a fancy term for making it look pretty) using the following technique: work with one hand on the inside of the edge, and one hand on the outside, and use the index finger of your inside hand to push the dough between the thumb and index finger of your outside hand to form a U or V shape. Continue the same motion all around the pie plate, spacing each about 1-inch apart. It's really a breeze to do but if you want to simplify it even more, then gently press the back of a fork all along the edges of your dough.

Save the other dough if you are only using one crust. It keeps up to 3 months in the freezer, wrapped in plastic wrap.

If your recipe calls for a pre-baked crust, you'll need to line the dough with tin foil and add something heavy, like uncooked beans or rice (they also sell pie weights just for that purpose). This keeps the middle of the dough from puffing up. Bake in a preheated 425°F. oven for 8 minutes. Remove the lining and weights, prick the bottom of the dough with a fork (make sure to prick all over the bottom) and bake another 8-10 minutes, or until the crust is golden.

Now you've got some of the basics for what will surely make many wonderful meals. Gather your family together, invite friends or those newly-moved-in neighbors you've been meaning to say hello to. Throw the dog a crumb or two as well! There's nothing more delicious than making memories around warm, buttered, biscuits or freshly-baked bread or savoring a bubbling berry pie — don't be shy with the whipped cream or vanilla ice cream!

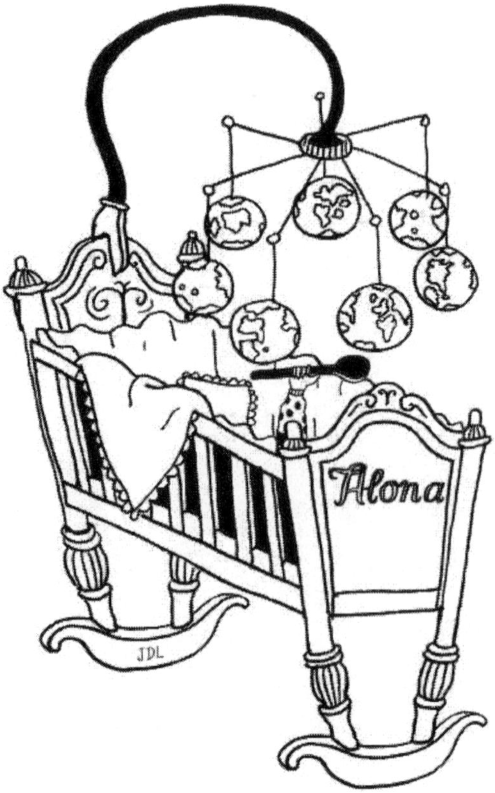
Alona
JDL

CHAPTER ONE

GROWING UP GLOBAL

Woo A Vegetarian: Marilyn's *Moussaka*

My father arrived from work proudly toting a dead goat. I was ten years old and my sister was eleven. It was an uneventful afternoon in our home in Venezuela until, of course, he showed up. My mother (who was from fine, gentile Pennsylvania stock and had already stunned her entire family by marrying *that crazy Israeli* and moving to a third world country) retained her composure and hid her utter shock. My father's eyes blazed with excitement and we all listened, spellbound, as he recounted his luck over receiving a goat instead of a much-needed payment for one of his portable face saunas he frequently sold door-to-door. It was befitting to my father, who was always driven by culinary gusto, to consider this trade favorably, even if it meant losing the telephone line when the bill wasn't paid.

I was young and wide-eyed and my father could do no wrong. His unbridled enthusiasm swept me up, and I was instantly raving about the exciting delicacy of goat that awaited us, something I had never savored and knew nothing about. My sister, being more pragmatic and less influential, was not so smitten. To put it simply, she was horrified.

"Goat?!" she squealed, as if her favorite Barbie doll had been decapitated and was simmering in the stew. "Who eats goat?" she continued to demand. And as all her 'i's' were dotted and 't's' were crossed in her culinary world, she quickly realized if a goat was too cute to digest then so were all the other cute animals she had been freely enjoying in her eleven years of eating. Without giving it more thought, her brewing, cobalt eyes hardened and she proclaimed in a loud, powerful voice:

"I will not eat meat again. I am a vegetarian."

I always held my sister high up on a pedestal, but after that declaration, I catapulted her right up there with Zeus. No meat? How? It seemed such a foreign concept: we were a family living in Venezuela in the early eighties where meat eating was a local past time. Not eating meat was like deciding not to breathe. Announcing this unachievable feat out loud made her an instant superstar for her impressionable younger sister.

I felt I should proclaim the same thing. After all, we were sisters through thick and thin and this felt like one of those thin moments she'd need me by her side, like the time I fell off the swing and scraped my back raw and she took care of me. Or the time I got lost in the snow on a winter trip and she shouted and shouted and shouted my name through the bitter Vermont wind. Or the countless times she'd help me catch frogs because they were too slippery for me to hold on to.

But I just couldn't do it. Thursday nights Mom always made that amazingly juicy filet mignon wrapped in thick, hickory-smoked bacon served with roasted baby potatoes and carrots bathed in a rich gravy speckled with fresh thyme. I couldn't forgo that dish.

And then there was my all-time favorite- the one request that rolled off my tongue each and every year when my mother would ask me what I wanted for dinner on my birthday: Shepherd's Pie. She would run the potatoes through a rice strainer to make them silky smooth and made sure there would be extra to seal in the rosemary-infused meat and keep it moist and tasty. How could I ever live without that dish?

And I hadn't even considered our Sunday afternoon ritual of taking a twenty-minute trip up the mountains of Caracas to the famous steak house appropriately named "*Belle Vue*" where tuxedo-clad waiters grilled infinite amounts of meat tableside, serving it on wooden cutting boards with generous scoops of an avocado-based sauce called *guasacaca*. No, I couldn't say farewell to that.

In the split second it takes for a ten-year old to make a life-altering decision I realized this was a battle my sister would have to fight on her own. Sorry. She had a reluctant look of doom on her face, almost as if she had regretted the impulsive comment that had now inevitably turned into a Position, but she was way too stubborn to take it back. I felt bad, I really did, but by then the undeniable aroma of curry had begun to creep its way into our household and the idea of goat seemed like a pretty good one after all.

My mother did her best to accommodate my sister's new life change. With every meal of succulent lamb chops or port-infused tenderloin, came a carb-exploding, mushy dish of mushroom lasagna or squash stew. She tried. She really did. But as I said, this was South America in the early eighties and vegetarianism was a horrible disability at best.

Twenty-three zucchini casseroles later, my sister finally caved and declared she was reverting to her meat-eating ways. She didn't seem to hold a grudge against me and my decision to abandon her

My Culinary Compulsion   5

to endless rounds of creamed cauliflower. We all celebrated with a family favorite: *moussaka*, a Greek casserole that is quite different from the many others that had landed on my sister's plate. Not only is it creamy and delicious, but it is loaded with meat as well. Lots of meat. Mom made sure my sister was served first. And life was restored anew.

Marilyn's Moussaka

A fixture in each *taverna*, this recipe was handed down to me by my mother, who did not have a drop of Greek blood in her, but instantly filled her kitchen with such tantalizing aromas of Greece that even the pickiest Greek God would have been happy. Mom created a clever twist to this dish by baking the eggplant instead of the traditional frying of the eggplant, allowing for its true flavor to shine (and giving your hips a bit of a break as well!)

 3 eggplants

 salt (to drain eggplants)

 2 tablespoons olive oil

 1 cup chopped onion

 1 1/2 lbs. ground lamb or beef

 1 teaspoon cinnamon

 1 diced tomato

 3 tablespoons tomato paste

3 tablespoons chopped parsley

1/4 cup white wine

salt and pepper to taste

1/4 cup Parmesan cheese (for sprinkling on top afterwards)

Béchamel:

2 1/2 tablespoons butter

2 1/2 tablespoons flour

2 cups hot milk

1/4 teaspoon nutmeg

salt and pepper to taste

1 egg yolk

Preheat the oven to 400°F.

Peel and slice the eggplants into 1/2 inch rounds.

Sprinkle with salt and allow them to sit for 15 minutes. Dab off excess juice with a paper towel, flip and repeat. (You will see liquid coming out of the slices, just pat that dry with a paper towel. Salt pulls out the juices that carry the bitter flavors sometimes found in eggplants.)

Bake on a greased cookie sheet for 10-15 minutes.

Reduce oven temperature to 375°F.

While the eggplant is cooking, sauté the onion in olive oil over medium high until the onions are translucent, about five minutes.

Add the meat and brown.

Add the remaining ingredients (except the béchamel ingredients).

Bring the onion/meat mixture to a simmer and then lower heat to medium/low and cook for 15 minutes. Adjust seasoning.

Put alternate layers of eggplant and meat mixture in a 9 x 13 greased baking dish, starting and ending with the eggplant.

Prepare the Béchamel:

Melt the butter in a saucepan over medium high heat. Add the flour and blend, mixing with a wooden spoon. When the flour begins turning golden, gradually add the hot milk with a whisk. Add salt, pepper, and nutmeg.

Reduce heat to low and simmer until sauce thickens, 3 - 5 minutes.

Beat egg yolk.

Stir a large spoonful of the sauce into the yolk and blend well. Pour this back into the whole sauce, stirring constantly.

Don't let the sauce boil again.

Pour sauce over *moussaka* and bake for 45 minutes, or until top is browned.

Remove from oven and sprinkle Parmesan cheese on top.

Serves 8-10

A Token of Time: Mom's Pineapple Upside Down Cake

As I grew older and adolescence became a pre-requisite for not hanging out with my parents, I'd still connect with them through all things food, particularly the culinary expeditions my mother and I would embark upon in the Caracas late day heat after school. I'd always say I'd allow her to pick me up in order to skip the hour-long bus ride home, but she and I knew better: it was the food and quiet company that drew me in.

Mom called our rounds simple errands, but, to me, they were joyous adventures in search of the freshest loaf of oatmeal bread or the perfect cut of filet mignon heightened by coveted one-on-one time together. Food was purchased in stations: for meat, one went to the butcher, for fish, the local fish shop. Cheese, breads, fruit, and veggies could be found in random trucks parked at precarious turns. Our favorite stop was in the lush neighborhood of Las Mercedes, where a cream-colored beat up VW van stood and its owner, an equally beat-up looking older man with a bushy white mustache, stood waving loaves of warm bread, sprinkled with fresh oats or bursting with whole wheat. Most of the time we'd buy two loaves because we knew one wouldn't make it home.

Sometimes Mom bypassed the fruit and veggies trucks and went to her favorite store: *Siempre Fresco* ("Always Fresh") where the equally fresh young Italian owner would pay a little too much attention to our needs, offering up free slices of papaya or guava to sample. The juice bar up front guaranteed a sampling of the products, my favorite being the refreshing *Batido de Patilla* (watermelon shake) that I'd guzzle while following Mom around a maze of floral aromas.

My mother always left *Siempre Fresco* with bagfuls of the tropical fruits which always included several pineapples. I knew one would be used for her Pineapple Upside-Down cake, a dessert she made to end a glorious evening, whether it be celebrating my sister's victory in basketball (*hip hip hooray!*) or dazzling my father's boss for dinner. This dessert was always loved for its flavor, but for me it was extra special: it served as a quiet token of prized moments shared with my mother.

Mom's Pineapple Upside Down Cake

For topping:

¼ cup unsalted butter

1 cup brown sugar

1 pineapple, sliced into ½ inch rings

For batter:

1 ½ cups flour

2 teaspoons baking powder

½ teaspoon salt

½ cup sugar

1 egg

½ cup milk

½ cup unsalted butter, melted

Preheat the oven to 400°F.

Prepare topping:

Melt the butter in a heavy frying pan or a cake pan. Add brown sugar and spread evenly.

Add pineapple in circular pattern.

Set aside.

Prepare batter:

Sift together, 1 ½ cups flour

2 teaspoons baking powder

½ teaspoon salt

½ cup sugar

Mix together the egg, milk and, melted butter.

Gently mix into the flour until combined. Do not overbeat.

Place on top of pineapple (the batter will be thick).

Bake until crusty on top, about 35 minutes. Cool on rack for 15 minutes. Invert onto serving plate. Serve immediately.

Serves 8

SIPPING LUNCH: 3-STEP ASPARAGUS SOUP

I am by nature a soup luncher. I blame it on my father. He sought out soups as the springboard to all his lunches, which, living in South America, always consisted of a full course meal of meat, sides, and salad, followed by a chaser of homemade lemonade. But soup always came first and always, as he insisted, piping hot. He'd then proceed to guzzle it with a delight and agility that left me mesmerized. I don't know how he did it, but I'd just be starting to decipher the flavors of that broth when he'd be done with it.

Lunchtime here in the States is another story all together. I am usually alone, running between errands and work, aware that soon I will begin/be picking up my kids and my role as Mommy will take center stage for the remainder of that day. I don't have the time nor appetite for a full meal, but the yearning for a hot and completely satisfying soup is there. It is a quick dip into a whole meal, a complex, nourishing dish that, when paired with a good, crusty bread, some butter, and a tall glass of lemonade, becomes a quiet reminder of home and all the comforts that implies.

3-STEP ASPARAGUS SOUP

This is quick, extremely easy, and very good. I use 5 ingredients.

2 tablespoons unsalted butter

1 leek, sliced

2 cups fresh asparagus, chopped into 1 inch pieces (*do not use the bottom 1 inch of the stalk, which has a lot of fiber*)

2 cups chicken broth*

salt to taste

Optional #5: A bit of cream if you're feeling frisky

*Now, I'd like to say I use homemade broth, I really would. That just has the ring of true culinary dedication. But, I am both honest and a realist, so I will tell you flat out that I don't. I use a bouillon cube (all formally French-trained chefs may gasp now). Yes, a chicken cube plopped into water. No time for anything else. And you know what, it tastes, not only fine, but DELICIOUS!

Here are the 3 steps:

1. In a heated pan (medium/high) melt butter and add chopped leeks and chopped asparagus. PAUSE: A word on leeks. They love to hide dirt so clean them well. To clean, just chop off the dark green and discard. Take the remaining white part and slice it in half, lengthwise. You will see it will fan out into many pieces. Make sure to run these halves under cold water, fanning the leek as you go so that the water enters into every crack and cranny, making sure to rinse it of any hidden dirt. But if

you miss a speck or two, no biggie. After all, who didn't eat a mud pie as a kid? (What, I'm the only one???)

P.S. If you don't have leek (I happened to find one shriveling up in my fridge) then go ahead and use onion instead, 1/2 cup, chopped.

2. Sauté until tender, about 5 minutes, stirring. Add broth and bring to a boil. Reduce heat to medium low and cook another 15 minutes, until asparagus is very tender.

3. Blend soup with an immersion blender and/or in the blender or food processor. (If you don't own an immersion blender, STOP RIGHT NOW, put the whole damn soup project on the side, and run out and buy one.)

Add salt, to taste. Add a dash of cream, if you'd like. Many people would now recommend you strain the soup, to eliminate any fiber (or texture) to the soup, but, personally, I quite like the soup to have the sense of body to it. If you don't, feel free to run the soup through a sieve or fine strainer. I just think it's one more thing to wash.

Serves 2-4

Recipe for a Memory: Oaxaca Cream and Jam

My mother's terrycloth robe appears in my thoughts every morning. If my eyes were to see such a thing today, draped on a dummy, let's say, I'd believe it to be horrendous: a plebeian mocha-colored sea of fuzziness, with a plain beige belt strap and a black trim. I can't think of any skin tone that would benefit from it, and most certainly not my mother's with her pale skin and salt and pepper hair. *So* not her color.

This was a sophisticated and fine lady we're talking about. Marilyn Dorothy Graham Flynn was grand. A graduate from Vassar, she was super smart and had the quality of a Hollywood star with sparkly eyes, a killer smile and the most graceful poise around. Black and white pictures of my father and her dating emanate her strength and beauty next to a puddle of mush and awe (Dad).

And this force that was my mother went on to tackle life with zest and courage: moving to the exotic country of Venezuela at a time when no one did such things with an even more exotic man (Jewish *and* Israeli!) who ripped her from her family's suburban Anglo-Saxon identity landing her in a tropical chaos of bananas and car fumes. But my mother embraced it all, every second of it, raising three girls in a rambunctious house she pretty much ran on her own while said husband traveled and traveled and traveled.

And then she began to cook.

A woman mocked for not knowing how to scramble eggs became the queen of cuisine: tackling thick and musty volumes of French Culinary Arts and Mediterranean cooking and melding those with the wonderful depths of her own imagination, making for unforgettable meals. I was blessed with an array of delicious soufflés, roasts, cakes, and her signature dessert of *Ile Flottante*, requested at every birthday dinner. I couldn't have asked for a better role model and mentor.

Except for her breakfasts. In that terry cloth robe. You could put her in the jungle, you could have her beat egg whites with the ease of a signature French chef, but some things were not to be messed with when it came to her routine: breakfast was one of them. For all the glamour, grace, beauty and adventure with which she tackled life, this woman ate the most boring thing each and every single morning: toast with cream cheese and raspberry jam.

"Mom, seriously? Again!" I'd say, half in shock, half disgusted, as my thoughts raced through the plethora of available, tasty breakfast offerings.

She'd look at me and smile, taking another messy bite out of her toast slipping with the sweet ooze created by the warm marriage of white and red goop.

"Don't you want an *arepa con queso guayanes*?" I tempted, thrusting the warm Venezuelan corncake nestling fresh white cheese. I was answered with another bite of bread and a savage dip of the knife into the jam.

I always found it unappetizing to reach for that jam, say for a quick PB&J sandwich, and find the insides of the jar tainted with white strips of cream cheese. There was only one culprit and I'd instantly go and complain:

"*Ewwww*, Mom, disguuuusting. Seriously, use *two* knives."

She was patient and kind and always quiet, throwing me a small smile I thought I understood but really had no clue what it meant.

I read: "*So sorry. Won't happen again, even though you know it will, time and time again*"

She meant: "*One day you will remember this. One day you will find yourself in your own comfortable robe, at your own table, eating your own toast and jam and cream cheese, and you will remember this.*"

That day has come. I am in Mexico. I can have the most elaborate breakfasts of eggs and tortillas and sauces and beans, and yet, I find myself longing for, *craving for*, my mother's breakfast. Each morning I turn into her: toast, raspberry jam, and a small but important adjustment: *crema de Oaxaca*, Oaxacan cream.

This stuff is for the Gods …and my waistline. I buy it off the local cheese truck every Saturday morning. The cheese guy pulls out a huge plastic bag, snips a hole in the corner, grabs a Dixie cup, and pours it in. He then puts a piece of plastic wrap over top and, if you are lucky, throws a rubber band over it to seal the deal. It's as simple as that. No FDA, no pasteurization, no questions asked.

The flavor that mesmerizes one's mouth is indescribable. Everything you know your arteries shouldn't have and more. And gosh darn it the thing goes *amazing* with raspberry jam and black bread! Mom was right on target with her combo and all I can think of is how much I'd love to share this with her right now. We'd send that Phili cream cheese out the door and create a new annoying goop combo with the *crema de Oaxaca*. I long to have my mother's palate dance with mine. I leave long white marks of Oaxacan cream in my jam. It's my tribute to her. It's my celebration. It's my acknowledgement: mother knows best, right down to the simple breakfast.

A Breakfast Suggestion:
Oaxacan Cream and Raspberry Jam Toast

Oaxacan cream is something my mother would have loved, and so will you! If you are anywhere near Mexico, you'll get the good stuff. If you are not, there are several creative and tasty alternatives, available in specialty markets and even in local supermarkets. Look for *Labne*, the Middle East's version of sour cream, if not, grab some plain Greek yogurt. Even fresh ricotta will work, but go for the whole milk kind, don't skimp out on the flavor with fat free! And you can also do it old-school, Marilyn style, and use her reliable favorite, cream cheese.

Toast your favorite bread: sourdough, multigrain, baguette, or a slice of plain ol' white (English muffins would be my mother's go-to choice in the States), then spread the two in whatever order you deem fit (Mom was more the cream cheese first, jam on top type.)

Take a bite, close your eyes, and enjoy!

For Peep's Sake: *Piña Colada* Ice Pops

Every holiday they seem to sneak past my culinary radar and invade the shelves of my well-groomed pantry, usually perched next to the rosemary chocolate and the bottles of Portuguese olive oil. I sigh in disbelief when I see them; their creative metamorphosis amazes me every time. After all, they are only reconstituted marshmallows, which is reconstituted sugar, but no matter what holiday, Halloween, Valentine's Day, or Easter, there is a *Peeps* for the occasion. And every single one of them enters my household.

I justify my insensitivity to this sugary fluff as a cultural bias. I grew up in Venezuela, where *Peeps* are non-existent. Instead, I hoarded bars of *Carleton* (a thin crispy wafer doused in dark Venezuelan chocolate) and guzzled down can after can of *Frescolita*, the local soft drink that boasts a neon red color and equally intense sweetness. Of course, my all-time favorite treat was the *raspao*, a street slush of ice and your choice of tropical flavored syrup (coconut, passion fruit, tamarind). These were my childhood glucose memories; marshmallow mush formed into pumpkins, chicks, and hearts is another story all together.

My daughter tells me that my lack of appreciation for *Peeps* is wrong, so very wrong. Of course, as she teeters along the dawn of pre-adolescence, it seems I am never even close to being right. But she is a culinary child, born with a whisk in one hand and a tasting spoon in another. This is the child that will bypass chicken nuggets shaped into stars for seared *foie gras* with figs and a Port reduction. This is the child who, at two, was thrilled to take a spoon to miso soup (extra tofu please) for breakfast while on a trip to Los Angeles.

She is my food prodigy, so sometimes, I do listen.

I watched her with her newest *Peeps* purchase: vanilla crème marshmallow hearts. She was giddy with excitement grasping the pink and red package that housed nine cramped foamy hearts sprinkled with colored sugar.

"Pleeease Mom, can I have three, pleeeease???" We were in the midst of our usual negotiations.

"One," I barked back.

"Two?" Her rebuttal.

"One," I barked back.

"Two, oh please, please, please," her desperate rebuttal.

"One," I barked back.

"Please Mom please, please, please, two, two, two, please! I'll do anything, please, two???" (This is never going to end.)

"Two," I say, just to see if she is listening.

She is, tearing the package open and barely giving herself time to smile before gulping two hearts.

As she skips away I approach the ravaged package, carefully scooping up one of the remaining hearts. Two are missing and the other seven are distorted and surreal, almost as if Salvador Dali's paintbrush had gotten ahold of them.

I am tempted to seek such giddiness and take a bite, but I know it will be an empty experience for me. This is not my memory. It is hers. Mine stands on the corner of a crowded Caracas street waiting for school to be out, housed in a portable ice cream cart with a hyperactive ringing bell and vocals shouting full force, "*El raspao, raspao, raspao, vengan pa' el raspao: tenemos parchita, coco, tamarindo, raspao raspao raspao.*" Like a racehorse bursting out of the gate, I'd charge down the hill at the end of the school day, dashing for a quick purchase before clambering on the bus for the long ride home. The five-second sprint was when I'd consider what flavor I was in the mood for, usually narrowed down to two: for sour I'd go for the tangy *parchita* (passion fruit); for something mellower, *coco* (coconut) would do the trick. If I felt like merging yin and yang I'd ask for the tartest of them all, *tamarindo* (tamarind) and order the bonus topping of *leche condensada* (condensed milk) which accordingly, would be drizzled all over the top.

This was no doubt the highlight of my day, when I'd be stuck in a glorious limbo of no-more-school and not-time-for-homework yet. All I would have was my favorite tropical fruit slushy and one hour of bumpy peace to enjoy it in. That sticky, mushy *Peeps* would never be able to transport me there. Carefully, so as not to distort the left ventricle more than my thumb already had, I placed it back into its pink plastic cage and left it to wait for its rightful owner who had her own set of memories and feelings attached to its fluff. It would only be a matter of minutes before she'd begin negotiating for more.

Piña Colada Ice Pops

This flavor wasn't an option for *raspao* when I was growing up! I'm sure I would have gotten it if it was!

3 cups cubed pineapple (fresh or frozen)

½ cup unsweetened coconut milk

½ cup cream of coconut (make sure it is well stirred!)

Special equipment: 8 (1/3-cup) ice pop molds and 8 wooden sticks

Blend all the ingredients in a blender until smooth. Pour the liquid into molds and add sticks. Freeze overnight.

Serves 8

Note: For the adult version, replace ½ cup of unsweetened coconut for ½ cup rum!

The Pleasure of Being Sick: Soft-Boiled Egg

It starts inconspicuously enough, like, when one of your kids turns towards you and sends a whole-hearted, sloppy sneeze in your direction. *'Okay, that was gross'*, you may think to yourself, but, being that it is your kid (and has inevitably crapped, puked, and pissed on you at some point in your bonding), you most likely will think nothing of it. And so you go on your way.

Your other child may cough on your food when you aren't looking. Dirty little fingers inevitably snag a bite of your chocolate cake (they never steal the broccoli). Whatever. Either way, one of these rugrats houses some sort of cold that is silently passed on to you. So that when you wake up three days later with your throat on fire, your eyes glazed and bloodshot and your head throbbing as if a Chau gong is banging ceremoniously declaring the arrival of your newfound illness, I can guarantee you, without a doubt, you can blame it on one of your children. And you don't even need proof.

When I was a kid, the world would actually stop if I was sick. People would flock to my side to tend to me as I wallowed in self-pity, not too thrilled about feeling lousy, yet happily basking in all the attention. It was a careful balance of perfection and lots of tissues. For eight hours, I became an only child bathed in excessive doting and not the forgotten last kid in a rung of three. Meals were instantly cooked up and presented on pretty trays splashed with tropical flowers: perfectly soft-boiled eggs nestled in delicate porcelain eggcups, bowls of homemade chicken soup, and freshly-squeezed orange juice arrived from me just thinking of them. Each dish was hot and soothing and blended with excessive dosages of salt, pepper, and love. Cars stuck in midday traffic would honk outside my window, and I would relish the thought of harried workers, rushing to their varied responsibilities while I basked in the serene and almost naughty pleasure of lounging in my comfy bed.

Today the world does not stop when I am under the weather, it seems to actually speed up. With two young children to care for and a weekends-only spouse, balancing the tissues with self-pity only gets me behind. I do get nostalgic for my past when Nyquil becomes my beverage of choice. I can almost smell the chicken soup Yoli simmered for me or the extra dose of hugs my mother would offer just to perk me up, but I have piano practice, karate and tutors to get to, and if I don't get going I will inevitably be more harried and stressed than I usually am. Still, a quick trip down memory lane is something I simply can't pass on, especially if this one takes all of four minutes. Tripping over laundry and discarded toys, I make my way to the kitchen for a revitalizing soft-boiled egg. It may not be served to me in a dainty eggcup as it was in my youth, but as I crack the top, douse it with coarse sea salt and fresh pepper and take that first nourishing, creamy bite, I am instantly transported to a moment made just for me filled with time, tenderness, and the simple comfort of a perfectly soft-boiled egg.

Soft-Boiled Egg

This is not brain surgery, but you'd be amazed how many people mess it up. Precision is key.

Bring to a boil 2 to 4 quarts of water, enough to cover a single layer of the egg by 1 inch.

Gently lower the egg into the water.

Simmer for exactly 4 minutes.

Remove the egg from water immediately.

Egg tip: Make sure your egg is room temperature, not straight out of the refrigerator (to avoid cracking). The best way to do this is to place the egg in a bowl of hot water for 5 minutes before using it.

To Serve:

Place in an eggcup (or shot glass, if you don't have an eggcup), wide end down. Use a spoon to gently crack the top of the egg. Peel off the tip. Using a knife, slice across the top to open the egg. Add the top of sliced egg into the egg. Season with coarse kosher salt and fresh ground pepper.

Toppings: There is nothing quite like a simply perfect soft-boiled egg with salt and pepper. However, sometimes you want to fancy it up. The sky is the limit on dressing up your soft-boiled egg!

Here are a couple of suggestions you may add to your egg: chopped chives, tabasco sauce, crumbled bacon, *chile* powder, crumbled cheese (feta or bleu cheese), caviar.

Serves 1

Three Moves Ahead: Bone Marrow Soup

When I was a little girl growing up in Venezuela, my nanny, Yoli, would whip up one mean beef soup.

Good stuff bursting with hearty meat bones glistening with bone marrow.

That makes it a winner, for those not sure.

She'd toss all sorts of vegetables laying around: carrots, potatoes, yucca. Then she'd grab a fistful of cilantro- she had tiny hands but generous fistfuls, always a good trait in a chef.

And then there were those meat bones.

Damn good things.

Ginormous.

Clinging with beef and filled with gold in the center.

"*Eso es lo bueno,*" she'd say, in a low whisper, pointing at the marrow while her eyes scanned the kitchen to make sure no one else was privy to her secret. And she was right.

That was the good stuff.

It was the first thing I'd go for, after hours of waiting, watching, and smelling that hearty soup simmer, its steady steam carving out swirls in the dense, tropical air.

Dinner came and I was joyous.

"*Dame el hueso mas grande*," I'd plead as she ladled. And because I was the youngest and played up the blue eyes the best, she would, she'd go ahead and plop the largest bone smack in the center of my soup bowl, filling it up to the rim with the caramel-colored broth which served as a moat housing an occasional floating yucca or carrot.

While others began with the broth I grabbed my fork and went for the kill, stabbing right into the gelatinous center of the bone and carving out the marrow. It would surrender easily to my assault and in a matter of seconds I gulped it down. Its warm, rich, beefy core filled me with happiness, topping my experience of beef soup before it had even really begun.

My father had more foresight, knew to plan his moves well in life. It was something his father taught him years before in front of a chess board, a trait that came in handy even when eating beef soup. *Always be three moves ahead.* He'd enjoy his soup the loudest, taking breaks with sips of lemonade or conversation and when he was done, the beef bone was left waiting, exposed, perfectly his.

That's when he'd go for the kill.

Unless, of course, he was distracted.

Perhaps by a set of pretty blue eyes.

His youngest.

She is so sweet that way, he'd find himself thinking.

Eyes can say it all.

"You want it?" He'd be compelled to ask. He couldn't help it. That question just drew itself out of him.

I'd give just a smile in return.

I never met the father of my father, but it turns out I had my chess skills as well. A word might break the spell that was cast and so a demure smile, ever so slight, curled its way around my lips, just to frame those hypnotic baby blues.

Three moves ahead and the prize was mine!

Placed gently in the center of my bowl, a partner to the other scooped out pawn, more gold ready to be enjoyed.

Bone Marrow Beef Soup

1 lbs. sliced marrow bones (If you don't see them, ask your butcher!)

1 lbs. beef shank (Beef shank will give you chunks of meat in your soup.)

1 large onion, peeled

3 carrots, peeled and chopped into 3" pieces

2 potatoes, peeled and quartered

½ cup squash, peeled and chopped into 2" cubes (or use 1 sweet potato, peeled and chopped into 2" cubes)

½ cup frozen yucca

A nice handful of fresh cilantro (What's a handful, you precision-thirsty chefs ask? Ummm, ¼ cup, ½, if you're feeling the love… By the way, save a teensy bit for garnish at the end to add some brightness, or chop a teensy bit more)

8 cups beef stock (Don't have time and want a good cheat? Use 8 cups water and 7 tablespoons of Better Than Bouillon beef stock. They sell this stuff next to the bouillon cubes in the supermarket. It comes in a jar: goopy, dark, and yes, my secret when I have no homemade stock lying around…)

Salt, to taste

Optional garnishes: minced onions, lime juice, picante (spicy sauce), additional chopped cilantro.

You're gonna love this: throw it all into a pot. Everything. One, two, three, GO!

Bring to a boil on high heat.

Now, reduce to a simmer (should be on medium).

Walk away and do everything you've been putting off (laundry, vacuum, do-I-have-to kid's algebra project, whatever). Or put your feet up and binge on your favorite show…

The soup should simmer a good two hours.

Take a peek now and again.

Give a stir, just so you don't feel neglectful. Move them bones around.

Sip, if you want.

If you have a teenager like I do, at some point a sample will be served, it always is. These children are perpetually hungry, and yes, it's all your fault, I hate you, you suck.

Somewhere along the way, add salt. You'll have to sample and figure that one out, everyone's salt needs are different.

Ladle into bowls in the following manner:

Big-ass bone first.

All the other stuff second.

Sprinkle with fresh cilantro.

Serve without any other garnish, if you are a die-hard bone marrow beef soup eater (cue in Husband). Anything else is sacrilege.

If you like surprising bursts and tangs of flavors that support, exalt, intensify your soup experience, sprinkle, squeeze, and squirt on the other stuff. That would be me.

Hey, either way, it's heavenly.

Of course, you'll be busy with the marrow first, if you've learned anything.

Serves 4-6 carnivores

CONTRABAND PIE: SOUR CREAM APPLE PIE

I didn't grow up around apples.

I grew up around mango and passion fruit and bright orange papaya.

Golden pineapples, enormous watermelon, and endless supplies of limes to be squeezed into every food and beverage.

And then there was the exotic fruit: the kind you rarely find in the States, but was commonplace in Venezuela:

Guanabana, guayaba, níspero, mamón.

But apples were impossible to find. Apples were high currency in my tropical country.

I remember biting into a large, bright red apple, so perfect it looked fake, like the ones I'd seen given to teachers in the movies. I was 24, living in the States, and had never had one before.

Getting apples in Venezuela in the 70's and 80's was complicated business. You had to know what *frutería*, fruit shop, would have them and when. Most didn't. Ever. In fact, most successful apple purchasing happened quickly and covertly from the fruit trucks: ancient vehicles groaning under the weight of way too much produce dangling precariously from rusted hooks or balanced miraculously in overstuffed plastic crates. The fruit trucks had known pit stops, usually around the second or third bend of one of Caracas' windy mountain roads.

My mother had connections with these fruit guys. I'm not sure how or why. I'm guessing her long legs had something to do with it, perhaps that milky white skin and those pretty blue eyes, or it could even be the musical, sing-song way in which she'd answer "*okay, hasta luego*" that captivated the vendors' hearts. Whatever her secret, she always seemed to know when they'd be selling apples, which were smuggled in from Chile, *solo para clientes especiales*, and hidden behind bunches of bananas and bags of oranges.

My mother was one of those special clients, and thus we were privy to her even more special dessert: Sour Cream Apple Pie.

My mother pulled out this show-stopper whenever she could. I think it was almost as a challenge to the traditional lattice apple pie we'd savor on our bi-annual trips to the States, a careful balance of apple and cinnamon goop. But those could never compete with my mother's pie, which rose as high as the mountainous road she'd traverse to purchase the rare and scarce apples. It was tricky to slice a piece without having it topple over, but my mother managed it just fine. Our neighbors were surely enjoying a delectable dessert of their own where one of the commonplace fruit may have played a central role. But the memorable transformation of the elusive Granny Smith was not one of them. This knowledge, as well as the layers of crisp, tart apples baked in a fragrant mixture of sour cream, cinnamon and sugar sealed this dessert as one of my all-time favorites, and my yearning for many visits to the clandestine fruit trucks.

Mom's Sour Cream Apple Pie

2 tablespoons flour

3/4 cup sugar

1 teaspoon ground cinnamon

1/8 teaspoon salt

1 egg, lightly beaten

1/2 teaspoon vanilla extract

1 cup sour cream

6 medium-sized tart apples (Granny Smith), peeled, cored, and sliced ¼" thin

1 unbaked pie crust (see recipe for Mildred's Famous Pie Crust on page xxix)

Crumb Topping:

1/3 cups flour

1/3 cup sugar

½ teaspoon ground cinnamon

¼ cup unsalted butter, chilled, cut into 1/4" cubes

Combine the flour, sugar, ground cinnamon, and, with a pastry blender or fingertips, blend in the butter until mixture is crumbly.

Preheat the oven to 400°F.

Sift together the 2 tablespoons flour, 3/4 cup sugar, 1 teaspoon ground cinnamon, and salt. Stir in the egg, vanilla extract, and sour cream. Fold in the apples and spoon into pie shell. Bake 10 minutes. Reduce the oven heat to 350°F and bake 30 minutes longer.

Remove the pie from the oven, and sprinkle the crumb topping over the top. Return the pie to the oven and bake at 400°F for 10 minutes.

Serves 8

My Own Private Grandma: *Pasticcio*

I want to think of my grandmother as a short, stout woman people could not help but gravitate to. She'd be a constant bustle of energy, always with a smile, her glasses unable to keep up with her pace, they'd *slip, slip, slip* down the bridge of her nose, only to be impatiently shoved back up to their appointed place. She'd wear a thin dress of paisley blue, which would sit proudly on her, unashamed of rolls or bulges that refused to be tamed. There'd be a delicate gold chain with a simple pendant hanging from her neck, nothing flashy, but rather a discreet amulet of her past: something she never talks about but I feel safe and secure seeing it there.

"Come here, *Pushka*" (she'd call me *pushka*, which is Yiddish for "little box", a nickname that didn't quite make sense to me but grooved its way through me nevertheless) and her petite but fleshy body would embrace me in a quick burst of zealous love which I'd happily swim in.

Of course, she'd be in the kitchen, but not in that traditional 1930's kind of way, but more as the conductor of an orchestra of many lives: weaving memories, nourishment, and love in her unforgettable brisket or chickpea soup or *ropa vieja*. She'd cook a patchwork of the different cultures and foods that have become my culinary language today. *Sopa de Mondongo*, tripe soup, because it is hearty and complete, and because she believes, as I do, that consuming soup for lunch should be required by law, no matter how hot it gets in South Florida. Flaky eggplant *bourekas* would lift my spirits in the middle of a slow week, and meatloaf, which she would refer to as *Klops*, would mark the end of the week, served with a heaping serving spoonful of creamy mashed potatoes. My serving would always boast an extra slab of butter.

I'd be her taster. I would have always been. From the time I was little until even now as an adult. My phantom grandma would always want my feedback on her recipes and concoctions: more salt, less garlic, a squeeze of fresh lime juice to bring out the flavor: she'd listen intently to my advice as if world peace depended on it, and in between tastes and commentary we'd prattle on about life, oblivious to the generation separating us.

This would be my grandma of choice. Of course, we all know we can't pick our family, and as far as grandmothers go, fate was not on my side. My Canadian-born paternal grandma passed away when my father was a teen. My mother's mother, a tall woman from Irish stock, died when I was barely three, leaving me with only fuzzy memories of my one encounter with her. She had brilliant blue eyes, and as far as I can make out, she did not really cook.

The mind is a spectacular thing, and, even though I may not remember where I put my keys five minutes ago, I am able to create, nourish, and feed off my own private grandma. She has no name (wouldn't want to offend Mildred or Agnes) but she has zest, and most importantly, she has great dishes. Her *Pasticcio*, by the way, is stellar. I don't know where she picked up that recipe, it's not like she's Italian, but each time I'd ask about it, she'd shoot me a wry smile, followed by the words: "Keep stirring the sauce," a sure sign that she kept a secret or two. It may take a bit of dedication, but the end result is well worth the trouble.

Pasticcio

Start with the Bolognese sauce:

    1 lbs. ground beef chuck

    3 tablespoons olive oil

    ½ cup onion, minced

    2 garlic cloves, minced

    ½ cup carrots, chopped in 1" cubes

    ½ cup celery, sliced

    ½ cup whole milk

    ½ cup red wine

    2 tablespoons tomato paste

    1 28-oz can whole tomatoes

    1 cup water

    1 beef bouillon cube

    salt, to taste

Make the Bolognese:

Put the olive oil into a large skillet over medium heat, and sauté the onions, garlic, carrots, and celery until the onions are translucent, about 5 minutes. Remove from skillet.

Sauté the meat until the pink is gone then add the milk and simmer for 5 minutes.

Add the vegetables and the remaining ingredients, raise heat to high simmer, then lower heat to medium-low and let cook, stirring occasionally, for 45 minutes.

Adjust salt.

Make the Béchamel Sauce on page 7.

Bolognese sauce
- 1 box of oven-baked lasagna noodles
- ½ pound smoked ham, sliced thick
- 2-4 cups shredded mozzarella
- Béchamel sauce
- ½ cup grated Parmigiano-Reggiano

In a square casserole dish, begin assembling your *Pasticcio:*

Preheat the oven to 375° F.

Create a layer of *Bolognese* sauce, follow by strips of noodles (make sure the noodles do not overlap) and then, slices of ham, and a sprinkling of mozzarella cheese.

Repeat until the layers reach ½ inch from the top (you should have either 2, or maximum, 3 layers)

Pour béchamel sauce over top and add Parmigiano-Reggiano cheese.

Bake until bubbly, 30 minutes.

Serves 6

Warming the Heart: Beef Okra Stew

When I was a little girl my family would leave our tropical home in Venezuela and head to Vermont for our winter vacation. My parents would rent a narrow chalet tucked in the corner of the woods and we'd cast ourselves in a winter wonderland production that managed to squeeze in every glacial activity imaginable during our two-week stay. Vermont, by the way, does winter hard-core. There's no messing around. *Everything* froze, even my hair.

My mother took those opportunities to warm us up in the kitchen. It was a cramped space that she worked expertly, offering a wealth of food and love to sustain my sisters and I throughout our chilly adventures. When we went sledding down the local farmer's hill, we were always greeted with her soothing hot chocolate. When we explored the woods in hopes of finding the land of Narnia (or at least the lamppost that would lead us to Mr. Tumnus) there might be a steaming bowl of chicken noodle soup waiting on our return. When we came home from a day of careening down the ski slopes, exhausted and slightly frostbitten, she'd present us with her best defense against record-breaking low temperatures: a hearty bowl of beef stew.

I loved this stew.

It made everything right in the world when I ate it, replenishing a tired body depleted from endless rounds on an icy bunny slope. We all snuggled around the rustic wooden dining room table with a front row seat to another awe-inspiring winter storm and I knew, at that very moment, that I had with me everything that mattered: my mother's delicious food, my family, and the absolute promise of another beautiful snowy day waiting for me tomorrow.

Somewhere along the road of parenthood, I began adding okra to my version of this stew. Okra is *mucilaginous*, which is just a fancy way of saying it can get quite slimy and gooey when cooked. I love this because it helps thicken the sauce and binds everything together nicely. Okra is quite popular in Middle Eastern cooking, where it is referred to as *bamia*, and used frequently to make lamb stew. Mom passed away before I perfected my okra stew, but several years ago my father, a Jerusalemite expat living in the Andean city of Quito, came to visit me in South Florida and was very pleased to see this familiar dish simmering on my stovetop. Vegetarians will be happy to note that this stew can be made with just the vegetables. Either way, make sure to serve it over some steamy rice or alongside a crisp green salad, and if you can snuggle up with your family to enjoy it, all the better.

Beef Okra Stew

1 lbs. stew meat

½ cup all-purpose flour

½ teaspoon coriander

½ teaspoon cumin

½ teaspoon paprika

1 teaspoon salt

¼ teaspoon pepper

1 cup onion, chopped

3 cloves of garlic, minced

3 tablespoons olive oil

1 lbs. okra, cut into 2" pieces (fresh or frozen)

16 oz. canned crushed tomatoes

3 potatoes (Yukon Gold work great), peeled and cut in fourths

¾ cup white wine

¾ beef broth (or vegetable broth)

2 tablespoons tomato paste

Combine the flour and spices in a gallon-sized Ziploc bag. Add the meat, seal, and shake until meat is fully coated.

Heat a large Dutch oven with a tight-fitting lid over medium-high heat. Add olive oil. Remove the meat from the bag, shake out the excess flour, and place in Dutch oven. Make sure not to crowd the meat in the pan! Brown the meat evenly. You may have to do several batches, adding another tablespoon of olive oil for each additional batch, and stir occasionally, about 5 minutes.

Remove the meat, set aside, and sauté the onions and garlic until translucent, 5 minutes. Return the meat to the pan and add the remaining ingredients.

Increase the heat and bring to a boil.

Reduce the heat to low, cover, and simmer for 2 hours, or until the meat is tender and done.

Adjust the salt and pepper, if necessary.

Serves 6-8

My Unforgettable Yoli: World's Greatest Flan

It was an incredibly kind gift to a college student barely starting out in life with a huge hunger for cooking and a scant budget to feed it. Yolanda, whom I had left behind in the tropical nest of my home in Venezuela to tackle independence at college in the bitter New England weather, made sure I left in possession of a brand-new blender, just as a mother offers her toddler a pacifier for a long and otherwise tormenting car-ride.

Every weekend I'd call back home to report to my parents on my budding adulthood: yes, I am learning my way around campus, yes, the philosophy professor is amazing even if the class is ridiculously large, and of course, I was making friends and good choices. But the chats I'd most look forward to were the brief and bright ones I'd have with Yoli:

"Como estas, mi amor?" How are you, my love? She'd adoringly ask, and her voice would lap over me like the syrupy molasses generously drizzled over her baked bananas, sticking to my heart and clinging tightly to it; it would inevitably break my streak of independence and I'd feel so very small and sad and lonely without my Yoli to guide and nourish me.

Just when I'd feel I was about to lose it, that it didn't matter if I knew the bus schedule of my new, foreign, city, or whether I'd decided on my major (again) she'd sense that, (because Yoli, who had helped raise me since the day I was born, could sense my every whim) and she'd gently ground me back to my own strength with her next simple but cleverly construed question:

"*Que preparastes hoy, mi amor?*" What did you prepare today, my love? And that would start it, just that: an explosion of quiet descriptions that connected us over miles of distance and cultures and weather, and I would tell her about her *Crema de Berros*, Cream of Watercress soup, that I had whirred to smoothness in the blender (*gracias Yoli*) and how funny that here watercress comes all fancy and shriveled in a pretty packaged bag. Both of us would grow quiet on the line imagining Arturo, the man at the *mercado* a five-minute walk from the house who offers up large bundles of earth-crusted watercress held together by nothing but a piece of loose twine. She'd share her latest recipe with me: she was a voracious reader and an avid cook and this time she'd learned how to up a traditional Nicaraguan dessert of *tres leches* by creating a *cuatro leches* - the fourth milk being coconut cream in addition to the traditional cow's milk, condensed milk, and evaporated. I'd try it when I returned for a visit, I'd promise.

What I would find, when I returned home, was flan, a luxuriously light, chilled custard with sugar caramelized to a deep amber gracing the top.

All the other flans I had tasted were wrong next to this one: too sugary, too dense, too hard. But Yoli's was perfect. And every visit home she'd show me how to make it. The last time she taught me, back in June 2008, I watched and absorbed with the usual enthusiasm, of course, completely unaware that this would be our final flan session together. Three months later, Yoli passed away from an unexpected and aggressive bout with cancer. I miss her smile. I miss her mischief. I miss the way she'd jump to life and recount crazy stories of my youth with such relish you'd think they'd happened only minutes ago. She carried the blueprint of my life with pride and never missed an opportunity to roll it out and share it with the world. I miss our conversations and our lively food connection, but when I make her flan, it is almost, almost, as if she is right there with me.

Yoli's Signature Flan

Yoli used to make her flan in a recycled saltine tin. She'd caramelize her sugar straight out of its dented bottom. On one of my trips back to Venezuela, when, I suppose, she felt my apprenticeship had earned it, she presented me with her beat-up tin: "*Para ti, mi vida*," she offered, beaming with pride. It felt better than winning an Oscar (I think!) – and, even though I had not made it on my own yet, just the love she radiated as she handed it to me assured me that I'd carry on her flan legacy wherever I went. To this day, I make my flan in her tin!

½ cup water

4 cups whole milk

2 cup sugar

6 eggs

1 teaspoon vanilla extract

½ cup dark rum

Preheat the oven to 350°F.

In a heavy saucepan, combine ½ cup water and ½ cup sugar over high heat. Bring to a boil, reduce to medium heat, and cook until the sugar turns caramel color. This, folks, takes a while. It's something that simply cannot be rushed! It's the secret to a great caramel: time. Patience. The sugar has got to bubble away, pretty much untouched (you can swirl it around 2 or 3 times) for about 20 minutes. What you are looking for is a deep amber color. A color that will put your body on high alert and you'll think, "Oh my goodness, I think I just burned this thing!" You want it to get that close. So just watch it like a hawk after minute 15, okay? Because I guarantee you, that puppy can go from talk-of-the-town stellar to bound-for-the-trash disaster in a split second. But you've got this: when the sugar is a dark copper, the bubbles of the sugar are slowing down in their popping, and the sugar looks like it's about to start smoking, that's when you'll take of off the heat.

Pour into an 8" round deep custard pan. Rotate so that the bottom is fully covered by caramel. Set aside.

In a big bowl, combine the remaining ingredients and whisk together.

Pour into the custard pan until it reaches the top (it should reach the very top) and place this pan inside a *bain marie*, another pan partially filled with water.

Bake until the custard sets, 1 - 1 ½ hours.

Remove from the oven and let sit for 2 hours. Refrigerate overnight.

To serve, carefully invert flan into a serving bowl.

Serves 10

Confession of Bologna Love: Biscuits & Gravy

Okay, so I lied. Sometimes it's not all about *foie gras* and truffle oil and *ganache,* sometimes it's about spooning out and gobbling up mayo from the jar and uncontrollable urges for black pepper potato chips (lots of them) and understanding that the ultimate source of a home comfort lunch can be, in moments of angst and trial and turbulence, yes, a *mortadella* sandwich slathered with that glorious mistress mayonnaise again (shun any light version) and a thick slab of hearty tomato on nothing other than a dense and overly processed slice of potato bread. Yes, I could do the *focaccia* or *kalamata* loaf or even multigrain your-colon-thanks-you-greatly stuff, but no, it's the mushy, soft, heavenly bread in the bag that will turn this experience into a religious one.

Bologna love begins early for most of us and I was no exception. I have few memories of those first years of school, but one crystal clear one is the delicious bologna sandwich that lay nestled inside my Six Million Dollar Man metal lunchbox. Eagerly, I'd bypass the sliced carrots, toss the tangerine, save the brownie for last, and pounce into my sandwich. Life was better with a bite of bologna.

I remember the first bologna confession I ever heard. It was from my mother, the most elegant and sophisticated woman on the planet. At 5 foot 9 inches, my mother, with her exquisite blue eyes and dazzling smile, was my own in-house movie star. As a child I constantly boasted about her and followed her every move and even though my father's short genes played the trick of leaving me at a mediocre 5"4, I was inspired to live a life full of grace and glamour because of her.

Cooking was no exception. It was the family joke that before my mother met and married my father she could not even boil water, an image that was inconceivable to my sisters and I, who, desperately trying to make sense of the world, would beg our father to retell the story of our mother learning to cook. My father, who normally did not have the best posture, would instantly perk up, puff out his chest, raise his chin, and pull back his shoulders, as he'd launch into his charismatic storytelling, complete with effusive adjectives and uncontrolled hand gestures, recounting how he slowly and patiently taught my mother the secret of scrambling eggs (slow fire, constant stir) during their courtship. It seemed fitting that the lesson in question revolved around eggs (my father makes the best omelet I have ever sampled) so, I assumed the tale simply pegged her as being a fast learner.

The woman I knew could certainly boil water and so much more. Our dinners were always sublime: from soufflés, to crêpes, to whole beef tenderloin wrapped in thick, smoked bacon (always served with her infallible scalloped potatoes) my mother cooked with the gusto and confidence of Julia Child. There was no culinary hurdle she wouldn't tackle and conquer. Our kitchen was always stocked with the finest ingredients and we were presented with a memorable meal night after night.

Which was why, when I moved with her to the States as a young adult, I was shocked to learn she loved to eat Lebanon bologna, a semi-dry, fermented sausage. I didn't even know what Lebanon bologna was and thought maybe it was some strange Middle Eastern trick around not eating pork. She also revealed her passion for Scrapple, a mush of pork scraps combined with cornmeal and buckwheat flour and shaped into a loaf. In an odd way, it all made sense: these items originated with the Pennsylvania Dutch and resonated with her humble Philadelphia beginnings. As she shifted into adulthood, marriage, and motherhood, raising us in a foreign country carried her away from the possibility of any American pork product bonding.

The two years I spent exploring the lost side of bologna with her in New York reinvented my mother in many ways. While we'd still enjoy perfectly chilled yellow label *Veuve Clicquot* champagne (Brut, of course) and eagerly explored the ever-bustling Manhattan restaurant scene, it was over packages of fried scrapple that she'd share forgotten stories of her youth now suddenly made available by these flavors.

It has been many years since my mother lost her battle to cancer and there are numerous moments in my day that tie me to her one way or another, but my quiet escapades with junky pork products is easily one of my favorites. Her Pennsylvania Dutch favorites are hard to come by in South Florida, so I resort to a southern favorite: Pork Sausage Gravy, which pairs nicely with buttermilk biscuits, and if you're feeling it, a glass of *Veuve Clicquot*.

Pork Sausage Gravy & Biscuits

1 16oz. mild sausage pork roll

2 1/2 tablespoons butter

2 1/2 tablespoons flour

2 cups hot milk

salt and pepper to taste

In a large skillet over medium high heat, brown the pork sausage, making sure to stir and break up the bigger pieces.

Meanwhile, melt the butter in a saucepan over medium high heat. Add the flour and blend, mixing with a wooden spoon. When the flour begins turning golden, gradually add the hot milk with a whisk. Add salt and pepper, to taste.

Reduce heat to low and simmer, stirring constantly, until the sauce thickens, 3 - 5 minutes.

Gradually add the sauce to the pork and stir to combine.

Reduce heat to low and cook for another minute.

Prepare biscuits.

Buttermilk Biscuits:

2 cups all-purpose flour

½ teaspoon baking soda

½ teaspoon salt

½ cup butter, chilled and cut into ½ inch cubes

¾ cup buttermilk

Egg glaze:

1 egg yolk

1 tablespoon cream

Heat the oven to 400°F.

In a medium bowl, stir the flour, baking soda, and salt until mixed.

Cut in the butter using a pastry blender or fork, until the mixture looks like fine crumbs.

Add the buttermilk and stir gently with a spatula, just until combined. It's okay if everything isn't completely incorporated.

Place the dough on a lightly floured surface and gently knead five or six times, just until the dough comes together completely. The less you handle the dough, the better!

Grab a handful of dough and shape it into a 2 ½" circle, then gently pat it down so it resembles a biscuit.

On an ungreased cookie sheet, place biscuits about 1 inch apart for biscuits with crusty sides, or place with sides touching for biscuits with soft sides.

Brush tops with egg glaze.

Reduce oven temperature to 350°F.

Bake 12 to 15 minutes or until golden brown.

Makes 8 biscuits

Split biscuits in half. Place 2 halves on a plate and top with about 1/3 cup gravy.

58   Alona Abbady Martinez

CHAPTER TWO

Ravenous Relationships

Love, City, and Pie: Banana Pudding Pie

I have often been asked for my Banana Pudding Pie recipe so here it is.

But not without a story first.

A story about a guy and a gal, (Husband and I) young and in love, living in that big wonderful island called Manhattan.

Oh, you've heard this story already?

Is Frank Sinatra crooning in the background?

So maybe I need to start it differently.

Like in a dingy narrow diner somewhere in the East Village, somewhere with a very dirty floor.

You wouldn't want to think about eating in a place with a dirty floor, but in this place, you'd make an exception.

I can't remember the name of the place.

It had a heavy wooden door the color of stale blood with a rusted bent pipe lodged in the middle of it as its handle.

Am I selling it to you yet?

No, huh.

Well, stick with me now, stay with the story.

Outside it was always cold. In my memory of this place, at least. New York City stories have so much more punch if it is grey, wet, and chilly outside; the trees in Central Park stripped of their beautiful green leaves.

Of course, we're nowhere near Central Park in this memory.

We're near a lot of city grime and honking angry taxicabs and this faded crimson door you need to dislocate a shoulder to open.

Inside there were eight booths.

The place was stuffy.

But not in a nasty *Damn-I-can-smell-your-feet* kinda way.

Stuffy in that *your-mama's-been-baking-pecan-pie-all-day* way.

Good stuffy.

There was real home-cooking going on for these eight booths parked on this dirty floor hidden by that heavy door somewhere in the lower guts of the city.

The place was always empty, by the way.

Husband and I would meet here often, weave our hectic, separate day into one solid thread that would join at the third booth to the left, our favorite.

I can rattle off the many dishes served here: Cajun Shrimp and Grits, Cornmeal-Dusted Catfish, Honey-Smoked Barbeque Beef Ribs. I'm sure they were all good.

Husband and I never found out, though.

It's a shame, you chastise.

And rightly so.

But there was a strategy involved here.

A need for space.

Because we had figured that after most folks (whom we never saw but trusted found their way here at some point) stuffed themselves on a main course, loaded up with sides of biscuits and collard greens and okra, there came time for dessert.

And at that point, as they placed their dirty napkin on their laps, maybe to hide the unbuttoned button, *because no one needs to know they're not really a 34 waist*, they'd yelp a teeny bit, cursing their impulsive need for meat or chicken or shrimp.

"*If only I hadn't eaten so much*," they'd wail in regret, and then, just because they were there already, and my goodness, how could you go there and pass on dessert, they'd have to order one to share amongst the table.

Order one!

Can you imagine that?

I've got to tell you about the desserts!

There was Peach Cobbler, warm and bubbly, oozing cinnamon and ripe Georgia peach and Red Velvet Cake that rose up shamelessly in moist layers cushioned by tangy whipped cream cheese frosting. There was fresh Blueberry Pie that reminded me of the pie my mother would make when we'd go up to Vermont for the summer and I would be a stubborn teenager determined to be bored and have a horrible time. All that would dissolve when Mom placed that freshly baked indigo beauty on the kitchen counter and I'd become restless and giddy as the 8-year old still trapped inside me and beg my mother to *please, please* cut me a piece now! She would, adding a hearty scoop of vanilla ice cream that magically pooled under the hot trance of blueberry, lemon zest, and sugar, forming a lavender puddle on the side of the plate.

There was Sweet Potato Pie and Chocolate Cake and, of course, there was Banana Pudding Pie, which was the faultless combination of heaven and earth with its fluffy meringue topping and its creamy rich banana pudding floating atop a buttery vanilla wafer crust. One bite and you'd be lost in three time zones of ecstasy: the airy kiss of meringue, the comforting sweetness of banana, and the crunchy chomp of cookies.

Can you imagine being forced to choose from one of these desserts? I'd give up a child easier! (Here, take *this* one...)

So the young lovers (Husband and I) had it all figured out, see.

We'd enter the place starving, sit at the third booth, and hit the desserts.

All of them.

The waitress's eyes bulged a bit the first time we did this.

"What, no dinner?" was all she managed to say.

"No dinner, just dessert," both of us answered in unison, reaching over the table and grabbing hands with a giggle.

Lovebirds, the waitress sighed as she walked away. *They'll never be able to handle it.*

That day we ordered five desserts.

And yes, we *handled it.* The Banana Pudding Pie was amongst the chosen.

The next week we returned and ordered three more, and the Banana Pudding Pie, because we both couldn't stop thinking about it.

The following week the waitress smiled at us and led us to our booth.

We had become regulars.

"Banana Pudding Pie and…," she asked, comfortable with our crazy scheme.

Husband and I looked at each other.

"We'll take two Banana Pudding Pies," we said in harmony, reaching across the table to hold hands and chuckle.

We weren't married at that point, wouldn't get married for another five years or so. But we moved with the ease and comfort of two people that had spent a lifetime together already. We'd definitely shared a lot of pies.

Banana Pudding Pie

For the crust:

    1 (12-oz.) box vanilla wafers, divided

    ½ cup unsalted butter, melted

    2 large bananas, sliced

For vanilla cream filling:

¾ cup sugar

1/3 cup all-purpose flour

2 large eggs

4 egg yolks

2 cups half-and-half

2 teaspoon vanilla extract

For meringue topping:

    4 egg whites

    ½ cup sugar

Set aside 30 vanilla wafers. Pulse the remaining wafers in a food processor 8-10 times or until coarsely crushed (you should have about 2 ½ cups). Stir together the crushed wafers and butter until blended. Firmly press on bottom and sides of a 9-inch pie plate.

Bake at 350°F for 10 to 12 minutes or until lightly browned. Remove to a wire rack and let cool 30 minutes.

Prepare vanilla cream filling:

Whisk together the sugar, flour, eggs, yolks, and half and half in a heavy saucepan. Cook over medium heat, whisking constantly, 8-10 minutes or until it reaches thickness of chilled pudding. Remove from heat and stir in vanilla extract. Use immediately.

Arrange banana slices evenly over bottom of crust. Spread half of hot filling over bananas.

Top with 20 vanilla wafers (filling will be about ¼ inch higher than top edge of crust).

Beat the egg whites at high speed with an electric mixer until foamy. Add the sugar, 1 tablespoon at a time, beating until stiff peaks form and the sugar dissolves.

Spread the meringue evenly over the hot filling, sealing the edges.*

Bake at 350°F for 10 to 12 minutes or until golden brown. Remove from oven and let cool 1 hour on wire rack.

Coarsely crush remaining 10 vanilla wafers and sprinkle evenly over top of pie.

Chill 4 hours.

Serves 8

A word of caution, or advice, or simply observation: You are going to end up with a bowl of fluffy, white meringue cloud. I'm talking TONS of it. Maybe panic seeps in as you wonder how the heck you are supposed to spread this meringue evenly over the 9" pie parameter. Don't let it! Remember this is meant to be tasty, not win any beauty pageants. What I do is plop all that cloud onto the middle of my pie and, with a spatula, work my way towards the edges. Make sure you seal the pie, in other words, the meringue and the pie plate meet. This is actually kind of fun: you are creating a package of goodness! Now, if you want to go all out and design swan figures on your meringue, more power to ya. But if you are like me, you will end up with one beautiful white blob, which you will eventually shower with cookie crumbs at the end.

Raging Bull

The first diploma I ever got hung proudly in the one place I felt people would truly contemplate it: my bathroom wall. I had worked hard to get it and wanted it fully appreciated. The space was small and with few distractions, so I imagined that as folks would go about their business they'd be happy to meet face to face with my accolade and undiverted, contemplate its scholarly script. Plus, it always got a response from the bathroom-goer. Nine times out of ten, any newcomer to my bathroom would exit with a surprised look and say, *'Really? Columbia University? Bartending?'* and (each time!) I would slowly smile and gloat, filled with pride and a sense of never-fading accomplishment because I had snagged a coveted Ivy League education, even if only in the unscholarly art of mixing the perfect *Orgasm*.

There were no all-nighters and brilliant professors behind that piece of paper. No moments where the world was reshaped through relentless academic efforts. Here, there was nothing groundbreaking, just a lot of drinking.

It seemed too curious a juxtaposition to ignore: harbored within one of the most prestigious and rigorous universities was a formal class on the making of drinks, and this was before mixology was in vogue. There was even a syllabus. I am not sure what drove me to take the class more: the free drinks, the promise of making great money, or that desirable Columbia University degree. It has been years since then, but I recall fondly many nights of *Madras Sunsets* and *Ruptured Ducks* and *Sex On the Beach*. The lecture hall would be crammed with eager students watching and feverishly scribbling recipes and concoctions they would later try on all their frat brothers. I brought my own guinea pig with me when I snuck in my boyfriend, whom I ended up marrying several years later. "I'll just act like I belong," he promised, assuring me that attitude and appearance were all that mattered.

The teacher (a slightly drunk older graduate student) would prepare each drink and then ask for volunteers to sample them. Invariably (and I assume in his efforts to "belong") my boyfriend's hand went straight up and the instructor must have appreciated his enthusiasm because he got the drinks most of the time.

As he chugged toxic mixes of vodka, Chambord, triple sec, and lime juice I'd quiz him on his experience. Was it too strong? Too sweet? Refreshing? How many could one enjoy? Ice or no ice? I'd zealously jot down his answers on my yellow bartending notepad, absorbing the drink through his palate. Occasionally I would venture and take a sip of the hard liquor, but my taste buds were always agitated by those attempts, craving much more the soft touch of a cool Friuli wine.

The class was a good three hours long and by the end of it my source of information, whose standard bar order was Diet Coke, was sloshed. My biggest challenge was always balancing his 6'2" 200-pound frame out of the classroom and onto the subway for the ride home. To his credit he was a happy drunk, always compliant and did little more than fall into a heavy sleep and wake up with a bad headache. Still, he was always game for more: insisting I needed to know if a *Mexican Mudslide* was sweeter than a *Blind Russian* (it's not), maintaining I'd have to understand each drink to learn them well, and he, graciously enough, would be willing to comply. It's all in the name of education, and an Ivy League one at that.

In the end it all came down to one recipe. In front of the entire class and a panel of five judges, I would have to pick one index card, amongst a sea of index cards of drinks, and mix it properly. This was my final ticket to that Everest of Academic Achievement: a Columbia degree. It had been weeks of flashcards and a very hungover boyfriend. I couldn't falter now because I knew we both would not survive another ten weeks of this. When it was my turn, I walked up to the stage filled with rows of rainbow-colored liquor bottles and turned to face the five stern-eyed judges, who appeared sober tonight, or at best, cleaned up, because of the suits and ties dutifully donned for the occasion. My fellow peers, a group of about 300 students, held their breath in anticipation. Would I get it right or would I fumble and pick up the Midori or the Bailey's or the go-to mistake of several defeated students before me, the forever favorite white rum? I turned to the judges and valiantly waited for their order. It was a *Raging Bull*. A grin spread over my nervous face as I pictured the image of Robert De Niro's beat-up one in the movie of that same name. I didn't share any of De Niro's demons, though. I knew what I was doing and assembled the drink as if I had made it every night: Kahlua, Sambuca, and tequila, in that order, expertly layered in a shot glass.

I presented the final product as if it were my millionth one, something I chased down with warm milk every night before bed. And I passed with flying colors. Attitude and appearance is key, all things I learned from my drunk boyfriend.

Raging Bull Cocktail

1 jigger (1 ½ oz.) Kahlua

1 jigger (1 ½ oz.) Sambuca

½ jigger Jose Cuervo Tequila

Layer in that order.

Serve to willing partner.

The Crimson Mistress:
Beets Roasted with Sea Salt and Olive Oil

I had all the intentions for a well-balanced meal. I had bought my veal scaloppini for an, albeit, politically incorrect entree, but after an instant sauté carefully paired with fresh lemon sauce, white wine, and plump capers even this milk-fed tender cow would understand why I had to do it. To go with my meat, I had lugged out my super-sized industrial rice maker, whose wide and shiny chrome exterior parallels that of a small car. It came from the top shelf of my garage, buried amongst the cemetery of culinary items I thought I couldn't live without (but turns out I can).

Getting to this rice maker takes some drive, but damn it, I wanted this meal to be perfect and that chromed beauty does wonders with my Basmati, a 20 pound bag I lugged home in a moment of weakness from Costco during one of my hoarding phases. The scratchy sack proudly proclaims these millions of grains (a steal at $9.99) are *"watered by the snow-fed rivers of these mysterious mountains"* and with the Oster Multi-Use Deluxe I swear I really can taste the Himalayan rainwater.

Crisp green beans beckoned to become the vegetable side dish for the event. Rinsed and cut into symmetrical 1 ½ inch pieces, they waited to be simmered in olive oil with some slivered garlic, onions and coarse sea salt and then to be topped with thick slices of Florida tomatoes that had ripened on my window sill. The meal was a simple one, but well designed and satisfying, where each dish got along with the other like a happy family.

And then there were the beets.

Just the way their lush, dark green stems peeked out of the brown paper bag was a tease. Immediately, I became distracted. I knew I should most likely close the fridge and continue with the safe preparations of my pre-planned meal, but I couldn't. I pulled the bag out of the fridge and removed them, exposing five dark purple curvy bulbs powdered in fresh dirt. Their primal presentation was exciting, a refreshing change from the pre-packaged, sanitized, smell-less food options we have grown accustomed to. I had been looking forward to my meal of veal, rice, and green beans but now all I could think about were these wild, lonely beets. I wondered what to do with them, what role they would play in the evening's culinary production. Somehow, they had to be included. Would I throw them into my green bean dish for a final crimson touch? Perhaps grate them raw on top of crisp Boston lettuce, bathing the whole thing with a citrusy vinaigrette?

Mingling them with the others seemed an injustice. I didn't want them to meet, didn't want the flavors to match up. I knew they would get along (beets are wonderful additions to so many dishes) but tonight, these beets felt special, they felt mine, and I wanted to enjoy them for who they are and not try to blend them into someone else's flavor.

I was filled with momentary guilt as I glanced at my lovely combo of veal, rice, and green beans waiting to be prepared. They seemed to smile in their bags and packages, promising that after a quick and painless preparation, I would be entitled to a very predictably satisfying meal. I knew this. I wanted to do this, but the dirt from the beet had already slipped under my fingernails and I could feel its grittiness pulling me in.

    I had to rinse these and give them center stage. Afterwards, I would turn back to the others. I decided to roast my precious beets. This would guarantee their flavor not be tarnished or altered but rather enhanced and celebrated. *It was all about them tonight,* I thought to myself as I carefully wrapped each one in tin foil. I didn't know what I would do with them after I roasted them. We were dancing this *paso doble* one step at a time, my beets and I. All I knew is that I needed to pop them in this 400° oven and wait for magic to begin to happen and just the thought of that made me so impatient and eager, I didn't think I'd be able to wait.

    A rich velvety fragrance filled the room thirty minutes later. It assaulted my senses and captured my heart and I found myself standing in front of my oven, mesmerized by that warm, earthy scent. I yearned to taste this smell. Under that spell, I wanted to be eating this source of earth, this root of life, right here, right now, and experience pleasure in a way I never had before. This crimson mistress had fogged my mind and senses.

    Barely pausing to put on some oven mitts, I pulled the baked beauties out and tore their foiled wardrobe off them, exposing dark, blushed skin. I envisioned presenting them at least a fancy home to sit centerpiece: perhaps some freshly snipped *arugula* with its sharp, peppery bite offering a cool contrast to the beet's mellow sweetness. I'd bathe them lightly with some roasted pumpkin seeds for that final crunch. Thick stalks of heart of palms beckoned as another alternative. I'd slice these into broad 2" rings and pair them with quartered hard-boiled eggs, fresh dill, and lime honey vinaigrette.

But in the end, I tossed all my ideas of culinary grandeur out the window and enjoyed them in the most immediate way a lover would: standing over my stove, beets barely peeled and quartered, I ate them straight up, only stopping on occasion to dip them in a Dijon vinaigrette I happened to have on hand. It was a delectable experience: one I had no control over, but rather allowed to control me.

I closed my eyes and ate and ate and ate. *'Keep some for later'*, I said to myself. *'Keep some for one of those salads'*, I begged. *'Stop this and fix your veal'*. But I couldn't listen to myself then. It was a lost cause. I hoped the veal would understand and would forgive me. I knew I had all the right intentions, but in the end, all the right intentions led me straight to a delicious dinner of roasted beets, where the only hints of the affair were the smile on my face and my crimson-tainted fingertips.

Roasted Beets

Preheat the oven to 400°F. Wrap six beets, washed thoroughly but not peeled, in aluminum foil and bake on a cookie sheet until tender when poked, around 45 minutes (time varies with size of the beets).

For those willing to wait a few minutes more, I offer this ethereal salad:

Roasted Beet Salad with Goat Cheese, Greens & Curry-Spiced Sunflower Seeds

2 roasted beets, chopped in 1" cubes

2 cups of your favorite greens (sweet pea greens or arugula works nicely)

2 ounces soft goat cheese, crumbled

1 ounce marinated artichoke hearts, drained

4 tablespoons curry-spiced sunflower seeds *(recipe follows)*

3 tablespoons honey-balsamic vinaigrette *(recipe follows)*

Curry-spiced sunflower seeds:

½ cup shelled sunflower seeds

2 tablespoons grapeseed oil

¼ teaspoon black pepper

1/2 teaspoon salt

1 teaspoon curry powder

1 teaspoon smoked paprika

¼ teaspoon cayenne pepper

In a small skillet, heat grapeseed oil on medium heat. Add seeds and sauté until brown, 3 minutes.

Meanwhile, mix the remaining ingredients in a bowl.

When seeds are ready, toss them in mixture until fully coated.

Toasted seeds will keep several weeks in an airtight container.

Makes ½ cup

Honey-Balsamic Vinaigrette:

Goes great with this salad…and many more!

½ cup extra virgin olive oil

¼ cup balsamic vinaigrette

2 tablespoons Dijon mustard

2 tablespoons honey (use your favorite- I love my local Florida orange blossom honey!)

1 teaspoon salt

½ teaspoon pepper

2 garlic cloves, crushed (use the side of a butcher knife or smash it with the bottom of a frying pan)

Place all ingredients in a vinaigrette pourer, or, if you don't have one, just use a plain glass jar. Seal. Shake! Shake! Shake! Use for all your salads! (There is no "correct" amount- some people like their salads extra soaked, other, super-duper dry!) Keep it in the fridge and just give it another quick shake when you want to use it again.

Makes 1 cup, good for one week.

Assemble salad:

Use your prettiest serving bowl! Place the lettuce mix as the base of your salad, then add pieces of beets and crumbled goat cheese. Top with curry-spiced sunflower seeds and honey-balsamic vinaigrette. You can either serve it like that or mix it all up before bringing it to the table.

Serves 2

Dancing for Dessert: *Ile Flottante*

Dishonesty is an ugly beast. Even more so when it rears its unsightly head between a man and his wife. Like last night. When I opened the garage fridge. Sparks flew. And not the kind that leave behind broken bedposts or sleepless neighbors (or both.)

"Did you... (pause, as a sense of betrayal/loss/shock glazes over me) ...was it you who?" (Pause again, more betrayal/loss/shock.)

"It's not what it looks like!" he shouted, a bit too automatically.

"I just went to the garage fridge to get some Parmesan cheese and I saw..."

"Look, it's just once in a while. It doesn't mean much, um, anything. Doesn't mean *anything* at all, really." His eyes look at me sharply, brow furrowed, muscles tense: this is the look of a scared man. And then a whisper, "I love you."

"So the *Ile Flottante* from last Wednesday..." I begin to ask in a loud voice, the shock quickly being replaced by anger. I feel my left eye start to twitch.

"Spectacular," he bounces back, hopeful. He is hopeful, I see it now. Hopeful this will end with just one compliment to distract me. Hopeful I will not dive into the gravity of the situation. Hopeful it isn't me, the gourmand, he is talking to right now.

"And the clementine *Clafoutis* from Monday was..." I trailed off, waiting.

"Phenomenal. Exquisite. I loved the tango between the creaminess and citrus."

He is reaching now. I know it, because he used the word tango to describe my dessert. Tango, the lover's dance. He could have said anything, but *he* chose the word. And if he knew anything, if he had any notion of this lover's dance, where bodies swoon sexually as one, *adelante*, the move describing going forward paired with *costado*, moving together to the side, this is a dance of communication, of passion, of lust... None of which was going down here next to the garage fridge. And yet he chose the word tango. These things do not happen by accident.

"Strawberry tart?" I bark. "*Dulce De Leche* Cupcakes?" I continue, my voice shrill. "My mother's extraordinary one-of-a-kind Lemon Freeze Pie? These mean *nothing* to you?"

The tiniest bead of sweat escapes from his disheveled sideburn and I wonder where he will take this next.

"Delightful. Scrumptious. Amazing. Memorable." He recites all these like a child studying for the Spelling Bee. "It's just that sometimes, I want a bite of Jell-O," he offers flatly.

"*Sugarless* Jell-O," I correct him, the image of this discovery in the garage fridge burning bright in my mind, not knowing which word is a worse crime in this culinary crisis.

"Sugarless. Jell-O," he concedes, defeated.

I throw a steely stare in his direction for added theatrics and realize a look of relief has spread across his face. A burden lifted?

A secret revealed? Would this mean that Jell-O would now parade freely amongst us? The thought of neon green, orange, and red plastic cups sharing space with my thoughtfully concocted creations in the main fridge was too much to bear and for a brief second I wished I had never gone looking for that wedge of Parmesan cheese.

"Fine." I huff. "Keep it in the back fridge," I command, laying a false sense of control over the situation. This is the dance he desires. Now he waves the white flag.

"Since you mentioned it," he offers, sauntering up to me and boldly placing his hands on my waist "that *Ile Flottante* sounds pretty good to me..." *Adelante!*

ILE FLOTTANTE (FLOATING ISLAND)

This was the presidential dessert growing up in my house: the one my mother made when someone important from work came over and my charismatic father wanted to make sure the deal was sealed with just a bit more dazzle, though he surely had plenty. I always thought it was terribly complicated to make, it effused such sophistication, but, I am happy to add that it is not only delicious, but simple.

- 4 cups milk
- ¾ cups sugar
- 2 teaspoons vanilla extract

6 eggs, separated

½ teaspoon corn starch

¼ teaspoon salt

¼ cup rum

Caramel:

½ cup sugar

¼ cup water

In a large skillet, bring four cups of milk to a boil over medium-high heat. Reduce to a simmer on medium-low.

Add 6 tablespoons of the sugar and vanilla extract and stir to dissolve.

Beat egg whites until soft peaks form. Add 6 tablespoons sugar, cornstarch, and salt and continue beating until peaks become stiff.

Use two large spoons to scoop up the egg whites and shape into ovals, dropping them into simmering milk.

Cook 30 seconds and then gently flip the egg whites over. Poach another 30 seconds.

Drain the egg whites on paper towels, letting them cool.

Strain the milk and pour it back into the skillet. Keep the heat on medium-low.

Beat egg yolks until light and lemon-colored and gradually pour into the milk, stirring constantly with a whisk. The custard should begin to thicken.

Add rum and stir another minute.

Pour the custard into a wide, shallow serving dish. Add the egg whites and chill at least 4 hours, preferably overnight.

Prepare caramel:

Combine ½ cup sugar and ¼ cup water in a saucepan.

Bring to a boil and reduce heat to medium-high, stirring until the sugar turns dark amber color. Keep an eye on it as it can burn quickly!

Drizzle hot caramel over the tops of the egg whites.

Serves 8-10 lucky people

FLIRTING WITH FLAVOR: CLEMENTINE *CLAFOUTIS*

When the word rolled off my tongue my dinner guest blushed and gently requested I not talk dirty to him, since, after all, we were both married and not to each other. As tempting and natural as it is for me to combine passion with food, my intentions tonight were purely innocent. Tonight I was merely dancing around my introduction for the French dessert I was eagerly pulling out of the oven, a dessert whose name alone guaranteed, at the very least, the same sigh of pleasure brought by a carefree Saturday afternoon romp in the sack.

"Cla-foo what?" my guest inquired, twirling his banged-up wedding band.

"*Clafoutis*," I clarified, explaining that the dish is pronounced "cla-foo-tee" and is a custard-based batter mixed with fruit, typically cherries. I emphasized that if pudding is the epitome of the American comfort dessert, then *clafoutis* most definitely should serve as France's, only healthier because of the fruit thrown in. I lost my guest at "tee", which was right and expected. And I noticed, for some odd reason, he was still blushing.

The minute this dessert, which is best served warm out of the oven, arrived at the table, everyone was silenced and dazzled. Mind you, this was one of those evenings where I had no clue what I'd produce for the meal's finale and had to come up with something good and quick in a hurry. *Clafoutis* is a reliable and phenomenal showstopper. The freshness of the dessert makes its shelf-life a nano-second, which is a good thing, because this treat usually gets gobbled up in one sitting. Oh, and your guests will be wowed beyond belief. They'll think you are a culinary genius, and as they look at that round, delicious dessert bursting with fresh fruit teasing through a gentle sprinkling of powdered sugar (there's something to be said about sprinkled powdered sugar on *anything*) they may even want to sleep with you. They certainly will think about lazy Saturday afternoons. So serve *clafoutis* at your own risk and wear your new undies, (because you just never know), and enjoy this spectacular dessert either way.

Clementine Clafoutis

(Adapted from Mark Bittman)

Exquisitely floral and smooth. Of course, *clafoutis* is a most flexible dessert and will work well with many fruits, so poke around your fridge for any forgotten ones: peaches, plums, or pears. Dried fruits (apricots or prunes) will also serve as proud stand-ins.

- Unsalted butter as needed
- 1/2 cup flour, more for dusting pan
- 2 eggs
- 1 tablespoon mayonnaise
- 1/2 cup granulated sugar
- Pinch salt

1 cup heavy cream

½ cup milk

6 fresh clementine's, peeled and sliced into 1" rings, about 3 cups

½ teaspoon clementine zest

½ teaspoon vanilla extract

powdered sugar

Heat oven to 350°F.

Prepare a gratin dish, about 9 by 5 by 2 inches, or a 10-inch round deep pie plate or porcelain dish, by smearing it with butter, just a teaspoon or so. Dust it with flour, rotating the pan so the flour sticks to all the butter; invert the dish to get rid of the excess.

In a large bowl, whisk the eggs until frothy. Add mayonnaise. Add the granulated sugar and salt and whisk until combined. Add the cream and milk and whisk until smooth. Add 1/2 cup flour and stir just to combine.

Layer the clementine sections in the dish; they should come just about to the top. Pour the batter over fruit. Bake for about 50 minutes, or until *clafoutis* is nicely browned on top and a knife inserted into it comes out clean. Sift some powdered sugar over it and serve warm.

Clafoutis does not keep; serve within a couple of hours of making it.

Serves 6-8

COCONUT LOVE: COCONUT CAKE

If I had another child it would be made out of coconut. Because anything made out of coconut is smooth and creamy and simply exquisite. It wouldn't talk back or whine or demand to be fed. It wouldn't wear diapers, strain mortgages, or keep me up at night with worry.

It would be tall and ethereal and covered in meringue fluff. The inside would be a rich, decadent buttercream frosting, and I would play with it, *play play play* with it on its own clean cake stand. I'd twirl and whirl and smooth and shape, and it would glisten and mold just for me.

My family would declare me nuts. *First she names raw poultry, then her appliances, and now this?* It may be too much for them, and they are a forgiving bunch. But they'd see the happiness in my eyes, and my children, wise beyond their years, would know that Mom wasn't replacing them with a coconut cake, she was just loving them more *because of* it. (The fact that she'd forgotten they passed their TV limit a half an hour ago was merely a bonus.)

But they love their mom, even when she sings (although they claim to hate her singing, they really do love it) and there she would be, cake scraper in hand, a bowl full of sweet fluffiness beside her, and her newborn baby cake growing and spinning and she'd be singing, not your ordinary lullaby - because such a child would demand something different - something more potent and self-assured, as this coconut cake would surely be, would summon something only

Ella Fitzgerald could pull off, a Cole Porter special of course, and she'd sing:

"You do (spin), something to me (spin, spin), something that simply mystifies me (more meringue topping now.)"

Eventually Husband would come back from one of his many business trips (oh don't ask me, I've lost track of what country he is in now.) But the important thing is he would return and he'd greet his two children with all the love and affection that he holds for them in his heart and builds with longing when he is away from them. And mid-way through that lovefest something would tug at him ever so gently, something in the pit of his stomach would whisper that he should look up, and he would, tenderly turning his eyes above his children's frame (not in a neglectful manner as he'd still have them clasped in his embrace) and there he'd meet her third child, now a big and proudly, deliciously, shaped coconut cream cake. His eyes would widen, fighting all the sleep his body ached for and his mouth would instantly shape itself into a miniature 'o' as the slightest greeting would escape his mouth and he'd croon, *"Ooooooh."*

And now he'd get up from his children, because he loves them dearly and they know that, but sometimes being tactful is a challenge for him and he'd hugged them and he *will* play with them later, he knew he would, but right now this coconut cake demanded his attention because he knew it was his wife's work of love and in it he'd find pleasures not found elsewhere. And so, without a second thought a sharp knife would be quickly in his hand and already digging its way through the coconut cake's tender interior.

He'd carve out the first piece and it would give way to his plate showing a pale and light complexion filled with coconut butter cream and framed in fluffy meringue topping. He'd bite and close his eyes, because one could not eat this with external distractions and he'd be absorbed in the impossible contrast of richness and buttery lightness all at once, and there was the coconut flavor, subtle but strong, and the foamy lightheartedness of the meringue topping with a tinge of something familiar, what was it, vanilla? And most importantly it was his wife, his wife and her passion for this cake, a cake she'd deem her third child, that embraced him strongest and filled him with warmth and love and soul. For he traveled everywhere and led a rootless life, but when he bit into that, her creation, he held on to her tightly, loving her completely and was home.

COCONUT CAKE

(Adapted from Celebrate! by the late and great Sheila Lukins)

For the cake:

    1 cup unsalted butter, softened

    2 cups sugar

    1 teaspoon coconut extract

    2 large egg yolks

    3 cups sifted all-purpose flour

4 teaspoons baking powder

1 teaspoon salt

½ cup milk

½ cup sour cream

4 large egg whites

For the frosting:

1 cup granulated sugar

4 large egg whites

½ teaspoon cream of tartar

1 tablespoon pure vanilla extract

Preheat the oven to 350°F.

Butter and flour two 9-inch round cake pans.

Prepare the cake:

Cream the butter and 1 cup sugar until light and fluffy, about 5 minutes. Add the coconut extract. Then add the egg yolks, one at a time, beating well after each addition.

Sift the flour, baking powder, and salt together in another bowl.

In a smaller bowl, combine the milk and sour cream.

Add one third of the flour mixture to the butter mixture, beating on low speed until it is incorporated. Add half the milk mixture and beat until incorporated. Repeat until fully incorporated.

In a separate bowl with clean beaters, beat the egg whites on medium/high speed until they are foamy, 2 minutes. Add the remaining 1 cup sugar, increase speed to high and whip the whites until soft peaks form, 3 to 4 minutes. Fold half of the whites gently into the cake batter, using a large rubber spatula. Then gently fold the remaining whites into the batter until just combined. Don't overmix!

Scrape the batter evenly into pans and cook until the center comes out clean, 25 minutes. Cool on wire rack for 10 minutes, then remove from pans and cool completely.

Split each layer in half horizontally with a serrated knife. Wrap the layers in plastic wrap and chill in the refrigerator for 2 hours or overnight.

Prepare the frosting:

Place the sugar, the egg whites, ¼ cup water, and cream of tartar in the top of a double boiler over simmering water. Beat with an electric mixer on high speed until very firm, 7 minutes. Remove from the heat and add vanilla extract. Beat until the frosting is cooled and holds a stiff peak.

As soon as the frosting is made, assemble the cake. Place 1 cake layer, cut side down, on a serving plate. Spread it with frosting. Repeat with 2 more layers (always spread on smooth side to avoid crumbs). Top with the remaining cake layer.

Immediately frost the sides and top of the cake with the remaining frosting. Swirl it on with a frosting knife. This cake is best served on the day it is frosted.

Serves 8-10

Confessions of a Serial Crust Killer: Blondies

Something strange started to happen along my mother-baker way.

I began cutting crusts off things.

All things.

And I love crust.

Crunchy, chewy, hearty, crust.

There's nothing quite like it.

But then I had children.

(Ahhh, it's always the children...)

And crusts started coming off.

Freely.

Wildly.

Unabashedly.

No one was safe.

It was the Reign of Terror all over again, only, instead of heads, it was crusts.

Perfectly good sandwiches, really, better with the crust, were decapitated, sneakily and with sharp knives.   No questions asked.

Battling the undisputed precision of Zorro.

One minute whole, proud units of flavor, the next, an emaciated, emasculated memento of its former self.

From there the cruelty continued and I moved on to baked goods.

Cute toddlers have a way of wrapping themselves around my heart and making me forget reason, a feature most potent when said toddlers are mine. Those grubby faces and clover honey eyes practically forced me to do it when they stared up at me and pleaded,

"Mommy, the one without the crust," signaling with a dirty finger the cube of brownie smack in the center of the pan.

And so I complied.

What else does a mother do?

And carved that one piece for the child.

Dug it out like an Aztec priest would dig out the beating heart of their bravest warriors giving themselves to their sun god atop the Great Pyramid of Tenochtitlan.

Sloppy like that.

People would cheer when that beating heart emerged into the sunlight in all its glory.

In my house, two children hooted with delight when the crustless gooey brownie finally came out.

"Yes, Mommy! Yes! Me too! Me too! I want that one!" The other grubby toddler now pointed to the partner brownie next to the vacant space.

You know how it is with revolutions.

It only takes one, then all the others follow.

So I spent years carving out the guts of my delicious concoctions.

Grandma's Famous Fudge Brownies.

Butterscotch Squares.

Jane's Lemon Bites.

Mississippi Mud Bars.

You name it. They were all destroyed Under the Influence of Clover Honey Eyes.

Until the day Husband stumbled upon the massacre I left behind.

Husband is brilliant, you see, you must understand this to understand fully what happened next.

He catches every detail of life.

Every.

Single.

One.

If the paint has chipped on the upper right hand corner of the far wall in your office, a room he rarely enters and you spend your entire life in, he will catch that.

If the woman three seats down in the doctor's waiting room, the one coughing incessantly into the plastic plant to her left, was

My Culinary Compulsion 97

your former boss's sister you both met once twenty years ago at a fundraiser, he will remind you.

And yes, if the butcher's wife isn't the killer, even though the movie has set you up to swear, to believe, to *know* it is her, but you've failed to pick up on the slight twitch in her left forefinger, a clue fundamental in realizing she was not able to proceed with the crime, why, yes, Husband caught the twitch the second it first happened and promptly let you know four minutes into the whole thing: *she didn't do it.*

Talk about a spoiler alert.

If you deduct a trace of annoyance in me, why, I'd be obliged to call you perceptive. But rest assured, my irritation is rooted in jealousy, nothing more, nothing less.

My office ceiling can be falling on my head and I would not notice.

My former boss's sister could have donated 20 million dollars to my personal cause and I still would not remember her.

And the killer? I would have been stunned to learn it wasn't the wife even after the big twist was revealed and the credits were done rolling.

For the most part, I consider myself fortunate to be paired with such a hyper-aware partner. It's good to have someone remind you to look up and notice how awesome the cloud formations are or that your accountant has begun parting his hair on the right side. And then, of course, there are the times when such hyper-awareness works in my favor.

Like now.

This time.

At the destruction of my Blondies.

Nothing was left on the battlefield but crusts.

All the plump crustless bodies were packed away in a Tupperware safely for the children.

Who were no longer toddlers, I may add, but rather gangly teenagers trapped in that odd vortex between child and adult.

Hopelessly addicted to their crustless goodies.

Husband sees the baking pan.

A pan whose scraps I am about to discard.

And observes.

Astutely.

Intelligently.

"Why, this is wonderful! You've left me all the crusts!"

And there was joy and a bit more twinkling in his eye fueled by That Feeling of Love.

You know the look when Guy and Gal first hook up and every action is accompanied by that adoring stare?

I was being stared at this way now. A stare that celebrated me as utterly and completely beloved.

He grabbed a long piece of cut-up crust and took a sizable bite.

"Hmmmm, perfect," he munched loudly.

He took what was left and dipped it in his coffee.

The piece was thin and long and crunchy with chunks of chocolate warming to a melt and the scent of spicy cinnamon filling the air as it gave way luxuriously to the steamy Arabica blend.

"Great idea," he concluded after wolfing down two crust pieces. "Make sure to separate the crusts every time!" He added, contentedly taking the last sip of his, now sweetened, mocha.

I could take this moment to clarify to him. To explain the History of the Crusts. How I didn't mean to do it, it all started with an innocent grilled cheese sandwich, years ago and now I just can't stop. How, unlike the butcher's wife, I don't have a twitch on my left forefinger. But, I choose not to. Adoration is intoxicating and I don't want to spoil that with a rambling explanation which would also highlight the apparent slip-up in his acute observatory skills I was just bragging about. Instead, I offer a sweet smile and make a mental note. Sometimes things are better left unsaid.

Blondies

Some like their blondies super-gooey. I like mine on the drier side: great for dipping into a morning latte!

1 cup sugar

¾ cup unsalted butter, softened

2 eggs

1 teaspoon vanilla extract

2 cups flour

1 teaspoon baking soda

1 teaspoon salt

1 teaspoon ground cinnamon

8 oz. chocolate morsels

¾ cup walnuts, toasted and chopped *(see page xxv)*

Preheat the oven to 350°F.

Beat the sugar with the butter until it is light and fluffy. You can never do this long enough, so, best to put it in your stand mixer and pop in that old Jane Fonda Aerobics VHS you have hidden behind Your Life.

Beat in the eggs, one at a time.

Add the vanilla extract.

Sift the flour, baking soda, salt, and ground cinnamon, or be lazy like me, plop it in a bowl and stir it around with a whisk. Same thing, I promise. Same enough, at least.

Stir into the batter.

Add 6 ounces of the chocolate morsels.

Stir in the nuts.

Place in greased 13-inch x 9-inch pan. Sprinkle remaining 2 ounces of chocolate morsels on top.

Bake 25-30 minutes.

Cool in pan.

Cut the crazy way: a long slice alongside the border of the pan (about ½ inch thick for the best crust pieces). Save these strips for coffee and great husbands. The inside will now be crustless, ready for spoiled children.

Makes 12 3" blondies

Triumph of the Toastmaster

I slipped into a food lover's coma this weekend, offering up a plethora of culinary clichés such as broiled lobster tails, filet mignon wrapped in bacon, and fresh strawberry tart.

Husband and I indulged with gluttony, but the fun didn't stop there: there were mounds upon mounds of slow-roasted asparagus in balsamic glaze, sea salt crusted baby gold potatoes, and baked grouper in creamy jalapeño sauce, all cooked to perfection. Our feasts were so excessive and exuberant that we barely had enough time to bat eyelashes at each other as we gorged in unison, only taking small breaks to sigh in contentment and comment on how much we loved the food (oh, and each other). It was a glorious two days and when it ended I felt blissful and renewed, even if it was with an extra pound or two on my waistline.

Kissing my man as he left for his weeklong work trip that following Monday, I couldn't help but bask in the good fortune of having both a soul mate that enjoys eating as much as I do and a fabulous oven to bake in. Dizzy with happiness, I skipped back to my boudoir (a.k.a. kitchen) where all this love happens and decided to continue the celebration with a batch of mini carrot muffins.

As the oven preheated, I sang to Lulu, my red hot mixer, and began whipping up the spicy mélange. Lulu was fast and efficient and soon the batter was tucked inside miniscule muffin tins and ready to be baked. All was well until I opened up the oven, muffin tins in hand, and was shocked to find it stone cold.

Had I forgotten to turn it on, I wondered to myself, knowing this wasn't true but not really surprised- what if dementia had set in early? I checked the electric panel and found that although it promised a 350° F heat, it was only delivering a cold hum.

The hairs on my neck stood up as my first warning, followed by shortness of breath and a feeling of doom in the pit of my stomach. This was the beginning of a panic attack. OH NO OH NO OH NO! I had envisioned many horrible things in my lifetime, but never my sleek, expensive, and indispensable oven not working for me! Who was I without the ability to bake?

Moving quickly, I ran through my limited technical expertise: flipping switches and fuses on and off, counting to ten before beginning anew, turning the broiler from low to medium to high, switching from baking to convection features; even prayer: *'Barukh ata Adonai Eloheinu melekh ha-olam...ha tanoor sheli lo oved?!'* But nothing seemed to reboot my oven back to life. The carrot muffins began looking glum and hopeless sagging in their tins.

Depression and anger replaced my failed repair attempts and I grew more frustrated with the expensive appliance that was supposed to stand by me for many more years to come. "But I made lobster tails!" I wailed, demanding an explanation. "Yesterday! How could this be?"

A kitchen can get eerily quiet when reprimanded and that is what happened to mine. Lulu stood still, her paddle still messy with raw dough. She dared not say anything, although I knew she was secretly disgusted by Oven's failure ('I would never let her down like that', her bright red sheen seemed to shout). Fridge just hummed, always happy to be a witness to disaster, but grateful not to be the cause of it this time (remember the leak in '02?), and then, off in the corner, next to the canisters of sugar and flour, was my beat-up, abandoned Toastmaster oven, carried from house to house with me like a chewed-up stuffed animal I no longer need but can't live without. It wanted to shout out a big "Hey look at me, here I am, here I am" but was afraid I was too angry to listen.

My muffin batter insisted I pay closer attention to my long-neglected alternative baking source, and so I turned Toastmaster's long-neglected dial to 350° degrees. Only one tin could fit, so it took quite a while to get them all done, but as I watched and beseeched all the Kitchen Deities to save my muffins, I recalled fondly how my cooking frenzy first took off years ago inside the cozy space of a toaster oven much like this one. My first apartment had a cramped kitchen with no stove, only two hot plates and an ancient Toastmaster with a broken handle. That didn't stop me from running full throttle on culinary zeal. Out of that miniscule space came many fabulous meals: freshly baked profiteroles, lemon meringue pie, orange roasted chicken, rabbit braised with tapenade.

As incapacitated posh Oven gawked on the sidelines, I gave Toastmaster center stage, baking tin after tin of deliciously moist and delectable mini carrot muffins. Just as I had years before, I poured all my culinary energy into this abandoned appliance, and, once again, it didn't let me down, giving me a scrumptious treat and a chance to reconnect with that youthful spirit that knows bigger is not always better. I knew Oven was miffed. She was fuming without even turning on. But in that moment, pulling out muffins at, perhaps a slower pace, but equally tasty, I was happy, I knew I'd be fine. Sometimes you've got to go back to basics, do away with the diva in your kitchen, and see how well you'll manage, how you'll even thrive.

Carrot Spice Mini Muffins

(Adapted from Kosher By Design, Susie Fishbein)

1 cup sugar

1 cup all-purpose flour

¾ cup canola oil

12 ounces baby food carrot

1 teaspoon baking soda

1 ½ teaspoons ground cinnamon

½ teaspoon ground nutmeg

¼ teaspoon ground cloves

¼ teaspoon ground ginger

¼ teaspoon allspice

2 eggs

Preheat the Toaster Oven (or regular oven!) to 350°F.

Combine all the ingredients in a mixing bowl and mix on medium speed for 3 minutes. (Alternatively, you can use a handheld mixer).

Place paper muffin cups into mini muffin tin.

Fill each cup until it is ¾ full. *

Bake 18-20 minutes (stick a toothpick in the center of a muffin and it should come out clean).

Allow muffins to cool for 10 minutes.

*Pour batter into a mixing cup and pour into muffin paper.

Makes 2 dozen mini muffins

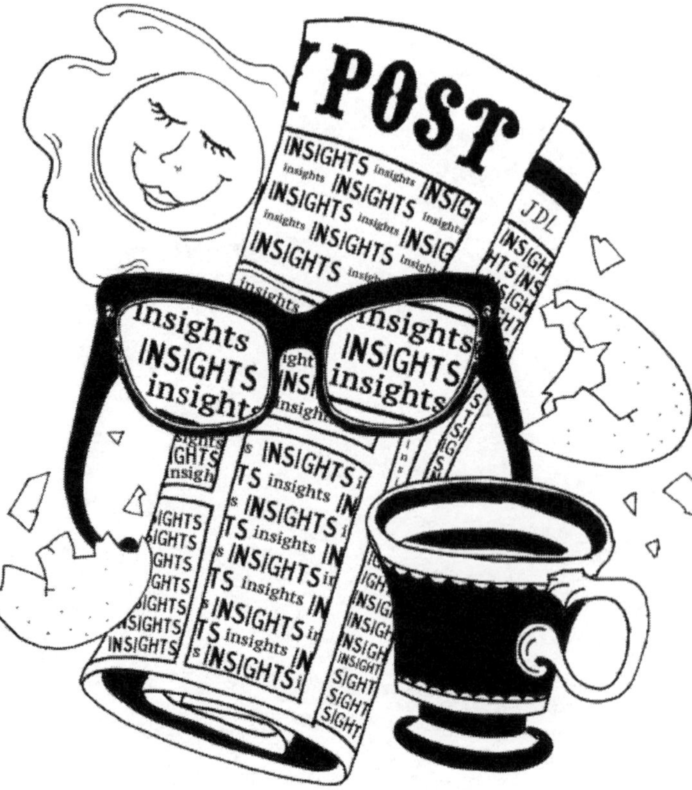
POST
JDL
insights
INSIGHTS
insights

CHAPTER THREE

Everyday Insights

Forget the Yacht: I'll Take a Steak

"I feel like running away to some foreign, exotic country...by myself," were not the reassuring words Husband (calling from the disconnected distance of Mexico) hoped to hear from his wife, but it was the answer he got nevertheless. Not even the award-winning Merlot he had brought back from a tiny, dusty vineyard visited in Argentina seemed to ease the strain of being the sole caregiver of two young children 24/7. Glass two was empty and the options had narrowed themselves to Turkey or Greece as destinations for my escape.

Husband was smart enough to sense that whatever reply he offered would invariably get him in trouble, so he spoke extra slowly, as if verbal speed bumps would guarantee him some sort of half victory in the conversation:

"...Escape ...to...a foreign...country? "

There was a second or two where he seriously questioned whether or not I actually planned to follow through on my declaration, and when he decided he believed me, I, for that split second, did too, instantly imagining myself being photographed by hordes of hungry paparazzi while I lounged around in a seven-million-dollar yacht off the coast of Mykonos. It sounded good. I already felt tan. Until I heard a six-year old squeal:

"ESCAPE TO A FOREIGN COUNTRY???" And was catapulted back to my reality: a suburban evening teeming with unmade beds, backed-up loads of dirty laundry, two highly energetic kids, and

Husband AWOL on another business trip. The only thing going for me was my dinner plans of Steak *au Poivre* with Watercress.

The first time I'd been privy to such a mix was in the dark, damp corner of *Le Coq D'Or* restaurant, a French culinary secret in a sinister, unforgiving street in Caracas. This was my parents' all-time favorite restaurant, and, after we braved the less-than desirable neighborhood, we'd enter the tiny establishment and be greeted by an art exhibit serving tribute to fighting cocks: a tradition still practiced in parts of Venezuela today.

Paintings and sculptures of all sizes lined the walls celebrating this disturbing cultural custom. I managed to disengage from the artwork, as well as the name of the restaurant, because I knew the culinary rewards far outweighed any ethical ones.

My parents began their experience at the overcrowded bar with a series of, what they described as, 'the best whiskey sours on this earth.' Then we would be seated at a small, dark booth where we'd all instinctively order the house special: Steak *au Poivre* with Watercress. The steak was served simply: swimming in a silky ocean of creamy melted butter and speckled with plump peppercorns, its red juices comingling with the crisp and pungent mound of fresh watercress served as the sole accompaniment. I remember closing my eyes as a forkful of crisp watercress mixed with the softness and full-flavor of rare steak. If you were lucky, you'd also get a peppercorn or two mixed in there. I would yearn to repeat that bite over and over and over again, asking my parents with predictable regularity when we would be returning to *Le Coq D'Or*.

I have no tributes to cockfighting in my home (if you don't count my children pitted against each other over the remote), but every once in a while, when the day has been a rough one and I peer out the garden window in search of the yacht, I settle my craving for escape with steak and watercress, just as they served in *Le Coq D'Or*.

Quick Steak *Au Poivre* with Watercress

- 2 marbled strip steaks, about 1 ½ pounds total
- 2 tablespoons whole peppercorns (can be black or combination of green, red, and pink)
- ¾ teaspoon kosher salt
- 1 teaspoon parsley garlic salt
- 4 tablespoons unsalted butter
- 1 tablespoon canola oil

For the watercress:

- 2 cups washed watercress
- 1 tablespoon extra-virgin olive oil
- 2 tablespoons fresh lime juice
- sea salt, to taste

Coat the steaks with the peppercorns, salt, and garlic salt. Heat 1 tablespoon of the butter and the oil in a skillet set on high heat and sear the meat for 1 minute on each side. Cook an additional minute each side for rare. Remove the pan from the heat and stir in the remaining 3 tablespoons butter until melted. Let rest for 5 minutes.

Serve on top of a bed of watercress drizzled with extra virgin olive oil, lime juice, and salt.

Serves 2

FLIP YOUR MOOD

Some people decompress after a stressful day by watching television. Turn on a half hour sitcom and forget their worries. Others, I imagine, fix themselves a stiff drink. *Do they still do this? Do people still fix themselves a stiff drink at the end of the day?* And then there's me: I sauté onions.

Have you ever tried this as therapy? You may put away your Prozac forever.

I slice long careless rings of raw onion, no chopping or, heaven forbid, *mincing* going on as this would only induce tears, and with the kind of day I had had, all I needed was a teensy speck of *allium cepa* juice to push me over the edge.

In any case, you know that kind of day, right? Stop. Remember yours. Okay. Grab an onion.

It's that rote movement that gets you started on the road to recovery, gets your body active while your mind begins to settle.

It feels calming to cut through an onion like this. Bet you never put so much attention on inattention. Are you trying it yet?

My pan has been heating up while I do this. Only because I have an electric stovetop and not a gas one.

I have an electric stovetop and not a gas one.

Electric, not gas.

Electric.

My Culinary Compulsion

Not gas.

Yes, I have issues with this.

I grew up with gas stovetops boasting little blue flames that instantly grew to fiery bonfires readily heating up skillets brimming with bubbly sauces, double smashed *patacones* or flash fried *parguito*. The options were endless. If the fire was too much, a quick snap of the wrist made it low and steady again, just like that. You'd need that for my mother's bittersweet chocolate pudding to come out *just so* or for Yoli's renowned *caraotas negras*, black beans, to have the ideal consistency (not too thin, not too thick) and let the flavor of fresh oregano really soak in. I took for granted the ease of such a switch until I moved to South Florida, which, with its beautiful beaches and its rich Latin American population, has numerous benefits; one of which not being the overwhelming poor choice of electric over gas stovetops.

Like an alien, I've lived amongst electric stovetop people and, even though I went out and bought myself the fanciest one, a sleek, modern slab of onyx with a German name I never know how to pronounce properly, I remain at a loss. The thing is *still* electric.

Which means it has about a one hundred and sixty-two second delay in heating up and cooling down, and that's sticking a "Mississippi" into every count.

This is why I've thrown my skillet on medium heat before I began my onion therapy.

Because even though I've had a rough day, rough enough to randomly slice through an onion, I know it will go to the dogs fast if I don't hear that satisfying sizzle sound when I toss my work onto the skillet.

Which is now, right after a quick coating of olive oil on the pan.

I've got a mountain of onion; I picked a particularly gigantic white onion.

I'm feeling better already.

The olive oil hangs out in a fancy glass bottle next to the stovetop; the two are always in cahoots.

Now you try.

The sizzle sound cracks the silence, scratching out any anger you may have, replacing it with relief, like reaching an itch in the middle of your back.

The aroma begins. First pungent onion, quickly followed by a more mellow, sweeter smell mixed in with the green fruitiness of the olive oil. This is the scent of promise and hope, possibly even redemption and glory. Can you smell it?

My son emerges from his bedroom, "Hmmm. It smells good, what are you making?"

Don't take this lightly, please. My son has discovered His Room. Goes in there now constantly. Locks the door. Doesn't realize I can pop that lock open with the screwdriver I keep close by in the kitchen drawer, but still, the door is now locked.

My Culinary Compulsion

But against all teenage protocol he emerges and engages in conversation with His Mother.

Sautéing onions will do that to a person.

What *am* I cooking? I hadn't gotten that far. The onions are turning into golden necklaces and I am inspired by my overwhelming feeling of laziness, my desire not to make much, just to feel better.

I crack six eggs in a bowl and quickly stir.

I slice up a peeled potato, razor thin.

I go to my garden with my big butcher knife and hunt for parsley, decapitating a small bunch hiding in the flowerpot I have outside.

I haven't told you this but these are also forms of therapy.

The onions are off the skillet now, set aside.

With the skillet still hot, I toss in the potatoes only after a new drizzle of olive oil, the magic elixir to this session.

The potatoes brown and crisp at the edges quickly with me turning them around once or twice. This is a tolerant dish: you can make mistakes, not pay close attention, walk away for something. Just make sure your flame or electric buzz is on medium-low heat.

In about five to seven minutes they look like nuggets of gold sparkling under clear river water. Pour the eggs in. Add a bit of salt and fresh pepper, sprinkle in the fresh parsley, the glistening onions and put a lid on the whole thing.

Remember, medium-low.

Let it sit there now for a bit.

This is a perfect time for that second glass of Chardonnay.

Sip and shake the pan slightly while the eggs set on the bottom, which again, takes about five to seven minutes.

Listen to me, you are now going to flip this whole puppy, like they do in the movies, only in the movies they don't spill a drop. You can spill a drop. You can make a mess. It's all part of our therapy.

Or you can cheat.

You can take a spatula, a monster spatula, if you have one, and flip this thing around like that. Or you can flip it face down onto a clean plate and then flip the whole plate back onto the skillet.

If I were you, I'd take a chance and try the movie flip.

It's all in the wrist, I know you've heard. You gotta shake the pan back and forth ever so lightly, then pop your wrist and kick the farther end of the pan up into the air gracefully so that the whole thing flies and flips in one flawless movement. Come on, make Gordon Ramsey proud…or at least give yourself a big shout-out!

One, two, three... flip!

Did it work? Or is your kitchen floor wearing egg?

Are you not laughing uncontrollably either way?

I hope you are. The point of all this was to get you laughing.

Hopefully though, the whole thing is somewhat intact on your skillet (or you have a very clean floor) because this dish, *which is*

My Culinary Compulsion 119

called Tortilla Española, is good. Real good.

Tortilla Española

The trick to this is time and a low flame- don't rush it!

1 cup of onion, sliced

1 cup Idaho potatoes, peeled and sliced thin

6 eggs

¼ cup extra virgin olive oil

½ teaspoon salt

ground pepper, to taste

In a large skillet on medium-high heat, add 1/8 cup of olive oil and the onions. Sauté for half a minute then lower the heat to medium-low and sauté gently for 10 minutes, until the onions are caramelized.

Remove from the skillet.

Add the remaining olive oil, raise the heat again, and place the potato pieces all along the skillet bottom. Sauté for a minute, then lower the heat to medium-low and sauté for 5-7 minutes, flipping the potatoes around now and then. The potatoes should brown lightly.

Beat the eggs in a bowl and add the salt and pepper.

Pour the mixture onto the skillet with the potatoes. Sprinkle on parsley and onion and cover.

Cook on low for 10 minutes, shaking the skillet every now and then so the tortilla does not stick.

Prepare to flip.

Remove the lid. Either using a spatula or a clean plate, or entrusting fate, flip tortilla (see story for slightly more precise instructions.)

Cook another 2 minutes and serve immediately, cutting in pie slices.

Serves 3

For the Love of Chopping: Yoli's Chicken

"Ya wannit in fourths or ya wannit in eighths?", he asked in an unequivocal New York accent resilient to thirty years of South Florida living. The man behind the meat counter was an oxymoron: tall and hefty with a scruffy beard and a mean stare, he held his cleaver delicately with fingers gracefully poised to attack the organic remnants of the chicken I ordered (I would name her Molly, but that would come later). The blade was sparkling, befitting of a Hitchcock scene or the prized collection of Daniel Boulud and appeared both perfect and mismatched with his once-white butcher's coat, now a patchwork of assorted animal DNA. This was a man that was tough but gentle and had the bloodstains to prove it.

"Miss? Fourths or Eighths?", he pressed, this time a bit annoyed.

"No. None." I responded. "I will do it myself."

His face fell in rhythm with his cleaver as a keen look of amusement and confusion temporarily drifted over his icy blue eyes. Was that a smirk I saw reverberate inside Big Butcher Man, almost as if to say this petite 5' 5" lady isn't up to the task of quartering his free range baby? Instantly I accepted the muted challenge and took an assertive step forward on my silver platform sandals (it's the only way I get to the 5' 5" realm). Like a rooster puffing out its chest, I took a big breath in and faced my 6' 4" burly rival with bravery and gusto, all the while looking him straight in the eye (after all, I have icy blues too.) A sudden urge to grab his cleaver and show this smug giant how well this *mamacita* can hack meat overtook me and I had to muster all the self-restraint of a compliant customer to hold me back from my attack.

Butcher Man sized up the crazy glare in my eyes and managed a quick "Suit yourself", while swiftly wrapping the prized poultry in butcher paper.

"Most definitely shall," I sputtered back triumphantly, appreciating the fact that making this man's job easier was, in our distorted duel, a victory of mine. I could go home and chop while his cleaver remained parked.

I would make the king of comfort food chicken dishes: Yoli's Chicken, our household's favorite of her chicken dishes. She'd smother the chicken in countless minced garlic cloves, then coat it with tangy Heinz 57 sauce and bathe it in Worcestershire and chicken broth. It was that simple. She'd always throw in chopped potatoes and together these and the chicken would grow soft and succulent, dripping with pan juices and producing a zesty and slightly spicy wholly unforgettable meal.

Yoli's Chicken became a signature dish in the Abbady household. Friends spending the night would silently hope that this would be on the dinner menu and relatives visiting from afar were always greeted with this favorite. It was the dish anyone who had spent some time with our family always remembered and would crave for years after. It was one of the many ways Yoli would quietly stay with you.

Yoli's Chicken with Potatoes

3-5 medium potatoes, peeled and cut into fourths

1 (3 ½ lbs.) chicken, cut up in eighths

6 garlic cloves, minced

½ cup Heinz 57 sauce

¼ Worcestershire sauce

2 ½ teaspoons kosher salt

1 cup chicken stock

Preheat the oven to 350°F.

Put the potatoes in a medium saucepan and cover with cold water by 2 inches. Salt the water generously. Bring to a boil over medium heat and cook the potatoes until tender, about 15 minutes.

Coat the chicken pieces with Heinz 57 sauce and Worcestershire sauce. Add the minced garlic.

Sprinkle with salt.

Place the chicken in the oven, skin side up, without the potatoes, and bake for 10 minutes.

Add the potatoes and baste with ½ cup of chicken stock.

Baste every fifteen minutes with stock, then with the

juices. Make sure to stir the potatoes around and to turn the chicken pieces around several times.

Cook 45 minutes.

Note: *This chicken dish can be made with a whole chicken as well - follow the same instructions, just rotate the chicken (yes, flip it upside down, sideways, and other sideways) every 25 minutes.*

Serves 4

Under *Abuela Margarita's* Circumstances:
Spaghetti *Tortilla*

I was at the airport waiting for a flight when I saw a kid hurdle-jumping seats by gate C29. He was a chaotic ball of energy, indiscriminate of whether the seats were occupied or not, he sprinted and jumped, kicking people, carry-ons, and shins in his path. Even though I was safely seated by gate C27, I found myself huffing and puffing and wondering in an indignant voice, "*Where the hell is that child's mother?*" as if I were the Queen of England and this eight-year old was competing on The Amazing Race inside Buckingham Palace. The severe judgement dissolved as my eyes scanned the room and landed on that poor, defeated, deflated, and, what's worse, utterly exhausted woman slumped on the chair nearby. *The mother.*

One just can't be mad at such outright collapse.

In fact, what I wanted to do was search my purse for some leftover Xanax, buy her a glass of chilled Chardonnay, and come to her rescue.

Husband had been one of those kids. Ask him. He'll take you on the tour of his scars and former broken bones. He'll tell you about the horses he "borrowed" to ride on his uncle's farm in Venezuela, the rooftops he jumped off of at his parent's house, and the endless array of apprehensive relatives he was passed on to like a hot potato.

Any relative that was witness to the tornado that was Husband as a child will smile, sigh, and offer the same vague comment, "Oh, yes, he was a handful!"

Both my children came out far more sensible than their dad. Still, they love to hear about their wild father. They beg for stories over and over again. By now, there are some standard favorites, like the time Husband snuck into his *abuelo* Pauxides's prohibitive cockfight in the colonial town of Curarigua and, while all were caught up in the excitement, stole the spectators' chairs, leaving stunned men with, not only the pain of losing a bet, but also of landing hard and unexpectedly on the cold, dirt floor. There are the hilarious stories of *abuela* Koko trying to tame her rambunctious and daredevil grandson over the course of an entire summer after he was put on an airplane, flown across the country, and dropped unannounced at her doorstep by his mom. The only warning she got was a phone call half an hour before he was to land, telling her, "*está en el avion*," : he's on the airplane. No name was necessary; it could only be Husband.

Every relative was volunteered (willingly or unwillingly) to deal with him, but it was his father's mother, *abuela* Margarita, who seemed to capture her wild grandson's spirit with her magic in the kitchen. Husband would postpone mischief to sit and watch and record, ever so diligently, his grandmother's preparation of breakfast. Wastefulness was a pet peeve of hers so Margarita relished creating memorable dishes with whatever was in the fridge. His favorite was her "*bajo las circunstancias*" or "under the circumstances" dish, an egg and pasta *tortilla* that he'd help make. Together they'd scour the refrigerator, where they'd find several kinds of cheeses, loads of parsley, cured meats, and any vegetable somewhat past its prime and combine them with leftover spaghetti and eggs. *Abuela* Margarita taught Husband that lots of freshly ground pepper is a Martinez must and the secret to getting the pasta crunchy is fast cooking at a high heat.

I met *abuela* Margarita once when we first started dating. She was frail, as expected for someone of 95-years, but her eyes were clear and her voice strong. She leaned towards me as I kissed her paper-thin cheek and whispered, *"Ya veo que lo vas hacer un hombre muy feliz,"*: I already see you are going to make him a happy man. I don't know how she knew this; our relationship was so new. Maybe she whispered that into the ear of every girl he brought to say hello, or maybe she knew by the way my hair had a slight floral scent of passionfruit or how my hand had the careless knife nicks of someone always contending with a chopping board. I was one who understood the need to create and share the making of a good meal; something she knew would draw and center her grandson for a lifetime.

ABUELA MARGARITA'S *BAJO LAS CIRCUNSTANCIAS* SPAGHETTI TORTILLA

- 2 cups leftover spaghetti
- 5 eggs, beaten
- 3 tablespoons olive oil
- ½ cup onion, minced
- ½ cup *Emmental* cheese, grated
- ½ cup Gouda cheese grated

¼ *Parmigiano Reggiano* cheese, grated

½ cup parsley, chopped fine

½ cup chopped ham or salami or combo of both

¾ cup chopped vegetables (can include peppers, mushrooms, celery, broccoli)

salt and pepper, to taste

In a large skillet, heat the olive oil on medium high heat and sauté the onions until brown, about 10 minutes, stirring regularly.

Add the pasta and heat up, five minutes.

Add the cured meat and sauté another minute or so. Add the vegetables and sauté an additional three minutes. Add the beaten eggs, parsley, and cheese and let sit until cooked, over medium heat, for about 5 minutes.

Flip the tortilla and cook it an additional 2 minutes at high heat. Add freshly ground pepper and salt, to taste.

Serve immediately.

Serves 4

The Golden Goddess

It was her presence that I first felt: a calm, beneficent, stillness that gently shifted my frazzled state and invited me to lap up the serenity that suddenly pooled around me. We stood side by side on a sullen Sunday afternoon in the checkout line of our local supermarket, of all places. Whereas I had barely managed to put on a bra, my hair was greasy, and my makeup was from yesterday, she was resplendent; I knew this even before I looked at her.

I was waiting impatiently in line, just behind a tiny octogenarian, decked out in flaming scarlet hair and a rhinestone-studded belt, who boisterously revealed that the secret to her hyperactive libido was the bags and bags of fava beans her frail but determined body was pulling out of the shopping cart and heaping on the conveyor belt.

"The beans' high levels of L-dopa increase sex drive," she announced to me and the lucky few also standing in line. The more she proselytized, the more annoyed I became, but I grinned and nodded respectfully, grateful for the culinary trivia but certainly not for the new imagery attached to it. *Why couldn't Channing Tatum have told me?*

Before our senior sexpot went on to expose other unsolicited secrets of her boudoir, I casually turned away to avoid further eye contact and first truly saw Her. She was dressed from head to toe in a golden silk fabric that gleamed glamorously even under the harsh neon light. It was a traditional sari that draped her cinnamon skin and hugged her tall and proud posture. The color was almost glaring: a yellow hue that would look unflattering on most people, definitely horrid on me, but suited her marvelously. The print had miniature flowers embroidered in ruby thread with even tinier hummingbirds sewn in dazzling turquoise. Her hair was thick and lustrous, and her eyelashes sparkled with glitter. Delicately balanced between her large eyes was a crimson *bindi*, the decorative Hindu mark that in her country proclaims her status as a married woman, but in this American suburb only added to her intrigue. I felt almost blessed to be in this strange woman's presence. I decided she was either a deity or a celebrity on the brink of breaking out into a splendidly choreographed Bollywood dance. No doubt her back-up dancers were hiding on aisles 6, 9, and 11. Why else would someone go through such strenuous beauty efforts to fix themselves up for a quick run to the supermarket, I thought to myself while noticing the gaping hole forming in my favorite Bruce Springsteen t-shirt.

But as our wait prolonged itself (it seemed grandma was talking about warm-up stretches instead of paying her tab), I realized she was just another ordinary shopper like me. Except for the fact that she was so very different. I wondered what secrets lay behind her dedication; what kind of woman got so decked out for a bag of rice? I wondered what kind of man waited for her return, was she proud of her bindi or bound to it? And then I wondered if this was her casual outfit, her Bruce Springsteen t-shirt, and if it was, what would she wear on an elegant night out? Of course, as I wondered I stared: part fascination, part awe, and part envy. Our local Dr. Ruth finally left and it was my turn at the cashier's. This mysterious beauty began placing items on the edge of the belt: cauliflower, plain yogurt, lots and lots of onions. My fixation with her grew and I felt like a lost puppy wanting to follow her to her house, for even though I knew nothing about her, the groceries sprawled on the conveyor belt behind mine promised a home that would always nourish with the gentle simmer of onion and curry and vegetables. A good *daal*, or a fine *aloo gobi*; a whirlpool of spices for the senses and a tranquil golden goddess to go with it.

She placed a bag of baby spinach on the belt and looked up at me. Her jet black eyes could have pierced through my bloodshot blue ones; I was blatantly intruding with my staring. But they didn't. They were soft and gentle and understanding, as if to read my agitated state and assure me my Sunday would bring the promise of tranquility and good food as well, even if I wasn't decked out in a beautiful gold sari. And with that, I became happy and smiled back because I knew she was right. Somehow, between the green peas and the eggplant, she had made me feel better. We never spoke. I paid and left, turning one last time to nod in her direction, a nod I am not sure she saw. But it didn't matter. She didn't need my acknowledgement, and, it turns out, I didn't need hers either. We were two women from two different worlds living through the same Sunday. That night, I was inevitably drawn to a simple dish of curried vegetables. I simmered my cauliflower and potatoes in a gentle sauce whose aroma permeated every corner of my house. Curry is like that. Its sultry presence lingers and makes you feel beloved and at peace, like the woman in the golden sari.

Aloo Gobi (Cauliflower and Potato Curry)

1 large head of cauliflower

2 Idaho potatoes, peeled and chopped into 1" cubes

3 tablespoons vegetable oil

2 teaspoons curry powder

1 clove garlic, minced or crushed

1 cup of slivered onion

¼ cup white wine

¾ cup water

1 diced tomato

2 tablespoons lemon juice

14 ounces (1 package) firm tofu, cut into 1" cubes

½ cup fresh peas

2 tablespoons fresh mint, chopped

1 teaspoon chicken bouillon powder

salt, to taste

Wash the cauliflower and break it up into small pieces. Microwave the pieces in a bowl with ¼ cup water for 3 minutes. Boil the chopped potatoes in salted water until nearly tender but not quite done, about 5 minutes.

Strain. Heat the oil in a large skillet over medium heat and sauté the onions, stirring constantly, until translucent, about 5 minutes. Add the curry powder and garlic and stir another 2 minutes. Add the cauliflower and potatoes and cook over medium-low heat until combined, 2 minutes. Add the wine and remaining water, raise heat to medium-high and simmer for 5 minutes. Add the tomatoes, lemon juice, tofu, peas, mint, chicken bouillon powder, and salt to taste. Allow the curry to simmer, covered, for 5 minutes. Adjust seasoning.

Serves 4

Rebel Without a Dinner

I want to tell you that I cooked something divine last night. That it was rich and velvety and luscious. That my palate celebrated each morsel and was awoken by the many layers of memorable flavor that left me yearning for more.

But I didn't.

What I did was not nearly as glamorous. Or romantic. Or exotic.

What I did was merely try to breathe. All day I focused on this task, in fact, attacking the mission full force with an arsenal filled with tissues, medications, homeopathic remedies and in the end, defeat. This head cold I've been sporting for the last three days outwitted all my attempts.

So savoring food was quite out of the question, sadly. And still, like a lost arm taunting an amputee, I craved the pleasure of eating. Albeit in between sneezes.

The children watched me with bemusement. They enjoy seeing their mother out of sorts. With Kleenex as my accessory of choice, I muddled around the kitchen deciding what to prepare, all the while croaking a very nasal rendition of Ella Fitzgerald's "I Love Paris" (no illness will ever stop me from singing, much to my family's chagrin.)

Since I could barely breathe (let alone savor), nothing seemed to fit the mood: too salty, too chewy, too healthy. And I didn't see the point in all the fuss if, in the end, it would end up being sorely misunderstood and risked being unappreciated by my numbed senses.

These are, of course, the moments my children adore most: the breakpoint, if you will, when all maternal instinct gets thrown out the window; concepts of food pyramids and broccoli and roughage lost in the wind, moments like last night when I'll suddenly declare: "That's it. We're having waffles for dinner."

Such an announcement prompted a serendipitous celebration complete with delighted laughter, and lots of skipping. For a second I had to stop myself and double check: *Wait, these are the same kids that are spoiled beyond culinary belief, with hefty dosages of exotic offerings (didn't we enjoy a marvelous Kashmir Lamb Curry the other night?)* They don't know how good they have it.

But offer up waffles with warm maple syrup and sliced bananas for dinner and they go nuts.

Bonkers.

Skip-happy.

So we broke the rules and enjoyed a breakfast dinner. I didn't have to worry about prep work- this stuff is seamlessly simple; the toughest part was plugging in the waffle iron.

Dinner was served and the kids bounced happily in their seats. The waffles were awesome, they assured me. I could not tell. I could not smell. But I could feel: soft, warm, and comforting, like the hugs I used to get from my mother when I was sick and she was alive to offer them. The outside was perfectly crunchy and the goo of syrup and smoothness of banana slices excessively soothing.

For one night, we were rebels without a proper dinner, but happy all the same: a flawless remedy for a sick or healthy palate.

SAM'S FAVORITE WAFFLES

Sam is my best friend's husband. He's a great guy, namely because he quietly and graciously accepts me as an integral part of his wife's (and hence, his) life. He also happens to be a fabulous cook! Breakfast is one of his specialties, from rainbow-colored pancakes to these unbeatable waffles.

- 2 eggs, separated
- 1 ½ cup milk
- 1/2 cup vegetable oil
- 1 teaspoon vanilla extract
- 1 3/4 cup flour
- 1 tablespoon baking powder
- 1 teaspoon salt
- 1 tablespoon sugar

Spray the waffle iron with non-stick cooking spray and let it pre-heat.

Using an electric mixer, beat the egg yolks until thick and lemon-colored. Continue beating, adding the milk, oil, sugar, and vanilla extract.

In another bowl, combine all the dry ingredients and add them to the wet ingredients, beating until smooth.

In small bowl, beat the egg whites until light peaks form and gently fold into the main batter.

Pour 1 cup of the batter evenly on the griddle. Bake for about 2 1/2 to 3 minutes (or simply follow your waffle maker's specific instructions).

Serves 4

Deciphering A Smile

This is the day that your headache won't go away, regardless of the amount of Advil you've wolfed down with a Tums chaser so you won't get an ulcer, with extra water so you're not left with chalk jammed in your teeth. This is the day you'll be stuck behind Grandma driving 37 miles per hour on the freeway and you will honk and curse like an idiot in a rush to go nowhere just because it's that kind of day.

You can't see her well, Grandma. She's shriveled down to a solid 4' 8" and that's including the lavender hair, but you could swear when the sun hits at an angle just so and you squint and look at her rearview mirror, well, you could swear that little old lady is smiling at you. Or at life. Or at something *you* certainly aren't smiling at.

We've all had these days but the grin on Grandma during mine threw me for a loop to the extent that when the steroid-happy 18-wheeler finally flew by me on my left side, allowing a window of opportunity to pass Grandma's cruising rate, I opted out and obediently chugged along behind her, suddenly wondering what the mind that held that grin was so damn happy about.

It could be her grandson's bar mitzvah she was going to, I concluded. She was so proud of that boy. Michael was her oldest of 12 grandchildren but he was her favorite (even if his hair was too long.) He had her smile, and she was pleased at how assertive and grown up he was becoming. He would be outfitted in an oversized dark blue suit and nervous as hell. But then her outfit was too casual for a bar mitzvah. I could see that from here (as I realized how precariously close I was to her Cadillac).

Maybe she was returning from bingo with the girls. Or bridge. Or some sort of social cliché for senior citizens.

She would spend a couple of hours of company, away from the solitude of her little apartment, together they'd drink English Breakfast tea (sometimes a shot of something to loosen the morning along) and many shared laughs. She'd almost always win too. Again, the smile: a dead giveaway of some sort of glorious happiness.

But then I noticed some bags poking out of her trunk, which I realized wasn't properly shut (time for me to back off a bit.) They were grocery store bags and it all clicked as I understood the smile. *Grandma was a cook, maybe even a baker!* She was having the whole clan over for brunch and it would be the typical spread with eggs and lox and bagels but what would make this meal stellar would be the ending: Grandma's killer Orange Cake. It would be moist and tender, with a slight kick to it, perhaps some of that Schnapps she'd share with the girls on bingo night (because now it made sense that she and the gals sat around yakking away over shots of something ridiculously sweet until late at night -no, these were not the *early bird special* ladies, no.) Of course, Grandma has class and shows it in this wonderful cake, this cake where she slips, not Schnapps (who mixes peach with orange, for crying out loud) but a dash or two or three of Grand Marnier, cognac all dressed up, the stuff my mother always had in the back of her liquor cabinet, the stuff she'd pull out for her orange cake too! I wanna drive up close to her now, way close, dangerously close. I want to do one of those Indiana Jones stunts actually, and somehow find myself climbing out of my car (yes, crazy things do happen on I-95) and land on her trunk (closing it with my weight), then climb right into her passenger seat. She would not be frightened. In fact, she'd roll her eyes at me and say, "Oy vey, you could get killed like that, you know?" And then she'd laugh and rest her liver-spotted hand on mine and grin again, grin and say, "Oh, but I'm glad you came!" And I would worry about the road, contending with a 90-mile-an-hour Grandma grasping her steering wheel with only one hand, but I would take the chance because I would not want the warmth and happiness she was sharing with me to leave. So I would grin back and say, as casually as I could:

"Orange Cake?"

And she'd wink, take her eyes off the road for a lingering second to look at me and reply:

"The best!", as a loud horn sounded and Grandma veered away from a panicked Smart car driver just in time to avert disaster ("Those aren't real cars," she'd add, as if that justified things) and then she'd continue, looking at me once more:

"You know the secret is..."

And I'd know, zipping down this crazy highway on the way to lift someone's heart with every buttery, citrusy warm slice she'd offer. The secret wasn't the careful blending of the dry ingredients with the wet (although this matters, yes it does) or the spiked glaze that must be spooned over the cake while still hot (so that it fully incorporates this flavor as the cake cools). The secret is the pleasure one gets, not just from creating these wonderful dishes, but with sharing them. *This* is the secret: the sharing. This is why I live in the kitchen; this is why I love to create dishes. Because I adore sharing them. It's all for moments like this - for moments I've imagined on a chaotic highway with a woman whom, I expect, feels the same way, and suddenly, I am not in her car any longer, I am not even driving behind her, but, I've managed to come up alongside her, and I too have taken my eyes off the road (for just a second) to look at her, and she looks at me, and at that moment we do smile at each other, me and this mysterious older lady who is on her way to who knows where. I want to shout out to her what the secret is. We both know it. But instead, I shout:

"Your trunk is open!"

She smiles, waves and steps on the gas.

Classic Orange Cake

1 cup butter, softened

1 ½ cups sugar

3 eggs, separated

2 cups flour

1 teaspoon baking powder

1 teaspoon baking soda

½ teaspoon salt

1 cup sour cream

grated rind of 1 orange

½ cup walnuts, toasted and chopped *(see page xxv)*

¼ cup orange juice

1/3 cup Grand Marnier

confectioner's sugar

Preheat the oven to 350F.

Grease a 9" tube pan.

Cream the butter and sugar until it is light and fluffy. Beat in the egg yolks one at a time until fully incorporated.

In a large bowl, sift together the flour, baking powder, baking soda, and salt.

Add to the egg mixture alternating with sour cream.

Stir in the orange rind and nuts.

In a separate bowl, beat the egg whites until they form stiff peaks. Gradually fold them into the batter.

Bake for 50 minutes. Allow to cool 15 minutes, then remove from pan.

Meanwhile, prepare the glaze:

Combine ½ cup sugar, the orange juice, and the Grand Marnier in a small pot and bring to a boil. Reduce heat to medium and allow to simmer, undisturbed, for

5 minutes.

Spoon over hot cake.

When cake is cool, sprinkle top with confectioner's sugar.

Serves 12

Uploading Peace: Challah

Yesterday my email server and I had a fight. It was a painful, emotional event that left me spent, angered, and uninspired.

I was asked over and over again to insert my password, a word or phrase I had casually selected months, maybe years before thinking it would be easy and simple to extract. The thing is, I can't remember what I had for dinner last night, so, how would I remember the name of the street I lived on?

Oh, I remember the street.

But how I wrote it is the tricky part. Stuff always gets thorny when you add another language to the mix, which I must have done, having grown up in Venezuela.

Did I put *4ta Avenida*?

Or maybe I translated it to 4th Avenue?

Perhaps spelled it out, Fourth?

Cuarta?

Or a clever play on words, "Forth?"

The computer announced I had too many incorrect attempts and locked me out.

I called the computer's customer service and spoke to a bubbly representative on the phone. A lady named Christy or Cindy, or something friendly like that. I pictured her with a blonde bob, a

My Culinary Compulsion 145

cerulean scarf wrapped around her slender pale neck and a pack of Hubba Bubba *Sweet and Sassy Cherry* gum on her desk in her tidy cubicle in Nebraska.

Of course maybe she was in New Delhi and just hid it really well.

Cindy was the center of the party back home. I just knew it. Meet her at Slowdown's on 14th Street for a couple of beers and some good music and you'll be laughing the whole night through with her, that girl's a trip!

Maybe it's Fourteenth Street.

Cindy couldn't help me at all though.

Just left me more frustrated and locked me out of the server for an additional 32 hours. We tried too many password combinations and failed. "It's for security reasons," she meekly read off her script.

Sage, calmer folk might preach this is all a good exercise from The Man Upstairs.

A reminder to slow down. Take it easy. Breathe.

Remind me there was once a time without email.

There was only a telephone, attached to a wire, attached to a wall that would ring if you needed something or someone, if you had to relay a specific message.

None of this constant texting and pinging and tweeting mindless matters.

Apparently, wisdom eludes me. I am in a bad mood because

Cindy could not repair my problem and has gone on and forgotten me. Is probably on her second Rolling Rock.

Or Kingfisher.

Making other people happy.

So I will do what I know will calm me.

I will make bread.

I will hear the methodic hum of Lulu, kneading with her magical hook, and then I will have a turn and roll and braid a beautiful challah and I will forget all the newsletters and junk mail that pour into my inbox: *10 Ways to Blast Through Stomach Fat* or *Top Secrets for Better Love* or *Prime Opportunities for Real Estate in North Carolina*. This is the bulk of my messages with only a sparse sprinkling of personal emails; a quick hello from a friend watching the frost on the leaves up north, a picture from a niece suddenly all grown up. I will put it all aside because I have to, because Cindy told me I must and I will focus on the scent of yeast and flour and silence.

The click the oven makes as it turns on.

The hum as it comes to life.

The pop from the baking pan buckling under the heat. This will soothe and ground me.

The bread will come out warm and soft and scrumptious.

Bread that has been made for thousands of years.

I will put a pat of butter on a slice and watch it melt into a puddle of delicious. I will not read an update on the caloric intake or the amount of crunches I need to do to make up for the moment I am about to enjoy.

Thoughtfully, I will eat, and taste, and chew, offline, and at peace.

Heart and Soul Challah

4 ½ teaspoons active dry yeast

¾ cup warm water

1 teaspoon salt

½ cup sugar*

2 tablespoons melted butter plus 2 tablespoons soft butter for bowl

2 eggs plus 2 yolks *(save egg whites for wash- see below)*

3 ½ - 4 cups flour

*I like my challah to be slightly sweet. If that isn't your thing, use ¼ cup sugar.

Wash:

2 egg whites

3 tablespoons water

½ teaspoon vanilla extract

¼ cup poppy seeds

In a bowl, sprinkle the yeast over warm water. Let stand for 5 minutes, until bubbly.

Beat the eggs and egg yolks with salt and mix into the yeast.

Pour into mixer bowl.

Add sugar, 1 cup of flour, and 2 tablespoons butter with the yeast mixture, using the paddle attachment, on medium speed.

Switch to the hook attachment and add the remaining flour. Beat on medium-high speed until the dough becomes elastic and forms a ball, pulling away from the sides of the bowl (6-8 minutes). Turn dough onto a floured surface and knead until smooth, sprinkling additional flour if the dough gets sticky. Your dough should be elastic and feel smooth.

If you don't have a mixer, follow the same steps using a large bowl and stirring 3 cups with a wooden spoon. The dough will become sticky. Lightly flour a work surface and sprinkle remaining flour on dough and begin kneading until the dough becomes smooth and elastic, about 5 minutes.

Place the dough in a large bowl coated with butter, cover it with a towel and let rise until doubled, 1 ½ - 2 hours.

Punch down the dough and divide it into 6 pieces. Roll the pieces into ropes roughly 1-inch thick and 16 inches long. Braid into two loaves, using 3 ropes for each braid. Place the braided loaves on a baking sheet, cover, and let rise for an hour.

Preheat the oven to 350°F.

Prepare the wash: whisk together the egg, water, and vanilla extract. Brush the tops of the loaves. Sprinkle with poppy seed.

Bake for 30 minutes, until the bread is golden and sounds hollow when you thump the bottom.

Makes 2 large loaves...or you can just make one supersized loaf!

Rounding Out the Day

The pizza dough was forgiving, ignoring my bad mood, succumbing to my careless hands; it folded, sighed, heaved, and bent. Just for me.

Nothing particularly bad had happened on that Friday. Just a gloomy, gray day filled with inane tasks which demanded something simple and comforting for dinner.

Something that would make your trainer, if you had one, shake his head in disapproval.

I have bags of lettuce and crisp radishes and cans of sardines, *yes, in extra virgin olive oil*, tucked away in my kitchen corners. Pledges of fiber and protein and cardiovascular health.

But like I said, the day had been a particularly dreary one that called for soft, mushy warm dough and lots of cheese.

After I formed my dough in an imperfect circle I was generous with the toppings, which began with a heavy dollop of tomato sauce I had simmered down to a tangy reduction.

It's an uncomplicated process, really. Anyone with half a brain, even an angry, tired brain, like mine was on this day, can do it.

Pureed tomatoes, minced garlic, dried oregano, and fresh basil.

You can mumble this while in *downward-facing-dog* pose in yoga class, if you take a yoga class.

I hear they are great stress relievers.

That sauce slipped happily over the dough and then, then the party began!

Mushrooms, which I had bought sliced and packaged, because I was nervous to be around a big knife on that day, were tossed on board. You add them to your pizza naked like that; they will wilt and roast into accomplished bronze versions of themselves. Or you can prep them in the pan first, like I did.

More minced garlic (once you start mincing you might as well), olive oil and thick salt, the type carved out of a resilient mountain somewhere in Turkey, are subjected to a quick sear in the frying pan under bright heat. If you have a gas-stove top, you will appreciate the therapy in this. Fire is hypnotic and effective with food.

If you are like me and are cursed with an electric stovetop, you will have to wait a bit for that pan to heat up under the controlled glow of technology.

I have lived at the behest of this glow for too many years to keep track of and still loathe it, still dream in blue and yellow flame.

So there go the mushrooms, sprinkled on the dough and sauce, they look so pleasing!

And here you can go off and do your own thing, that is the best part of this type of an evening. Everyone has their own canvas of flavors, individuality is celebrated and roasted in a wickedly hot oven.

My mood is feeling pretty darn meaty so I pile on some minced smoked ham and thin discs of pepperoni; stuff I'd normally sidestep, my mind usually heavy with guilt over the after effects of too much grease and empty calories.

But not tonight.

Tonight I look the other way and load up.

Because it is one night, a Friday night no less, the start of a weekend, the opener to fun times.

Hearts of palm await.

Many people shy away from these, simply because they have no clue what they are. Heart of palm is a vegetable harvested from the inner core of coconut trees.

In Venezuela, waiters with white gloves in the fanciest restaurants would present them to me as a child, in miniature oval dishes cloaked in a rich and creamy sauce, smothered with grated Parmesan cheese and broiled so a toasty crust formed on top.

This was an all-time favorite dish and lingering memory of mine.

I sprinkle the ivory discs on the dough and smile.

The pizza is ready to be doused in cheese.

Shamelessly doused in cheese.

There I go.

It rains, like the torrential storms that would randomly descend on Caracas, flooding streets, causing *derrumbes*, calamitous landslides that would halt the already congested roads for hours; it rains.

On those days I would love to be home, in my room, sitting on my windowsill, looking outside while protected inside, close my eyes and inhale the humid and fickle tropical breeze mixed with tumbling earth.

Today I smell cheese.

Shredded mozzarella cheese, to be exact.

Stuff that will melt and ooze and turn gooey and make life one with the universe.

Just like that.

The pizza is popped in a preheated oven of 375°F and ten minutes later, magic emerges.

My not-perfectly-round pizza appears perfect.

The mushrooms glisten, the ham has curled up and browned at the tips, the hearts of palm are golden, I can't even see the pepperoni, and the cheese, as vowed, has melted all over the place.

This is now an exceptional day.

Do-It-Yourself Pizza

For the dough:

- 1 cup warm water
- 1 package active dry yeast (2 ¼ teaspoons)

2 ½ cups all-purpose flour

1 tablespoon sugar

1 teaspoon salt

3 tablespoons olive oil

For tomato sauce:

1 14oz. can of tomato puree

2 garlic cloves, peeled and crushed (smash it with the bottom of a skillet or a heavy knife)

1 teaspoon dried oregano

4 fresh basil leaves

In a medium bowl, dissolve the yeast in the warm water. Let stand until bubbly, about 10 minutes.

Stir in the flour, salt, sugar, and oil. Mix until smooth. Let the mixture rest for 5 minutes.

Turn the dough out onto a lightly floured surface and knead for 5 minutes. If the dough gets too sticky, go ahead and sprinkle some more flour (up to ½ cup). Roll the dough into a round; cover it loosely with dishcloth and let it rest for 30 minutes. Using a rolling pin, roll the dough out into a large circle - most large pizzas run between 14 to 16 inches in diameter. The larger the pizza, the thinner and crunchier the crust. I also highly recommend using a pizza stone (which would have to be preheated in the oven for 30 minutes). It's not too big an investment and it really makes a difference with the crust!

Transfer the crust to a pizza pan or stone, dusted lightly with cornmeal.

To make the sauce:

Put all the ingredients into a small pot and bring them to a boil. Reduce the heat to low and simmer for 30 minutes, stirring occasionally.

Prepare your pizza:

Preheat the oven to 375°F.

Using a ladle, add the sauce (about ¼ cup per pizza) and spread it around using the back of the ladle.

Add your desired toppings and bake the pizza in a preheated oven for 10-15 minutes, or until it is golden brown.

Let the baked pizza cool for 5 minutes before serving.

Makes 12 slices

Lazy Cook – Roasted Zucchini Soup

It turns out I'm a lazy cook.

Shhhhh…don't tell anyone!

Yes, people think I'm productive! Energized! A fiend in the kitchen!

But I'm not.

I really don't like to work.

What I do dig, what I go nuts over, what I toot my horn about, is good food done effortlessly.

When my kids were little I could be found in the drive-through line of certain fast food restaurants.

Hey, I know, that stuff will kill you; I myself haven't eaten it since 1985.

But, remember, I said I was lazy, not perfect, so sometimes incessant whining and car chair kicking from bratty toddlers with low blood sugar got the best of me and that was the only thing around.

My toddlers are now teens and thankfully actually listened to my relentless preaching about the hazards of consuming such crap. They've both moved away from Combo Meals and nestled right up with me on more gourmet culinary choices.

"Mom, I'm only ordering escargots tonight, but the big portion, okay? I want lots!" my son informed me on our latest visit to our local French bistro.

"Jeez, Mom, you're so lame. You haven't made octopus in, like, forever!" my daughter reprimands while rolling her eyes and clutching a bag of tentacles at the Italian market.

There are many requests, from many parts of the globe: *Bobotie*, the South African casserole with meat, fruit and nuts, *Moqueca De Camarao*, a stew of spicy shrimp with coconut milk which hails from northern Brazil, *Ajiaco*, the hearty Colombian chicken soup with avocados and sour cream, and of course, *Arepas*, the staple Venezuelan cornmeal cakes which we stuff with cheese for our go-to emergency dinner on extra-hectic nights.

Don't let *exotic* fool you. These are tasty and effortless dishes.

Whatever the meal, there's usually a roast vegetable involved. There's not much to it, just lay out the veggies, drizzle with olive oil, salt, maybe some Herbs de Provence, and you're off! Yes, it does take a smidgeon of time, but I've got the whole thing timed so that they roast while I whip up dinner.

Zucchini is a favorite choice. Roasting takes about 20 minutes to produce golden flavor-filled slices that the kids munch on as if they were chips! And it makes an incredible soup, by the way, for those low blood sugar moments when kids, even big ones, become whiny and cranky. It's quick, fast, and super easy. Music to the ears of a mom and a lazy cook.

Roasted Zucchini Soup

For the roasted zucchini:

1 ½ zucchinis (about 6-8)

6 tablespoons olive oil

2 teaspoons Herbs de Provence (if you don't have, you can use 1 teaspoon thyme and 1 teaspoon oregano)

salt and pepper, to taste.

For Soup:

2 shallots, minced (if you don't have, use ½ cup onion, minced)

2 tablespoons olive oil

1 cup roasted zucchini plus a few slivers of roasted zucchini for garnish

2 cups chicken stock

¼ cup heavy cream

salt and pepper, to taste

Roast the Zucchini:

Preheat the oven to 375°F.

Slice the zucchini into ¼ inch rounds. Place the zucchini slices into a bowl, and drizzle with 3 tablespoons of olive oil, tossing lightly to mix well. Line the baking sheet with aluminum foil. Spray the foil with non-stick cooking spray and spread the zucchini into a single layer.

Bake until golden, 20-25 minutes.

Make the Soup:

Sauté the shallots in the remaining 3 tablespoons of olive oil over medium heat, until golden (5 minutes).

Add the roasted zucchini and chicken stock and bring to a boil.

Reduce the heat and simmer for 5 minutes.

Blend the zucchini mixture in a food processor or blender, until smooth.

Return to the pot and add cream and salt and pepper.

Serves 2-4

FABULOUS GREEN PRETTY: CHEESE AND HERB OMELET

My mornings aren't pretty.

Somewhere, in some Disney movie, a beautiful, rested, princess awakens to warm glowing sunlight and an exciting, fun-filled day. I think there is a blue jay or two involved as well.

That's not me.

I wake up in pitch blackness to iPhone Marimba harmonizing with an annoying mosquito who's locked in on my jugular for its early morning snack.

It's five o'clock in the morning when this all goes down.

I am not much of a morning person, but I choose this early hour to rise because the house is quiet and calm. That *calm-before-the-storm* calm, but still, quiet and calm.

The dog doesn't even get up to greet me.

He lies in the living room smushed up between the coffee table and the couch, four paws dangling upwards engaged in a light trot. He is chasing a squirrel in his sleep. He wakes up momentarily and spies me passing, something I must do in order to get to my morning coffee. I'll get a quick look-over from him, a small tail wag if it's a good day, but then, it's off to sleep for him again. Apparently, imaginary squirrels are more interesting.

I use this time to wake up on my own terms, not fueled by hurried teenage morning demands *("Where's my shirt? You took my*

My Culinary Compulsion

charger!!!! Mom, my hair is frizzy and it's all your fault!")

Those will come later.

No, at five, it's just me and my dormant inspiration, which will hopefully come to life after a sip or two of my double shot of *Ristretto*.

Of course, just as I feel my fingers begin to fly on the keyboard, convinced it's the grand makings of America's next literary success forming, six o'clock arrives and I must stop and become A Mother.

It's downhill fast after that.

Many of you join me in these trenches every day. You know what I'm about to say, what needs to be done:

Children to wake, dishwasher to unload, dog to take on walk (or if you're me and think you're outsmarting everyone, dog to let out in backyard), children to re-wake, school lunches to be made (*don't forget I don't like anything with preservatives Mom, don't give me that weird pasta salad again, it smells funky*), find the missing hairbrush (*yes, it's all your fault again*), be a Crisis Clothing Consultant (*Oh my God this skirt makes me look so* [fill in the teenage-blank]), try to tame younger child's unruly curly hair, get breakfast going, let dog in, see the mud-crusted paws, kick dog back out and wish you'd just taken him on a walk instead, scream at children: *We're leaving in five minutes!!!*, be reminded by said children that breakfast hasn't been served, serve breakfast, rinse dog's paws with hose and dry with towel so you can let the barking beast back in, scream about all the things children need for school and somehow get out the door intact and on time.

It goes a little like that, right?

Some days the screaming will be directed at different issues, obviously.

I can't write an exact script.

But you follow.

And this is all before seven o'clock in the morning.

I think Cinderella's bird started chirping her to happily wake up around eight-thirty. Maybe nine.

If you were paying close attention you would have noticed I skipped feeding myself in all that craziness.

And I don't know about you guys but I need to eat.

I'm one of those types you want to stay away from when hunger kicks in. *Cranky* is putting it nice.

Unfortunately, I'm also one of those whose stomach wakes up precisely 2 hours and 17 minutes after I've awoken.

2 hours and 17 minutes puts me on the freeway with my coiffed, fed, and dressed children headed north for the 25-minute drive to school.

So, you see, somewhere in between making the appropriately-scented lunch for school and towel-drying a dirty dog, I have to prepare myself some kind of breakfast I can quickly take and eat on the road so that I can save humanity from the monster that will inevitably emerge if I don't.

It's usually toast.

Because that's quick.

And easy.

I'm good, though, you'd be proud. It's sprouted, whole-grain toast.

I'm not sure what the heck that is but I know it's healthy.

Plus, there's some quote from the bible, or Psalms, or something on the packaging, which makes me trust it more.

I'll slather it with a dollop of organic peanut butter.

As I do this I think of those flat-ab chicks on the covers of *Self* or *Women's Health*. The ones that have sweat dripping down their bodies for artistic effect? They all snack on this type of thing, the articles always boast. I look nothing like them, you realize, but for that instant, as I spread my overpriced peanut butter made from sustainably farmed peanuts, I imagine I do.

On special days, when, for some weird hiccup, I have an extra three minutes, I'll go all out and prepare myself an omelet. With a hot skillet, this takes a minute and a half, tops. My obsession lately has been herbs. All kinds, all together, and an omelet serves as a delicious platform to showcase their bright flavors.

I heat up my pan and chop herbs snipped straight from my garden. Basil. Cilantro. Parsley. Stuff I use generously but usually separately all get thrown in there before the morning dew has had a chance to dry off.

Chives. Scallions.

Really, whatever else I find that is green, goes.

A bit of red onion, for extra crunch, but not sautéed or anything: raw.

Husband would hate this, he's not much of a raw onion eater, so it's a good thing his work has him traveling and away from home most of the time. Back when I was a student living in Israel, there was a restaurant I'd frequent in the city of Jaffa. Can I call it that? Can I call it a restaurant? There were, maybe, three rickety tables, at best. And absolutely no health code inspections going on there. The only thing on the menu was hummus, which, I remember to be the best hummus I've ever had. It was served with the prerequisite pita and then, almost as if it were a prize, a whole, peeled raw onion. The trick was to chase each bite of hummus and pita with a big bite of salted raw onion.

No one would go near you for the rest of that week but it was worth it. It was amazing.

Okay, the skillet is hot! The beaten eggs go in, followed by all the great green goodness and a slice or two of cheese to seal the deal- Swiss, Gruyere, or Emmental, please.

I wrap it up into my omelet package then wait for it to cool a minute or two before I cut the finished product up into perfect squares and throw the whole deal into a Tupperware for the road.

The end result is perfect: a healthy, cheesy omelet bursting with peppery tastes of fresh herbs and crunchy onion that keeps the monster at bay and gives me time to re-energize and regroup. It's even good at room temperature, in case I'm busy screaming at the kids on the car ride and don't have a chance to get to it right away. By the time I get back home it is almost nine o'clock, just about when I should be seeing some blue jays and feeling happy and inspired.

Herb Omelet

Have more fresh herbs you want to add? Go ahead! Play around with your greens! Chives? Scallions? It's all good!

The trick is a hot skillet and speed and not honing in on perfection! Seriously, Jacques Pepin isn't watching! (And if he was, he'd still enjoy your energy and fearlessness!) If your omelet breaks, no worries! If it spills, who cares? It will be tasty and that is what counts! One final note: if you don't care for omelet ooze, then keep it on the skillet a bit longer!

- 1 tablespoon extra-virgin olive oil
- 2 eggs
- 1 tablespoon water
- salt and pepper, to taste
- ¼ cup minced raw red onion
- 2 slices cheese or 3 tablespoons shredded (Swiss, Gruyere, or Emmental)

3 tablespoons parsley, chopped

3 tablespoons cilantro, chopped

3 tablespoons fresh basil, chopped

Crack the eggs in a small mixing bowl, add water and salt and pepper, to taste.

Heat the skillet over medium high.

Add the olive oil when the skillet is almost smoking hot.

Slowly pour in the egg mixture. Add the cheese in center and sprinkle with the herbs: the chives, scallions, onions, or whatever else you've got going.

Cook a few seconds, until the edges of the egg become a bit firm.

Flip both sides of the omelet shut with a spatula (like closing a book!) or just fold the whole thing in half. Either works - the idea is to get all the gooey, tasty stuff in the middle!

Flip the packet around and cook for another minute or so.

Serves 1

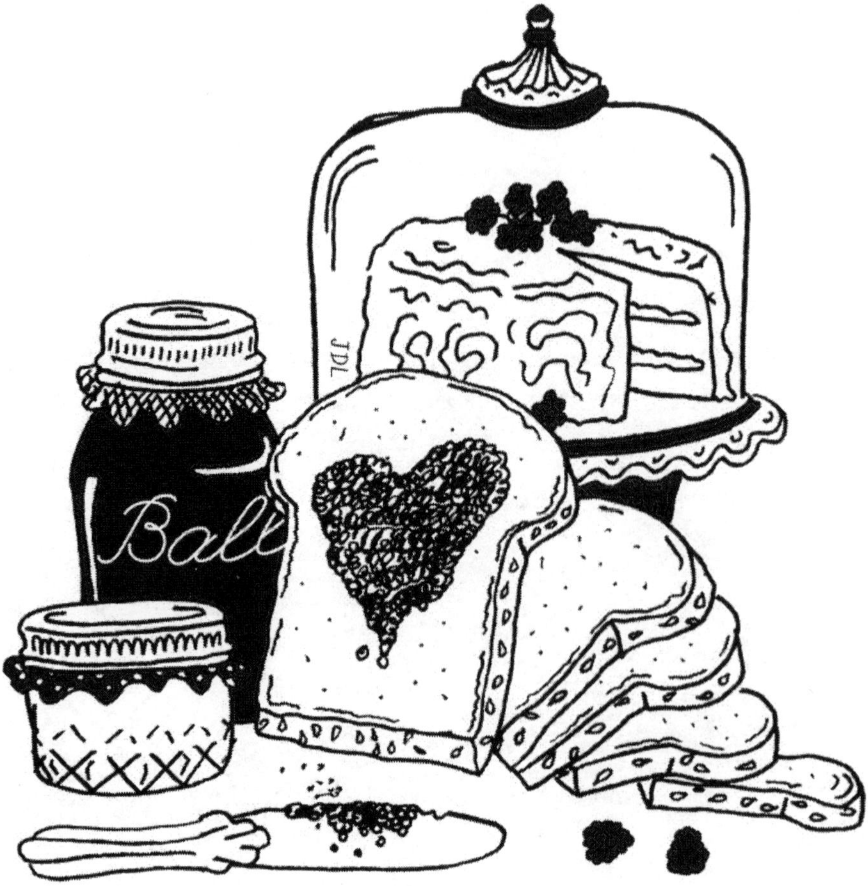
Ball
JDL

CHAPTER FOUR

MOTHERHOOD CRAZY

Risking Juvi for A Piece of Pie: Chocolate Pie

I knew from the six-inch label riddled with artificial ingredients that this was a bad idea. It was anyone's guess if, muddled amongst the additives and preservatives, was an egg or two, even if from an extremely non-organic hen. Still, my daughter's birthday celebration eagerly awaited and according to her it could not be commemorated without our local grocery's mammoth sheet cake spray painted with glorious images of the latest cutie pie from the hottest Disney channel show.

"Are you sure you don't want me to bake you a cake?" I wheedled, knowing, in the back of my head that I must be supportive of whatever her wants and needs are and be flexible at this significant time, because after all it was her birthday.

I watched her lanky body standing next to me and duly noted that she was on the cusp of adolescence, which promised an assortment of rebellion. It could be pierced body parts, neon orange hair or late night stays in strange places and thus, now would be a good time to practice that much supportive I'm-there-for-you-you-can-always-talk-to-me Mom vibe because it was a quick hop from cake choices to hoodlum hood if I played my cards wrong. So yes, knowing, in a theoretical sense how much was at stake here, I forced my best smile and tried, really tried, to embrace the idea of this impostor cake participating in my daughter's merriment. But I was betrayed by my mind, which spun with all the chemicals such a cake assaulted the sacred world of baked goods with, and my smile just wouldn't stick.

I looked at my daughter and already she had grown. It would only be a year or two before the curves would start to pop out, then the dark eyeliner, then...

"Any cake you want, I promise!" I barked out suddenly very afraid.

Of course, I was referring to my generous offer to bake her any type of cake she wanted, but being the good lawyer-in-waiting that she is, she saw the loophole and pounced on it:

"Any cake? Well I want this [Disney channel pop star dude] cake with two layers of chocolate and chocolate pudding filling in between."

"Okay," I sulked, feeling like a failure for selling out to over-processed goop in the name of pre-adolescent concord. I might have just saved her from a treacherous trail to juvi, but still, my heart sank. Transferring minimal baking ethics that require not ingesting anything whose label I can't understand was part of my Basic Culinary Legacy and I had fallen short, and quickly.

Her eyes lit up with excitement (or was that just victory? I couldn't tell) as she eagerly rattled off to the baker all the prerequisites for her artificial birthday cake, which, I noted, included generous strokes of neon yellow and orange. And even though she stood on the brink of authorized rebellion, she sensed my angst and curled her arm around my waist, whispering in her most reassuring tone, "It's okay Mom, it will be good," to which I could only respond with another feigned attempt of an equally artificial smile.

Her birthday came and with it all the excitement of her party and its festivities. Throughout it all, the cake sat waiting to be enjoyed, watching the birthday girl savor her day and hoping a cue to cut its chemical contents would soon be called. As the mother, I knew it was my duty to serve her cake. But I simply couldn't.

'I'll leave it up to her,' I reasoned with myself, knowing it was unrealistic and unfair to place such weight on an overscheduled party girl. And so, socializing led to hairstyling led to playing led to dancing led to dinner out led to more dancing led to a long movie with popcorn and sleeping bags and snoring girls and absolutely no cake.

The next day after the last of her friends left, she wandered up to her overlooked sugar teenage idol and half-heartedly said, "Mom, we forgot to eat this."

"I know", I said, this time sporting a true grin, the product of both relief and sheer happiness.

"All the same" she continued, watching me closely, "It's probably old by now" she stated, knowing that with all the questionable ingredients in there it could last until she turned 22.

"I'm more in the mood for one of your things, anyhow", she offered, giving me appropriate time to let those words sink in.

"Really?" I asked, unable to contain my excitement.

"Something really great. Something to celebrate being ten. A chocolate pie, maybe."

No sooner had she said that I was bouncing around melting chocolate and separating eggs. I caught sight of her in the corner of the kitchen. She was watching me and smiling, savoring her own private victory and sharing in mine.

Vivian's Sinfully Rich Chocolate Pie

No pie beats Vivian's, a dear friend with an equally crazy mommyhood life. Somehow, between running her own business, raising three kids and two dogs, she came up with this recipe!

Crust Ingredients:

1 7-ounce package of *Galletas Maria* (found in Hispanic section of supermarket)

½ cup of unsalted butter (melt and let cool)

Using a food processor, pulverize the *Galletas Maria*. Add the melted butter and press it into a pie pan to form a pie shell. Put the pie shell in the refrigerator, to harden and set for about 20-30 minutes.

Pie Ingredients:

4 eggs, separated

4 tablespoon milk

1 teaspoon vanilla extract

10 ounces of bittersweet chocolate morsels

Melt the chocolate morsels in a double boiler over medium heat. Once they are melted, whisk in the milk and reduce the temperature to low. Continue whisking to cool the chocolate mixture to warm, then add 4 egg yolks and the vanilla extract, whisking vigorously until the sauce becomes glossy. You don't want the egg yolks to cook like scrambled eggs. Don't have a double-boiler? Googling what that is right now? Don't worry! It's just a pot sitting inside another pot filled with some water, enabling steam to cook whatever is on top. This can also be achieved by placing a smaller saucepan or a metal mixing bowl over a saucepan that has water in it.

Using a handheld mixer or a standing mixer, beat the egg whites on high speed until soft peaks form, about 3 minutes.

Gently fold the eggs whites into the chocolate mixture (still in the double boiler on medium-low heat) a little at a time until the mixture is smooth and the egg whites have been fully incorporated and are not visible.

Stir for another minute.

Spoon the mixture into the pie shell you prepared and place the pie back into the refrigerator for at least 4 hours, preferably overnight, until well set and firm. Take out of the refrigerator about 15-20 minutes before serving.

Serves 8

This pie is rich and pairs wonderfully with homemade whipped cream. I like to place dollops of that over the servings of pie.

* See recipe for *whipped cream, on page xxvi*

Deconstructing a Blackberry

"Oooh, what are *those*?"

We weren't brushing through thick, quiet forests on a peaceful summer's Vermont afternoon like we should have been, like the way my sister and I did when we first asked that same question thirty years ago, so I felt a pang of regret that my son was cheated of the experience.

No, we were in the middle of an artificially-lit and climate-controlled supermarket, our shopping cart haphazardly parked between wilted bags of once perky arugula and a pile of rock-hard peaches claiming to be from Georgia (but any good Georgian peach would have laughed at the suggestion that these aroma-less, sterile impostors were one of their own.) It was there that I discovered the pretty Canadian box bursting with blackberries and my son, ever the fruit zealot, beamed at the bubbles of blackness, cooing in wonder and curiosity.

"These are blackberries," I force myself to answer in my calmest and most believable voice. I could still sense Champ, the horse I'd request to ride every summer in Vermont, pulling at the bit, eagerly wanting to jump the next log (we weren't allowed to jump on trails, but Champ and I were both little daredevils when paired together) and the only time I'd hold him back was when we'd encounter those thick bushes speckled with tiny, tart blackberries, one fourth the size of these ones, but packed with double the flavor. Still, that was thirty years ago and I wasn't going to spoil it for my son, no matter how sweet my memory or how shocking the size of these babies.

It didn't take much for him to love them, and love them instantly. He didn't even need a horse, or the story of one (I tried; he seemed bored). And so, we began buying blackberries. Lots of blackberries. Dollars and dollars' worth of blackberries: they can become rather expensive coming from Chile, or New Zealand, or anywhere but the mountains of Vermont, where they are a well-kept secret. It became his fruit of choice, his *food* of choice, which isn't hard for a self-proclaimed fruit eater as he is. Stacks of small plastic crates filled my fridge and for weeks I found myself running back to that neon-lit, refrigerated corner of the supermarket for more.

My son is a no-frills kind of guy and would eat them straight up, stalling only for the mandatory rinse I insisted on giving them. But that was it. I, on the other hand, become restless enjoying fruit in its naked state. I must do something to celebrate the tart yet sweet taste with an earthy undertone that hooks you and keeps you coming back for more. Eating them straight up feels too quick a commemoration. So, my mind began to wander and inevitably led me back to the mountains of Vermont. I recall my mother making heavenly blackberry pies during those long summer days spent in the Green Mountain state, but I didn't want to compete with that memory so I went for the next best thing: my mother's stellar coffee cake, to which I added a swirl of fresh blackberry compote nestled within the cinnamon center.

My son seemed a bit irritated by such manipulation. He is only six but already has mastered the curled lip. "Why are you messing with excellence?" he seemed to wonder when he realized the baked goods were created from what he felt was his private refrigerator stash. But then again, he is only six and it usually doesn't take much beyond the word "cake" to bring him around. This time seemed no exception. He was perfectly content enjoying a slice of warm fruit-laden perfection crowned with a buttery, streusel topping, as long as it was served with a side of blackberries, fresh and exploding with summer flavor.

Note: I confess, I let the blackberries get the better of me. I tested all sorts of recipes for this piece. It came down to two: my mother's coffee cake, which, as I mentioned, won my son's heart many years ago, and, this other invention: Sour-Cherry Berry pie. I'll be honest. That one happened by accident. That one happened because I was cleaning out the pantry (simply because one of the drawers was jammed, it's sadly not a regular habit of mine to organize... anything!) The culprit jamming the drawer was a forgotten can of sour cherries that had fallen and lodged itself in the back wall behind the bread flour and the industrial-sized jug of Lebanese olive oil I buy from the Middle Eastern market down the road.

"One can!" I sighed, because I knew if I wanted to make a gloopy, diner-style cherry pie, I'd need two cans, but I wasn't committed enough to the idea to go out and buy a second can. Instead, I remembered all the fresh blackberries beckoning in the fridge. And so I made a new pie: a Sour Cherry Berry pie. And it was spectacular. I offered it to several testers who LOVED it and insisted on the recipe.

"That one's gotta go in the book! That one's gotta go in the book!" they chanted with berry-rimmed lips. So I was torn, you see, between two great desserts: Mom's classic coffee cake (with a

My Culinary Compulsion

memorable blackberry addition) and this pie, which is also, so good! But again, it is another pie. There's a chocolate pie and an apple pie and a banana pie in here, so the obvious question became:

Am I over-pie-ing it in this book?

Is there such a thing as over-pie-ing it, anyhow?

I slept on the question and woke up the next morning to a breakfast of champions: a slice of Sour Cherry Berry pie and a slice of Mom's Sour Cream Coffee Cake with Blackberry Swirl. Both go great with coffee, if you're wondering. I thought about it some more, and realized there are some things you just shouldn't have to pick between, like Paris vs. New York, Marvel vs. DC, and great desserts. And so, at the risk of setting the pie balance askew here, I am listing both recipes because they are both fabulous, quite different, and equally delicious.

COFFEECAKE WITH BLACKBERRY SWIRL

½ cup unsalted butter, softened

1 ½ cup sugar

2 eggs

1 cup sour cream

2 teaspoons vanilla extract

2 cups flour

1 teaspoon baking powder

1 teaspoon baking soda

¼ teaspoon salt

1/3 cup pecans, toasted and chopped *(see page xxv)*

1 teaspoon ground cinnamon

For Blackberry Swirl:

1 cup blackberries (can use frozen if you don't have fresh)

½ cup sugar

1 teaspoon lemon zest

1 tablespoon lemon juice

Preheat the oven to 325°F.

Prepare blackberry swirl:

In a small saucepan over medium-high heat, bring the blackberries and the sugar to a boil.

Reduce the heat to medium low and simmer, stirring, for 5 minutes. Using the back of the spoon, crush the blackberries as they cook.

Remove from heat and add the zest and lemon juice.

Set aside to cool.

Prepare cake:

Beat the butter and one cup of the sugar until fluffy. Beat in the eggs one at a time.

Stir in the sour cream and vanilla extract.

Sift together the flour, baking soda, baking powder, and the salt and stir into the batter until smooth.

Spoon half the batter into a greased 9" square baking pan.

Combine the remaining sugar, nuts, and ground cinnamon and sprinkle 2/3 of it over the batter.

Add the blackberry swirl on top of that.

Top with the remaining batter then sprinkle with what is left of the cinnamon-nut mixture.

Bake 50 minutes.

Makes 9-12 pieces

SOUR CHERRY-BERRY PIE

1 unbaked pie crust (see recipe for Mildred's Famous Pie Crust on page xxix)

1 14.5 oz. can red tart cherries

1 cup blackberries (fresh or frozen)

½ cup sugar

3 tablespoons cornstarch

1 tablespoon lemon juice

1 teaspoon zest

Preheat the oven to 350°F.

Drain cherries and reserve juice.

In a saucepan, stir the cherry juice, sugar and cornstarch and cook over medium heat, stirring constantly until the sauce thickens, about 5 minutes.

Add the cherries and blackberries and cook another 2 minutes.

Remove from heat and add the lemon juice and zest.

Pour the filling into the pie crust.

Bake for 35-40 minutes, until the crust browns and the filling is bubbling. You may want to cover the edges with aluminum foil for the last 10 minutes to prevent the crust from getting too brown.

Allow the pie to cool completely before serving (that will help the filling thicken properly).

Serves 8

Becoming an American Jew: Ginger Kugel

Religion did not play a big role in my upbringing. I'd venture to say it was nearly non-existent. We were the odd, token Jewish family in an unquestionably Catholic South American country that seemed to have more churches and saints than homes. And we seemed just fine like that. My father would joke about his father (a man of iconic stature I'd grown up hearing stories about) who would most likely be turning in his grave at the sight of his son frying up Sunday's bacon. And yet, he'd smile, fry on and offer up another story about Isaac Abbady's critical role working with the British government in Palestine, only to end the story with a plateful of the tastiest bacon (the secret, he claimed, was a low flame and lots of patience). If my grandfather was turning, I couldn't hear him over the crunch.

Still, my stamp of Jewish identity seemed an inherent right to me. Born to an Israeli father, my life was woven with colorful stories of *Abba* (Hebrew for "father") and his youthful adventures as a Boy Scout romping through the still-forming confusion of Palestine and then later, Israel. My father is a real *sabra*, a term (I wear proudly as if my own) used to describe native-born Israelis. He'd come alive, vividly narrating his tales of growing up in Israel that drew me into his world and kept me there. Every year my family and I would make our annual summer trip to Israel, where, aside from excessive cheek pinching from over enthusiastic relatives, our father would point out the landmarks of his many stories and even attempt to relive some with my sisters and I: taking us on the skidding snake trail up to the peak of Masada, the Jewish fortress high on top of a mountain overlooking the Dead Sea, huddling with us in the small kiosk on a crowded Jerusalem street which served as a meeting point for skipping school, sunbathing on the overcrowded beaches in Tel-Aviv. Each had helped make my father who he was and in turn, each helped draw me closer to him.

This was how my Jewish identity was formed and joined itself easily to the kaleidoscope of my unconventional upbringing as a child raised in a Latin country by an Israeli man and an American (converted) woman, a life spent brushing shoulders with diplomat's kids and army brats that came from any corner of the world you could name. It all seemed quite normal to me.

When I started my own family in South Florida I realized I had a huge American Jewish cultural gap. Just as I couldn't bond with college buddies reciting episodes of *Starsky and Hutch* (I only caught snippets of it on our winter visits to the U.S.), I couldn't navigate through the American Jew's pronunciations of Sabbath, Yom Kippur, or Rosh Ha Shanna. There have been many other adjustments coming from a secular Israeli-international background to a South Florida Jewish one, and times where I feel I don't quite fit in. But then again, it is a feeling I have carried with me one way or another my entire life and strangeness is strangely familiar to me.

My adaptation to the food customs has been a huge success as I eagerly embrace the American Jewish obsession with brisket, *kugel*, and *tzimmes*: delicious prerequisites for being a good American Jew. The pronunciations and prayers may take some time to figure out and I am grateful for my unassuming, progressive rabbi as well as the unbridled excitement and enthusiasm of my kids. This is their reality, this is their Judaism, and I am gratefully cooking my way along, ready for and happily partaking in, the ride.

Ginger Kugel

I am indebted to Roberta Berry for this fabulous recipe!

Noodle Kugel:
- 1-pound medium egg noodles
- 1/2 cup unsalted butter, softened
- 1 (8-ounce) package cream cheese
- 8 ounces sour cream
- 6 eggs, slightly beaten
- 1 teaspoon vanilla extract
- 1 cup sugar
- 1 (8-ounce) can crushed pineapple
- 1 tablespoon fresh-grated ginger

Crumb Topping:
- 3/4 cup crushed cornflakes
- 1/4 cup sugar

2 teaspoons ground cinnamon

4 tablespoons unsalted butter

Preheat the oven to 350°F.

Bring 4 quarts of water to a boil, and cook the noodles about 10 minutes until slightly overcooked. Meanwhile, combine the butter, cream cheese, sour cream, eggs, vanilla extract, and sugar in a food processor (or mix with electric mixer). In a small bowl, combine the pineapple with ginger and mix well. Drain the noodles and place in a bowl. Add the cream cheese and egg mixture and pineapple/ginger mixture and mix well. Transfer to a greased 13 x 9 x 2-inch glass baking dish and refrigerate overnight. If you are short on time, you can freeze the kugel for 30 minutes, and then bake.

Make crumb topping:

Mix together the crushed cornflakes, sugar and ground cinnamon.

Spread the crumb topping evenly on top of the kugel. Dot the top with bits of butter and bake for 1 hour or until golden brown.

Serves 8-10

A Day in the Life of Not Saving the World:
Salmon *en Papillote*

A long, long time ago, in a galaxy far, far away, there was a very stressed out and overworked mom.

It dawned on her she could not save the world. Could she boast to fighting crime on the streets all day? No. Could she claim to seek justice in the highest courts of the land? No. Could she offer to better humanity with countless selfless hours of teaching our future generations in the classroom? Not that one either.

Nope, this is just one plain ordinary mom whose day encompassed the following (very glamorous) events:

Drag herself out of bed at the ungodly hour of dark. Curse Husband for being gone on yet another business trip.

Prepare separate lunches for two demanding palates (hold the bread for him, extra mayo for her, peel and slice the cukes for him, minuscule cubes of apple for her lest it get stuck in the braces - *and it better be Granny Smith because it's the only one sour enough for this sour-flavor-lover.*)

Imagine Husband strolling through the streets of Sofia. Feel blood pressure rising.

Try not to kill Child #1 who pops out of bed just as oh-so-tired-mom shuffles past her room en route to the espresso machine. (Note: espresso has not been consumed yet. *Not even smelled it yet.* You'd think Child #1 would get it by now: DO NOT ENGAGE WITH

AFOREMENTIONED MOTHER PRIOR TO INTRODUCTION OF COFFEE.)

Child #1 wakes up fully charged/energized. Dives right in as that first cup of Joe is being poured. "Mom, where's my uniform skirt? Mom, do you want me to play you that new song I was talking about yesterday? Mom, do you think today after school you can get me the tap shoes because my recital is in two weeks and the shoes Ms. Cindy saw me wear are too tight and Ms. Jenny said Ms. Cindy thought Marcia's shoes were the same brand and Marcia cried to Ms. Jenny because…." And on and on and on.

Sip Coffee.

Wake Child #2 up.

Prepare two completely different and equally demanding breakfasts for aforesaid children because THEY THINK THIS PLACE IS DENNY'S OR SOMETHING…

Child #1: Sunshine Breakfast: two eggs, over-easy, two slices of lightly toasted and buttered bread, sliced in exactly 5 rectangular strips (take crust off) spread around the egg as to portray rays of sunshine. (No joke. Waiting for this to not be cool anymore, but, apparently, at age 12, it still is.) Bacon on the side, semi-raw (any sign of crunch and it is rejected.) Tater tots, mushy, not crunchy, and a bowl of sliced bananas that are consumed with the same dramatic flair as if they were cyanide cookies.

Child #2: *So* not an egg eater. Oatmeal, made just right: creamy, not clumpy, with just a smidgen of brown sugar and a light dusting of cinnamon. Otherwise it's no good. Bacon: extra crunchy, i.e., one notch below burnt. (Anything less and it is rejected.) Two pounds of fruit. Don't bother giving Child #2 less than that. He'll just ask for more. Raspberries & blackberries are top choices, but will always accept any.

Then, three hours are gobbled up by The Black Hole of Time. And Errands:

Grocery shopping, photocopy making, mailing of important documents in pending preparation for move to foreign country (just a small stress factor), tending to The Phone Call That Never Ends, meeting with school teacher (#2 not listening again), gas up the chauffeur-mobile (again).

And off to *Le Alliance Française* to try and learn French (*pour quoi pas?*)

Three hours of brain frying. Utterly exhausting mental workout. Is it because I am old or was learning EASIER when I was YOUNGER???

Race back to pick up Child #2 from school.

Harass #2 about doing homework.

Afternoon snack for #2 (cheese tortilla roll, *froid*), cucumber slices with ranch, sliced apples (peeled).

Drive Child #2 to tutor. Zip back to Bus Stop of Child #1 for pickup. Zoom back to tutor with Child #1. Drop off.

Accept "Don't be late" as the closest resemblance of affection from a soon-to-be teenager.

Reluctantly head over to gym for body's sake. Because somehow, somewhere along the way, fifteen pounds crashed this party.

Exercise very unhappily. (And no, it never feels good, not before, during or after, dammit.)

Pick up Child #1 and Child #2 from tutor (late).

Assaulted by numerous complaints on the injustices of their lives.

Appear sympathetic.

Drive home with two zapped and hungry children.

Dinner?

What's a gal to do?

Salmon en Papillote!

It's simple, tasty, fast, and guilt-free!

Plus, perfect chance to savor *superherodom*, albeit within the small but intense confines of the family. Even Child #1, i.e., *Child Who Does Not Eat Vegetables*, eats vegetables when this dish is made!

Command children to assist.

"*En Papillote*" is just French-fancy for parchment paper – a mess-free, healthy method of steaming fish (or whatever protein you choose.)

Cut the parchment paper pieces into hearts (oh the fun!), coat with butter (keep an eye on craft-happy #1) and then pile on the diced veggies.

A fun, family moment is happening here. (Curse Husband for missing fun family moment.)

Seal up packages and pop them in the oven. They'll cook with their own steam, offering packets brimming with flavor and goodness that is delicious and healthy.

Child #1 & Child #2 are clueless to health scam.

They just think it's cool, and by default, maybe Mom is a bit cool too. That's as close as I'll get to saving the world today. And it's good enough for me.

Salmon en Papillote

3 6 oz. pieces of salmon

4 purple potatoes, sliced paper-thin

1 carrot, peeled and sliced into thin rounds

1 zucchini, sliced paper thin

¼ cup red pepper, diced

2 sprigs fresh thyme

2 tablespoons unsalted butter, softened

Sea salt and pepper to taste

Take a piece of parchment paper, fold it in half and cut out a heart shape. Open the paper and coat it with some butter. Place a row of potatoes on one side of the fold. Place the fish on top. Add the remaining ingredients and top with a little bit of butter. Fold the paper closed (as if making an empanada) and seal the paper by folding one corner and working the folds all the way around the paper.

Repeat with the other fillets.

Place in a preheated 350°F oven and bake until done, approximately 10 minutes.

Open the packet carefully! Beware of the steam. Enjoy!

Serves 3

A Fruitful Name: *Dulce De Mango*

As a parent, you want to try and stay optimistic.

You want to believe in your child/children…no matter what.

You want to be their advocate.

Their cheerleader.

The one that is always on their side.

I try to do this for my daughter and my son.

So when the latest member arrived, the baby mango tree I acquired several years ago and nothing happened, well, I kinda started to wonder.

I reminded myself that some children are late bloomers. I, in fact, was one of them. Recalling less-than-fuzzy memories of junior high school locker room angst, I told myself to chill out and be patient. My baby tree would produce mangoes when good and ready.

That first summer passed. There was no fruit to be had.

Still, I cheered on.

I decided to name the thing and hoped that would spur it to grow a bunch of well-adapted, comfortable-in-their-skin, much-loved, succulent fruit.

The name had to be just right.

Naming my children felt way easier. My daughter's name was

one I'd always loved and knew I'd use years before she even came into the picture. It's a good thing Husband dug it because there was zero wiggle room in the choice. For my son, we tossed around a few options before deciding on his, which then felt immediately right.

The mango tree was different. It just stood there in the sun.

Matilda?

Betsy?

Dianna?

I settled for Hilda, after Hilda Carrero, the leading lady in the soap operas I was addicted to growing up in Venezuela. She was glamorous and graceful and played characters who managed to succeed against all odds and get the incredibly hunky, rich guy in the end. Naturally, I figured such a name would inspire mangoes.

I forgave my Hilda for the hiccup of no fruit, as her Home Depot label had promised, and waited patiently for the next summer.

And the next.

And the next.

"Something is wrong with Hilda," I moped to Husband.

"Who?" He asked in his best *careful-to-not-get-in-trouble* voice.

I explained about Hilda and what was going on, hoping he'd offer some scientific advice.

"Hilda Carrero?" was his reply. "Didn't she die really young? Cancer or something?"

I called him an idiot. Because this man gets off on Friedmann Equations and Boltzmann's Entropy Formula. He can explain all the ins and outs of the supermassive black hole astronomers discovered, the one that is 12 billion times as massive as the sun. He can recount, in detail, the Duke of Wellington's success in the Battle of Waterloo (I can sing you the entire Abba song.) But he cannot, for the life of him, recall or keep up with anything to do with pop culture. Wasn't it just last week that he'd asked me, *"Kardashian? Who are they?"* I imagined Hilda Carrero was alive and well, living a quiet retirement in the penthouse of some luxury condominium in Aventura, Florida.

After insulting him, I ran to Google to learn that he was correct.

Cancer had claimed the life of the beautiful, graceful, successful, *love-conquers-all* actress years ago, when she was just fifty years old. I took a moment to pause and thank her for all those hours I spent pining over her feathered haircut, tiny waist, and unwavering power over men. Then, I went outside to have a chat with *my* Hilda.

Because everyone could use a pep talk when they find out the person they were named after perished much too soon and mango Hilda was bound to find out.

It could have been the time of day, but she looked a bit withered.

Down and out.

Not so lush.

So I did what a good mom does and I cheered her on:

You have great qualities!

Such poise!

You're strong and healthy!

(And take this extra sprinkling of fertilizer, for good measure.)

Still, a few more summers passed and Hilda remained fruitless.

The cheering subsided. The obsessive fruit-checking disappeared. I bought (and killed) other, smaller plants: basil, tomato, even lettuce.

It's not her, it's me, I concluded, resigned to the reality that my produce would come from the sterile bins of the supermarket.

Until this spring Hilda woke up full of flowers.

At least I think they were flowers.

But I didn't want to get my hopes up too high.

Maybe that was some sort of freakish Florida spider web all over the thing.

One never knows.

Summer approached and my son came running inside from the garden one afternoon screaming.

"Mom!!!!!!!"

My blood pressure dropped as I did a quick check for wounds, blood, missing body parts, dilated pupils. Nothing. He seemed fine. A bit of a crazed look, but, otherwise, fine.

"Mom!!!" He shouted again, jumping.

"What? What is it? Are you hurt?" I screamed back at him.

He didn't need to say more. He turned his head towards the garden and my eyes followed him, past the pool, beyond the cemetery of failed produce, culminating in the lone mango tree, now proudly bearing the little beginnings of fruit.

"Mangoes!" We both shouted, hugging and screaming like we'd guessed the price of the washing machine on *The Price Is Right*.

We ran over to Hilda to bear witness. My son counted ten mangoes, the size of kumquats (I tried and failed at those too) and the coaxing began anew.

Every afternoon I'd visit Hilda. I'd sing to her. I'd tell her about my day, which, at times sounded as crazy as some of those *telenovelas* I obsessed over as a kid. Slowly but surely, the mangoes grew. From babies, to teens, to adults, from dark green to hues of purple, orange, and yellow. A sunset of love and sweetness in my very backyard.

Husband's Dulce De Mango

4-5 ripe, but firm mangoes, peeled and sliced into chunks

1 cup red wine

1 cup *papelón*, also known as *panela*; raw, hardened sugar cane juice (found in Latin specialty markets). You can also use dark brown sugar instead.

3 whole cloves

2 tablespoons vanilla extract

2 teaspoons ground cinnamon

4 tablespoons unsalted butter

3 tablespoons lime juice

Place the mango pieces in a skillet and cover with red wine. Add the sugar and bring to a boil. Reduce the heat to medium and add the remaining ingredients, except for the lime juice. Simmer until the liquid thickens slightly, 15-20 minutes.

Remove from heat and add the lime juice.

Can be enjoyed hot or chilled - over vanilla ice cream!

Serves 4

Repairing Motherhood Strains: *Labneh* Chicken Salad

The wee hours of the night were spent holding a screaming seven-year old as he shrieked and squirmed in horrible pain. *What is a mother to do with such pain?* You tell your kid he will be fine, the Advil will kick in, the antibiotic will kick in – and you want to offer love and full force of confidence and assurance as you are The Mother (*and Mother knows best, right?*) but he will not, cannot, be held. He cannot be contained through his pain that has suddenly and ravenously devoured that little body and you watch a million tiny crystals shatter in you, as something tremendous breaks and your mouth dries up; you cannot help him at this very moment and so you plead this episode (which you later find out to be a ruptured eardrum) will soon end and allow his exhausted small self to fall into forgiving sleep so that you can let out that breath you've been holding in all day; carefully exhaling so as not to disrupt the delicately woven web of his well-being at this particular point in time.

You feel incredibly helpless but you are not hopeless. The Advil does kick in, the fatigue takes hold and you are left at long last with a sleeping child, his small fists clenched, his flustered panting the only remnant of the pain that kept him up just minutes ago. A sense of relief begins to absorb you right along with hunger: violent, tactless hunger, because you realize in all this time you've not had a thing, not even a sip of water.

The appetite is loud and angry and doesn't take your neglect well. You need something full and filling, rich and creamy, sweet and savory with a crunch as well; something to engage all your senses and distract you from what has left such a rattled stamp. And so you shuffle over to your refrigerator in the darkness of night and hope you will find the unfindable in there.

This is like a woman in search of her perfect mate: it just ain't that easy (for you've read countless articles about this, listened to Oprah and her clones; you are in touch). But in this case you are amazed at how in tune you are with yourself, for, gleaming amongst bowls of oranges, egg crates, and the faithful tub of mayonnaise, sits your Creamy *Labneh* Chicken Salad begging for a midnight rendezvous. It is sweet, savory, crunchy, and velvety all in one and it is yours for this night.

A smile replaces the furrowed brow that has been your uniform all evening. And even though it is 2 a.m. and you are tired beyond words you now dash, dash I say, for a spoon, grab that entire bowl of creamy deliciousness: the tang of the Middle Eastern sour cream delicacy of *labneh*, the sugary assurance of golden raisins and plump grapes and the steadfast American crunch of celery and, selfishly and content, you eat by the glow of the kitchen fridge.

LABNEH CHICKEN SALAD

Labneh is a yogurt cheese with Middle Eastern origins but I like to call it heaven's version of sour cream. Thick, rich, and creamy with a certain tanginess, it is often enjoyed in the Mediterranean simply served with a drizzle of olive oil and warm pita to scoop. This salad works great nestled inside a crunchy baguette with some greens and a couple of slices of extra sharp cheddar.

2 chicken breasts, pre-cooked* and chopped into 1" cubes

½ cup *Labneh* (available in Middle Eastern markets)

½ cup mayonnaise

2 tablespoons fresh lime juice

1 teaspoon dried dill weed

3 tablespoons onion, minced fine

2 celery ribs, sliced

½ cup red grapes, sliced in half

½ cup chopped walnuts

½ cup golden raisins

sea salt and pepper, to taste

*Chicken that has been cooked in chicken soup works fabulously, or leftover roasted chicken you've been wondering what to do with.

Whisk the *labneh*, mayonnaise, lime juice and dill weed together in a bowl. Add the remaining ingredients and adjust the seasoning. Refrigerate, preferably overnight.

To make a sandwich, spread a generous portion of the chicken salad on your choice of bread, and garnish with mixed greens and thick slices of extra sharp cheddar cheese.

Serves 4

Not Promising Anything: Deal-Breaking Chocolate Cake

Monday's are the days I schedule in empty promises.

Last week is behind me and the new week lies ahead.

Calorie-free.

It happens every time. I tell myself on Monday how great I will be this week.

This is the week I return to the gym.

This is the week I begin to shun bread.

This is the week of salad.

No cake. No sugar.

When my son was in his last year of elementary school he was handed a fancy thick document and asked to take it home.

"What is this?" he demanded in a very inconvenienced tone.

I had barely pulled up to the school car loop when he tossed the four-pound document on my lap.

"It appears to be some sort of guideline or school code," I said, reading the bold black title that said "SCHOOL CODE."

My son couldn't be bothered. He had too many pressing matters, like reaching the next level on his video game or filming his latest comedy skit, the one where Robin gets asked to the dance but Batman doesn't.

"Yeah. Just sign it in the back and return it the next day," my daughter, the wise and older veteran of the same school, casually informed us from the backseat without even looking up from her phone.

"Well, we might want to review it first," I suggested, flipping through the pages quickly before shifting into second gear. I said this not because I yearned to sift through academic bureaucracy, but because it was *The Parental Thing to Say*, like when you tell your child not to eat all those Oreos ten minutes before dinner (and then you sneak in a few as you put the package away.)

That night we did read it. Or rather, I read it while my son made every effort to look extremely disinterested.

"Where do I sign?" he interrupted after each paragraph.

When we finally got to the end, I showed him the long blank line that awaited his signature. It was such a grand moment, the first time his John Hancock was officially requested, I felt we should use several pens to gift the lucky spectators, just like the president does, but then again, there was only one line to sign and only one spectator: our equally bored dog.

"Here you go, buddy," I said, handing him the *BIC Ultra Round Stic Grip* ballpoint pen I had gotten on sale at Walmart, suddenly feeling proud and a bit sad.

He perked up, grabbed the pen, and meticulously wrote his name with inflated loops and slanted lines.

Just as he was done, he paused and looked up to the sky, deep in thought, before resuming his ebullient cursive. I was confused, he'd already written his whole name.

"Whatcha doin'?" I asked casually.

"Signing," he responded triumphantly.

He turned the document towards me and sure enough, there was his name, the one I saw him write.

Along with a few extra letters: *npa*.

"NPA? What's that?" I asked.

"Just taking precautions," he clarified, evading the question.

"What precautions? What does NPA mean?" I persisted.

"*Not promising anything*," he announced with a smug smile. "That way, I'm covered. I signed. There's my name. But I'm not promising anything."

From that moment on, anytime a signature or commitment of any kind was required of him (apparently once you enter middle school you sign a lot of stuff), it was always followed by those three letters, npa: a quick and optional escape.

Which brings me back to my Mondays and my empty promises.

I have all the best intentions, I do.

And I am good on Mondays, I promise.

Even Tuesdays. Maybe not rock solid, but there I go.

Wednesday is another matter altogether. It's not called hump day for nothing. You either get over the hump, or you don't.

My mind's pretty much caved by Wednesday. I start daydreaming in sugar.

And by Thursday, it's all over. I need cake.

A cake I will love and will love me back. A cake that will make me feel whole and human and alive, much more so than a stick of celery or a set of squats. There's a chocolate cake that captured my heart years ago. It is easy and fast and moist and delicious. It is so painless to make it serves as the perfect temptress to my weekly promises of fitness and health.

Maybe I should write myself a contract to sign every Monday. With three little letters added to the end.

Deal-Breaking Chocolate Cake

    10 tablespoons unsalted butter, softened

    2/3 cup unsweetened cocoa powder

    ¾ cup milk

    2 cups cake flour (page xxiii)

    1 ½ teaspoons baking soda

    ½ teaspoon baking powder

    ½ teaspoon salt

    1 ¾ cup sugar

3 eggs

2 teaspoons vanilla extract

Preheat the oven to 350°F.

Grease a 9 x 13" pan

In a small bowl, whisk together the cocoa powder and 2/3 cup boiling water.

Add the milk.

In another bowl, whisk together the cake flour, baking soda, baking powder and salt.

In a mixing bowl, beat the butter and sugar until fluffy. Add the eggs, one at a time. Beat in the vanilla extract. Then, with the mixer on low speed, add the dry ingredients, alternating with the cocoa mix. Beat until smooth.

Place in your cake pan and bake 25-30 minutes.

Serves 12-16

Quick Chocolate Frosting

2 oz. semi-sweet baking chocolate

2 tablespoons unsalted butter, softened

3 tablespoons milk or espresso or rum

1 ½ - 2 cups confectioner's sugar

Melt the chocolate over a double boiler or in a microwave (follow the specific instructions on your microwave). Cool and add to the butter. Beat with a mixer, adding milk (or) espresso (or) rum. Slowly add the confectioner's sugar until creamy.

Tip: I prepare this cake as a sheet cake because it's simple and straightforward. However, this cake can also serve as a showstopper extra pretty and perfect layer cake. Just bake it in 2 9" round pans and double-up on the frosting. You'll need about ¼ cup frosting to put on the top of one of the (already cooled!) cakes, then gently place the second cake on top and use the remaining frosting on the outside!

Stories, Lessons, and Brownies

"Mom, you should make *this*," my teenage daughter announces, flashing her phone in my face for a heartbeat, enough for me to catch a towering cake of six…seven…layers with sparks and enough fondant to rebuild Pompeii.

"Or *this*…" she adds before I can respond, again a quick show of something neon and rotating. "Of course, I like this one," she continues, this time not even bothering to show me. "Although I'd swap out the peanut butter flambé for chocolate mousse. You know how I feel about peanut butter, Mother."

It's fantastic that the worldwide web is at our kids' fingertips. Great, really. So much to learn out there, information made accessible to all. But, sometimes, ignorance is bliss, particularly when one has a child obsessed with the most complicated food preparations and an, while flattering, albeit inflated, trust in her mother's culinary abilities.

Which is how I end up being accosted with baking feats that should, at least, earn me a spot on The Food Network's *Chopped*.

I don't get that, though.

What I get is a lot of sugar and flour and egg all over the place, battles with multiple kitchen appliances, silent cursing, extra rounds of chardonnay, and a girl that, so far, I haven't managed to let down.

Still, I kind of hold my breath when I see my daughter approach me with that iPhone clasped tightly and that excited look on her face. *Oh God what baking coliseum am I being thrown into now?*

"Mom," she begins and I find myself closing my eyes, as if a Coconut Cream Pie is about to come flying in my face. "Today I'm just in the mood for something simple," she goes on. (*Note: simple is a relative term, some people find a 5k to be simple. I can't even jog around the block.*) "One of your classics." (*Note: she has a tendency to distort reality. That Transformers cake that took Buddy Valestro and his team four days to make may have turned into one of my classics in her mind.*)

I am waiting to be hit by the Coconut Cream Pie.

"Mom, can you please make Grandma's Brownies today?"

"Yes! Grandma's Brownies!" The other child chimes from across the room. "I love Grandma's Brownies!"

I almost collapse when I exhale. I touch my face. There is no pie. There is no mountain to climb, there is no award to be won. There is just the simple and comforting pleasure of baking my mother's signature brownies. They are rich and chocolaty inside offering the slightest crumbled crust on the outside: the ideal balance of fudge and cake. My children never had the pleasure of meeting my mother, but in as best as I can, I share with them tidbits of her- with stories of my childhood, valuable lessons and insights she gave me, and, of course, this time-honored chocolate treat.

Marilyn's Brownies

1 cup unsalted butter

4 oz. unsweetened chocolate

4 eggs

2 cups sugar

1 cup flour with a pinch of salt

1 teaspoon vanilla extract

½ cup toasted walnuts, chopped (optional)

Preheat the oven to 350°F.

In a double-boiler, melt the butter with the chocolate. Using a hand-held mixer or a standing mixer, beat four eggs until thick and lemon-colored. Add sugar. Stir in the vanilla extract. Add the chocolate/butter mixture. Gently fold in the flour, and stir in the nuts. Bake in a greased 13 x 9 pan for 25-30 minutes.

Makes 12 3" brownies

Free Range Motherhood: Potato Chip Fritatta

A mother has free range to get desperate. You moms out there know what I am talking about. It goes pretty much like this, or at least, it did for me...

Non-mom declaration:

When I have kids they will never drink Coke.

Mom reality:

Only two cans dear. You have to eat some dinner.

Non-mom declaration:

My children, MY children of all children, will never step foot in a McDonalds!

(I can hear my sister-in-law's laughter all the way from Omaha on this one...)

Mom declaration:

Gimme a Mighty Meal, double bacon cheeseburger, extra fries, Coke, and maybe another cheeseburger.

So you get it. Maybe I was a bit idealistic. Maybe I wanted to be like Dianne Keaton in that baby movie and live in a big barn house in Vermont and make my own baby food from scratch (the million-dollar business and cute veterinarian being a nice bonus.) But life gets in the way and, I dare say, even I, a professed food snob, get desperate from time to time with a bit of greasy, preservative help.

Take the whole vegetable conundrum for instance. My daughter won't go near them. Not with a ten-foot pole. Not with a ten-foot pole loaded with M&M's on the end. Nothing. No can do. And I have tried. I did charts, rewards, sneaky stuff like those famous spinach brownies (*'They taste weird, Mom, can't you just make your normal ones?'*)

I resorted to cute and crazy. Mixing it up a bit. Living outside the box. My daughter is a box girl. There are rules and WE FOLLOW THEM. And so, if I break one it's a big deal. And the girl keeps track, I tell you. I can't slip up one bit because she's there to call me on it: *It's Tuesday, Mom, you usually have the laundry folded by now. Why isn't it on the table? Monday is your bill day, why are there so many envelopes unopened in the front desk? Don't forget Mom, it's Friday, ice cream day. We go every Friday.* I'm telling you she is relentless about the order of life and trip-ups are unacceptable.

Except when they work in your favor. Like serving up potato chips for dinner. Potato chips no less! Oh the rebellion! She wigged on that one. So much so that she didn't realize the vegetables lying underneath. And thus, gobbled the whole thing up and even asked for more. This is a small victory for me and all mothers out there (we are all smiling and nodding our heads now.) So, you may think it irrelevant or cheesy but it works. Take some eggs, throw veggies into them, shred cheese, dump it all in muffin tins so they bake individually and look too precious, and sprinkle crushed potato chips on top and you've got yourself a potato chip frittata that will make the most stubborn anti-veggie kid smile and ask for more.

Mom declaration:

Forget hard-and-fast rules: leave room for Cute and Crazy.

Remember: more battles are won with potato chips than logic.

Potato Chip Frittatas

A great dish for breakfast, lunch or dinner!

5 eggs

2 tablespoons heavy cream

½ teaspoon salt

1/8 teaspoon pepper

1 tablespoon olive oil

1 leek, sliced (about ½ cup)

¼ cup onion, diced

1 carrot, grated

½ cup zucchini, diced

¼ cup mushrooms, diced

¼ cup shredded cheese

potato chips (I used French fry-style, but you can use regular chips as well)

Preheat the oven to 325°F.

Whisk together the eggs, milk, salt and pepper. Heat the oil in a skillet over medium heat. Add the leek and onion. Cook until tender, 3 minutes. Add the zucchini and mushrooms and sauté another 3 minutes. Add the carrot and cook for 1 more minute. Set aside.

Grease a 6-cup muffin tin. Divide the cheese among the cups, then add the vegetables. Pour in the egg mixture until each cup is ¾ full. Don't overfill, the egg will rise as it bakes! Add a small handful of potato chips on top of each. If you have more egg and veggies, just fill up more muffin tins!

Bake until cooked through, 12 to 15 minutes. Run a knife around the edges to loosen.

Serves 4-6

Cooking up a Dream: Thyme Roasted Chicken

Julia Child's breasts were leaning on the speckled white linoleum table in lopsided fashion. It figures; I was in the presence of the icon of American cooking and all I could focus on were her breasts.

"Dear, just a touch of black pepper will give it the bite you need," she volunteered with a kind smile.

The room was small and musty. It was late at night and the light had a congenial glow to it. I didn't know the day or the year, or the five other people huddled around her for that matter. All I recognized was the table. It was the same one that graced my family's ancient kitchen in Venezuela thirty years ago. The one with the cheap, dented chrome border. How Julia's breasts ended up resting on it was beyond me, but I wasn't about to question that now.

Her masculine, oversized hands tore away rhythmically at the Boston Bibb lettuce, briskly assaulting the leaves, leaving them finished in customized 2-inch shreds without them even having a chance to notice. Almost as if the lettuce came that way. A child's cry pierced through the comradery of the room instantly shaking us from the intimacy of these four walls of culinary opportunity. I grimaced and bit my lip, pissed off because the kid was mine. The cry grew louder and was accompanied by a pestering *"mama, mama."* As much as I wanted to be with Julia, I knew I'd have to leave.

"Excuse me, I'll be right back," I offered, feeling sorry for myself.

The five strangers and Julia looked up momentarily and gave me a diluted, empathetic smile: each one the merrier that they had no children to tend to at that moment. They sipped their wine. It was chilled. And good. I could just tell.

I left the room and entered a world of darkness, void of details or occurrences, just emptiness and lost time. When I returned, the lettuce was already delicately resting inside the bright red porcelain bowl. Come to think of it, it was the same bowl my mother had used for my sisters and my monthly haircut. This very bowl would lie inverted over our heads as the blunt scissors battled against our rebellious hair. My mother was perseverant and determined as she worked her way around the rusted frame, leaving us looking like five and six-year old Ringo look-alikes.

But now the bowl was brand new and held no remnants of our fashionable past, another detail I chose not to question. And as I admired its bright metamorphosis, the child began to cry again. This time the stares I received from those around me were not so patient. The kid was bothering all of us and I'd better fix it.

"Right back," I assured them, making a quick exit stage left towards my nondescript world of darkness that cut me off from all of Julia's extraordinary food moments (was that an anecdote on her first sampling of *boudin noir* I was missing?).

I knew parenting would be difficult and thankless, but this was one of the most difficult and thankless days I'd experienced. As soon as the anonymous kid of mine was silenced, I returned from exile.

"Place them gently, like so," Julia explained, casually arranging a dozen oysters that had been coated lightly in a fluffy buttermilk batter and flash fried in hot oil. "And now we pour the warm garlic-thyme vinaigrette," she instructed, automatically producing it from behind her on the white counter. Dishes were passed around and as I lined up to receive my portion of goodness that damn kid started wailing full force.

"Damn it I want my salad!" I demanded out loud, while those around me now shifted into complete aggravation and a lack of sympathy for my situation. If it boiled down to Julia's salad and my child's malaise, the choice seemed obviously simple to me. Be that as it may, I was being watched, so I put down my plate and headed out towards my destiny as all the '*ooohs*' and '*ahhhhs*' over the salad chimed in the background.

When I returned I was disheveled, distraught, and disconnected. The room had changed even though it looked the same. The circle around Julia had closed a bit and I was no longer a part of it. The salad was gone and the closest I could come to sampling such a divine marriage of earth and ocean was the scent wafting in the air for my nose to be teased by. Julia had moved on to another story, a time when she and Jacques Pépin prepared a simple roast chicken dinner together. She was cradling a bumpy, raw chicken in her hands as she spoke, holding it upright, as if introducing it to its audience. (*Fredericka, I would call it*, I thought to myself. My ritual of naming my dinners had been inspired by Julia's intimacy with her food). After describing the suspiciously simple method of preparing the chicken, Julia miraculously produced the finished product from behind her again. And as she set the chicken down on the table for all those around her to enjoy, she did another wonderful thing: she paused, smiled, and waved those large and friendly hands of hers from side to side to signal that the circle be reopened to include me again. The people began to part like the Red Sea, and I was instantly embraced by Julia's warm smile framed by a stunning roast chicken. At that moment there was no crying child, no darkness, no interruptions, just Julia, an unforgettable dish, and I. It was a magical moment that ended all too abruptly on a dark morning at 5:14 am when my alarm clocked buzzed to attention, socking me out of my wonderfully delicious slumber with Julia Child. I cursed into my pillow and waited for a kid to start crying.

THYME ROASTED CHICKEN

I learned of this simple and delightful roast chicken recipe while listening to the iconic French chef, Jacques Pepin reminiscing about his good friend Julia Child in a radio interview. This was one of their favorite dishes created together. The gravy is my mother's, and pairs beautifully with it.

- 1 whole chicken (4 to 5 pounds)
- 3 tablespoons olive oil
- 1 ½ teaspoons coarse sea salt
- 1/2 teaspoon freshly ground pepper
- 4 sprigs fresh thyme

For the Gravy:

½ cup white wine

1 cup chicken broth

3 tablespoons flour

salt and pepper, to taste

Preheat the oven to 400°F. Rinse the chicken and pat dry. Place 2 whole sprigs of thyme inside the cavity. Rub olive oil all over the chicken. Chop the remaining 2 sprigs of thyme and sprinkle over the outside of the chicken. Add the salt and pepper.

Place the chicken breast-side-up in a baking pan, and place in the oven. Roast for 20 minutes. Flip the chicken breast-side-down and bake another 20 minutes. Stand the chicken upright* and roast another 20 minutes. Turn the oven off and let the chicken stand in the oven for 10 minutes.

*Use an empty soda can or food can to prop the chicken up by placing this inside the cavity and resting the chicken on it.

Prepare the Gravy:

Remove the chicken from the baking pan and place on a cutting board. Add 1/4 cup white wine to the baking pan and place over high heat, scraping the bits in the pan with the wine. Pour this into a saucepan, add another 1/4 cup white wine and 1 cup chicken broth and bring to a boil. Lower the heat until the sauce comes to a simmer. Mix 3 tablespoons of the wine with 3 tablespoons of flour and slowly add to the sauce. Simmer for 2 to 3 minutes, or until thickened. Add salt and pepper to taste.

Serves 4

A Mother's Promise: *Babaganoush*

Rich hues of purple beckon me. The market in Mexico is full of colors today: fire orange for zucchini blossoms, crimson red endless mounds of tomatoes, and rich coal-colored piles of avocados that promise a buttery light green inside. I could gather them all and on most days I do, but today I go for the eggplants- they are the perfect size- nothing too pretentiously large, smooth and shiny with a dark skin as mysterious as the pond in Vermont I'd dive into freely as a child. These babies are mine. Today I will give them center stage.

I take them home – just two is all I need, and the ritual begins. It is a slow process- I must gently char the outside over a low flame on my gas stove (*yes, I am in Mexico, in Mexico I have a gas stove!*), easing in the smoke that will give my dish its distinctive flavor. My young son watches me in awe and confusion. I am doing exactly what I tell him not to do. I am playing with fire. But this is different, I guarantee him. This is *aubergine* and I am making *babaganoush*. I figure if I speak in foreign tongues I might lose him. But he is curious and stubborn like me and insists on clarification. So I tell him. It is a favorite Middle Eastern dish of smoked eggplant to be scooped with freshly baked pita.

He isn't buying what I am selling. The smooth plum-colored skin is getting withered and cracked, its hue turning a tarnished black. Chips of burnt skin fall off revealing a scarred cream interior. *This can't be good*, my son thinks.

But I promise him it is. I will crush and mince fresh garlic, squeeze tart lime and sprinkle coarse salt and add it to this mix and this will be good. Like your grandfather's father ate in the dusty hills of Palestine before there was a state of Israel. Like your grandfather scoops messily while reading the newspaper and listening to Brahams. Like your father did as a young soldier on weekend break in *Ertez Israel*, the land of Israel. This will be good.

I will take this withered warrior of an eggplant and make a hero out of it. I will slice it in half and gently scoop out the smoked pulp. It will give to my spoon and splat out onto my bowl. It will look ordinary but it will taste extraordinary. The flame I've gently subjected it to has left it with a magical smoky taste. And it will dance with those three simple ingredients. If I feel frisky I will drizzle some extra virgin olive oil (like a good Middle Eastern, this is reflex) and my fresh pita will scoop up this goodness and know something else is missing. One other ingredient I have forgotten.

Chopped parsley.

Finely minced. So as not to interrupt but to add a spicy bite. Another reflex a *sabra's* daughter ought never forget.

And it will be perfect. It will dance in your mouth and your mind will beg for more, your stomach content and dazzled. All this over purple shine and blurry black and white photographs of forefathers and more forefathers – all of which shared this dish that today, my son, you share. In the crowded city of Mexico, you are instantly on that dusty hill in *Eretz Israel*. This is what a drizzle of olive oil, a squeeze of lime, and an eggplant can do. I promise you. I promise you.

BABAGANOUSH

2 eggplants, medium size

2 tablespoons lime juice

1 garlic clove, finely minced

2 tablespoons flat parsley, minced

2 tablespoons extra virgin olive oil

salt, to taste

Over medium heat of a gas burner, char the eggplants- rotating regularly. You can also do this on a BBQ grill or you can broil them in the oven on a baking sheet, turning eggplants every 5 minutes. Make sure to use aluminum foil on your baking sheet as these guys will get messy! Skin should be blistered. Be patient, it can take up to 20 minutes, and be prepared: things will get smoky!

Allow the eggplants to cool for 5 minutes.

Cut the eggplants lengthwise down the middle and scoop out the pulp into a bowl. Mash with a fork. Add the remaining ingredients.

Chill and serve with pita bread.

Makes 2 cups

You Can't Beat Yellow Dye #5: Macaroni and Cheese

"What kind of sauce is this?" they asked in unison with scrunched eyebrows, ignoring the bead of sweat that had formed on the nape of my neck from my constant whisking. I turned around to face my two young children, looking aghast, noses upturned (cute noses albeit). "It's the wrong color," they persisted, insisting that I reply to their unanswered question.

"It's homemade," I threw at them like a confident Aborigine hunter throws a boomerang in the dead of a quiet summers' heat. This one would surely come back to me.

"I don't like it," the little one said without skipping a beat, derailing my life's mission of teaching these suburban brats to appreciate good food, i.e., *my* food.

"Try it," I urged with authoritarian bravado. I knew I'd need to pull all the stops and get their tiny hands to activate their tiny forks to scoop a bit of my mac-and-cheese into their mouths. A little bit of *"because I said so"* parenting was in need here since, after all, this so-called mac-and-cheese was not blindingly neon in color, so, following their line of reasoning, it must be bad.

The two accomplices turned and looked at each other in silent conference. *Do we struggle with our demented mother or do we eat?* their gaze asked. Whatever they'd decided to do, they decided to do it together, that much I could tell. If they've learned anything in their young lives it was this: when Mom gets that angry glazed look on her face we'd best stick together. If there is a food product involved, they tended to silently clasp hands to solidify the alliance.

Resistor 1 and Resistor 2 quietly turned back to their steaming bowls filled with creamy macaroni and, with the timing of an Olympic synchronized swimming team, reluctantly scooped. I exhaled and relaxed my grip on the whisk. I knew I had won. All I needed for victory was this one chance. One taste and they'd be mine, for how could my meal, and nurtured to creaminess with love and wholesome ingredients, be overturned by neon yellow dye #5? It was just a matter of getting them this far, and, obviously, my pissed-offness had gotten them this far. I turned my back to them and smiled.

Score:

Mommy: One

Kids: Zero

Until...

"...I don't like this", Resistor 2 whined.

"Yeah, me neither," Resistor 1 chimed in.

And then in graceful unison - I wasn't watching them but I knew they were holding hands, "This stuff is gross..."

Now I know they are only nine and six and I should have had plenty of time to grow elephant skin as a mother of a nine and six-year old. But I haven't. Since my oldest learned at fifteen months that tofu soup was admissible for breakfast in certain countries, my children have been nurtured in a constant cloud of *Osso Bucco*, Shrimp and Scallion Pancakes and Rabbit Braised with Kalamata Olives.

It's just the way it is in my household; so, accepting my version of Macaroni and Cheese should be no exception.

But apparently, it was. I could not compete with the big proud world of Kraft, and as the children pushed their elbow macaroni from side to side, they looked at me ambivalently and now remorseful, sensing my hurt.

"Mom, can we have more chicken?" one offered as an olive branch to my culinary ego.

"Yeah, the chicken, Mom. The chicken is good. We'll have more of that," the other begged (interesting how they work as a team only when it is convenient to them, I noted.)

I let go of the whisk and with it any hopes of culinary enlightenment for my children. I turned to them and was faced with their gaze, as warm as the Cranberry Pear Crisp I had planned to bake.

"All right," I relented.

Score:

Kids: 10 (out of 10)

And with that, I scooped some chicken onto their plates, making a note to offer up my mac and cheese when they were a bit older. It was nothing exciting, just leftover *schnitzel* from the night before, but they gobbled it up and watching them do so inevitably led me to smile.

Purist Mac and Cheese

2 cups elbow macaroni

6 tablespoons unsalted butter

3 tablespoons flour

1 ½ cups whole milk, heated

12 oz. extra sharp Cheddar cheese, grated

1 tablespoon Dijon mustard

1 teaspoon salt

1/2 teaspoon ground pepper

Bring 4 quarts of water to a boil, and cook the macaroni until tender, about 10 minutes. Drain and return to the pot. Reduce the heat to low. Add 4 tablespoons of the butter and stir in gently. Set aside.

In a small pot, melt the remaining butter on medium heat. Add the flour and stir with a wooden spoon until the mixture turns amber in color, 3 to 4 minutes.

Slowly whisk in the milk and stir until thick, 2 – 3 minutes.

Reduce the heat to low.

Add the remaining ingredients and mix to combine.

Adjust the seasoning. Add the cheese sauce to the macaroni.

Note: *If you like your mac and cheese a little "looser" you can stir in up to ½ cup hot milk in the end.*

Serve immediately.

Serves 4

Jam Crush: Apricot Jam

There's a woman I've never met whom I love.

Dearly.

And with unwavering reverence.

Catholics pray to saints; Buddhists burn fragrant incense.

I worship Husband's former roommate's mother, whose name I don't even know.

I imagine her slender and fit. The type of woman who doesn't look her age, who gardens and rides a pastel-colored bicycle into town. Her bicycle has a wicker basket for the baguette or two she brings back from her trips to the local market along with bunches of earth-covered peppery radishes, plump strawberries, and bright orange carrots whose leafy tops leave a trail on the ride home like a healthy adaptation of Hansel and Gretel's breadcrumbs.

Of course, Husband's former roommate's mother sports a tan.

Not that leathery *too-many-years-sizzling-on-a-beach-towel* tan, but that healthy-glow tan, the one that comes from endless rounds of tennis, hiking, and kayaking, things involving pure air and strong lungs.

I look to her son, Matej, for clues about her. He is handsome, charming, smart, and youthful, with a mane of golden hair and a movie star smile that makes it hard for Husband and I to keep up on who his current girlfriend may be. He is generous, kind, and thoughtful, all of which serve as a nod to his mother, whom I surmise, raised him that way. This is enough to already like this woman, to allow my imagination a one-way ticket into her home, where we'd have many absorbing conversations by a crackling fireplace while stirring risotto laced with fresh-picked yellow morels or sipping a glass of chilled Rebula wine.

But the adoration really began when I got her jam.

It came, several years ago, in a Mason jar wrapped in an old washcloth with a single scribbled word on its red-checkered top: *marelice*.

"Here," Husband said while pulling it out of his carry-on after one of his many trips home. "Matej sends this to you."

I grabbed the jar carefully, like when Indiana Jones first took the Golden Idol off its booby-triggered pedestal in *Raiders of the Lost Ark*. I don't speak Slovenian, but, from its deep golden hue, I knew what it must be and my heart fluttered with joy.

"It's from his mother," Husband added. "Her *world-famous* apricot jam."

There are few things I'd give my first-born up for but *world-famous* apricot jam is certainly one of them. Said first-born would probably go willingly, so tired she is of hearing me complain over the years about how impossibly difficult it is to find a properly made apricot jam. Most of my apricot-jam-eating-experiences are cloaked in the following whines:

Too sweet!

Not apricoty enough!

Wrong texture!

She can tell you that list goes on and on.

But here was a homemade apricot jam that was bursting with promise.

And did not disappoint.

I knew from the first spoonful, when the balance of acid and sweet shimmered in my mouth. After that I kept finding excuses to pull out the jam. My breakfasts became decidedly Parisian with the mandatory croissant and, of course, the irreplaceable apricot jam. In the afternoons I took to being a Brit, taking 4 p.m. breaks for a spot of tea and a scone which I'd dutifully slather with, yep, Husband's former roommate's mother's jam.

The jam was given elite shelf status in our fridge and guarded with the same scrutiny as Fort Knox.

No one in the household was allowed access.

If anyone dared ask for some, they'd be met with heavy resistance on my part (*"Jam? You're more of a Nutella fan!"*), many sighs, and many attempts at redirection (*"Here, have this bag of chips. You aren't a fruit eater, remember?"*)

Then, the inevitable happened and I ran out. Teaspoon by teaspoon, scrape by scrape, lick by lick, the jar practically squeaked.

My interest in Husband's former roommate's travel plans back home to Slovenia suddenly increased. He had left after university, settling half way around the world in a crowded, Mexican metropolis for a two-year job stint that went on and on.

"Your mother must miss you," I coaxed.

"You need to stay connected," I urged.

"Don't forget everything us mothers do for our sons," I whimpered, hoping to successfully weave in a thread of guilt that would get him on a plane home.

Remember though, Matej is a good man; his mother made him that way.

He is kind and thoughtful and warm.

Which makes him a good son.

A son that travels back home frequently.

And luckily, brings me back a jar or two of his mother's *world-famous* jam.

"One day I want to meet your mom," I tell him. "I want to be in her kitchen and watch her make her jam," I say, not sharing with Matej that I would wish for a matching pastel-colored bicycle with a market-filled basket as well.

Mirjana's Apricot Marmalade

2 ½ pounds apricots

4 cups sugar

Rinse apricot and slice in fourths, removing the pit. Place them in a large bowl and sprinkle sugar. Cover and refrigerate overnight.

Place apricot/sugar mixture in a pot and bring to a cook over medium flame, stirring constantly. When the mixture begins to boil, reduce heat to low and let simmer for 20 minutes. Remove from heat, place in sterilized jars and allow to cool.

If you don't have access to fresh apricots but have got the craving for apricot jam, here is another delicious recipe using dried apricots:

Dried Apricot Jam

   6 cups water

   2 cups dried apricots

   1 cup sugar

   1 lemon

   2 tablespoons fresh lemon juice

OPTIONAL

Some people enjoy more complex flavors in their jam. If you are one of those, you may add 1 cinnamon stick, 2 cloves, and 2 cardamom pods to the whole process. You would do this by placing the spices in a muslin bag (yes, they sell these on Amazon) and plopping it in at the very beginning of the jam-making process (with the apricots, sugar, and water.) I personally like to be socked in the face with pure apricot flavor.

Place 6 cups of water in a pot with the apricots and sugar. Raise the heat to high and bring to a boil.

Once boiled, reduce the heat to medium, slice ¼ of the lemon into very thin slices and then into pieces, and add to the pot.

Cook over medium heat, uncovered.

After 20 minutes, using a potato masher, mash the apricots and lemon together, leaving bits and pieces (this will make it more like Husband's former roommate's mother's jam).

Let simmer another 10 minutes, undisturbed.

Check to see whether the jam has thickened enough by taking a spoonful and plopping some on a plate. If it plops to your liking (i.e., it doesn't soup all over the place but, rather, sets exactly how you'd imagine it should on a perfectly crispy croissant) then it is ready. If not, cook just a little bit longer. Once thick enough, remove from heat, add the lemon juice, and let it sit until it cools. Place in sterilized jars and keep in the refrigerator.

Makes 4 cups

Baking Through Grief: Vanilla Raspberry Cake

I suspect she will never be the same. The road bore humid secrets of the night before and the sky was a solemn blackish blue. In an unfathomable twist of fate, while that darkness turned to dawn, her son was hit by a Jeep Grand Cherokee and the day began with immeasurable heartbreak.

There is no sense to such a senseless act. There is no sense to a child, all of sixteen, being taken away from his world, which, by all accounts, was one filled with thrill and adventure. I visited her in her home and it was adorned proudly with photographs detailing all of her son's explosiveness and zest. An image of a young child, all of seven or eight, comfortably propped on a huge motorbike bathed in crusted mud. Another of the same child, reeling in a supersized fish, with an even bigger grin.

A photograph catches me and begs me nearer: it is a close-up of him sporting a wildly long and bleached-blonde Mohawk. He is probably eleven in that one, and, where the hairdo could easily serve as the centerpiece of that image, it is not. It is the warmth and promise of his smile that has brought me closer. It is the sparkle in those eyes that demanded me to stop. And think. And look closely. '*I am alive; I am happy*', those eyes say confidently and fearlessly.

Death is the uninvited visitor in our lives that always manages to show up and we are never sure what to do with. This teen's passing has touched me to the core, has made me grab onto the soft, small hands of my own children and hold on tight. There are pictures everywhere, you see. So many pictures. So many memories. And the promise of a life that remains unkept. And his mother's eyes that have hardened and I don't know how they will see life as sweet again.

We all deal with grief in our own personal way. Mine, of course, is through the kitchen. It is the turf in which I feel most comfortable, where I best know my way. I made a cake. For my friend, and for her son. I beat the sugar and butter for a long, long time. It needed time and care, just as a small child does. I didn't want to rush this cake. I wanted it to be just right. Some cakes call for a more impersonal approach: dump all the ingredients in one big fast hello and beat them hard and fast for three minutes, pour into their respective pans and bake them, and that is the end of that. I love those cakes. They are convenient, quick, and good, but this time, it didn't feel right. I wanted to savor making this cake, carefully divvy its contents and gently introduce them to make a grand batter.

Lulu, my hot red mixer, understood. She churned diligently and produced the fluffiest butter/sugar mixture as I stood numbly watching her paddle go round and round. Mostly things work just as I intend in my kitchen, and that soothes me. Once the cakes are baked and cooled, I begin to assemble them, first carefully slicing them into thin layers then dousing them with simple sugar to seal the moisture, then adding the raspberry preserves and finally, the whipped cream topping.

I can't seem to shake the images from the collage of photographs at my friend's house. Images of youth and hope and adventure churn into a sad loss under the hum of Lulu. Still, I hope her son would think this the perfect cake for his mom and the thought of that gives me solace. I spin the final layer of frosting, making sure to have my cake spatula at the perfect angle so as not to create any imperfections. I carefully mark the pieces using the back of a bread knife and go about creating the final touches with a French tip and some fresh berries. I turn and pipe and assemble as if this cake were my practical test for *Le Grand Diplôme*. All the while I think of this boy that I never knew who has died, and I think of his mother, who has touched my life and that of my children with all her spunk and creativity and fun.

The cake is done and is indeed perfect. I know she will never be the same, how can she? She has lost her son. But I bring her the cake anyway. It is round and sweet and filled with richness. She places it on the table, next to the photographs. I hug her and, once again, express my condolences. "That kid, he has such a sweet tooth," she tells me through her tears, as if expecting him to come tumbling down the stairs.

Raspberry Vanilla Cake with Whipped Cream

This recipe will produce enough for 2 cakes. Don't fret! If you don't want to invite extra relatives, just wait until the other cake has fully cooled, wrap it tightly in plastic wrap and pop it into the freezer. Now you have a delicious dessert-in-the-waiting: all you have to do is allow it to defrost and proceed with the frosting, filling and assembling instructions.

For the cake:

    3 cups flour

    1 tablespoon plus 1 teaspoon baking powder

    ¾ teaspoon salt

    2 ¾ cup sugar

    1 ½ cups milk

    2 teaspoons vanilla extract

    1 ¼ cup plus 2 tablespoons unsalted butter, softened

    5 large eggs

For the filling:

    Simple Syrup*

    1 cup seedless raspberry jam

    whipped cream (see page xvii)

    *made by taking equal parts of water and sugar and boiling down for five minutes

    Decoration:

    Berries

    Sliced almonds

    Preheat the oven to 350°F.

Grease two 9" cake pans. In a large bowl, combine the flour, baking powder, and salt.

In a separate bowl, combine the milk and vanilla extract.

Using an electric mixer, cream the butter and sugar until fluffy, about 3 minutes. Add the eggs, 1 at a time, and beat well. On low speed, add the flour mixture alternating with the milk mixture. Mix until fully incorporated.

Divide the batter equally between two cake pans and bake for 35-40 minutes, until a tester inserted in the center of the cake comes out clean.

Cool the cakes 10 minutes in the pans, then invert them onto a cake rack. Cool completely before assembling.

Each cake layer makes one cake. If you are going to make just one cake, wrap your other cooled layer in plastic wrap and place it in the freezer for another time.

Now you are ready to assemble the cake. Perfectionists will demand you slice each layer into three thin layers. I'm good with two: two is just delicious. Three, for me, is more like when your mother-in-law comes to visit. Then you try three.

To slice your cake layers, you'll need a big serrated knife, like a bread knife, and a steady and straight hand. To make a two-layer cake, you'll need to slice straight across the middle of the cake layer: don't go up, don't go down! Go straight! All the way across! To make a three-layer cake, you will need to cut the cake layer into thirds. Brush each layer with simple syrup, then thinly coat with 5 tablespoons of jam. Top with ½ cup of whipped cream. Place the second layer on top, and if you are making a three-layer cake, repeat with the next layer.

Cover your top layer with whipped cream. Add nuts and berries as decoration.

Makes 2 cakes

244   Alona Abbady Martinez

Chapter Five

Tasting the World

DO YOU *VONGOLE*? LINGUINE IN CLAM SAUCE

I always crave carbs when it rains. Maybe it's my "hunker down" caveman instinct that calls in carbohydrates for the energy to ride out the storm. Or maybe it's just that I love pasta so much that I will find any plausible excuse to eat it (caveman instinct is a bit of a reach, I admit.) Since I am not nearly as committed to my exercise regime as I am to my culinary drive, I like to compromise with a seafood pasta dish that is fast, delicious and light. That way, even if a torrential downpour (or occasional drizzle) prevents me from driving to my sheltered gym (slick roads would make it too dangerous, I am sure), I won't have the guilt of devouring pasta with loads of creamy calories.

Enter *linguine alla vongole*. *Vongole* is Italian for small clam. When I talk *linguine alla vongole*, I refer to white *vongole* sauce. Red *vongole* is its crimson counterpart: a thick tomato-based sauce that can easily swallow up this mollusk's delicate flavor. White *vongole*, however, is all about the clams. The trick to this dish is all in its simplicity and freshness. The fresher the ingredients, the better. No one understands this better than Mark Bittman, whose column *The Minimalist*, I fell in love with years ago. From 1997 to 2011 Mr. Bittman created spectacular dishes using just a few ingredients and even less time. Many of his recipes have become staples in my home, and his *linguine alla vongole* won the hearts of every family member the first time I made it. His secret is in sautéing/steaming the clams in olive oil and garlic before adding anything else, and true to his nature, what follows is short and easy, perfect for those short on time but high on expectation when it comes to mealtime. This is one of those tell-tale dishes I always order at restaurants to see if they get a thumbs up or not. Making a *vongole* sauce properly is the sign of a sure winner.

Linguine Alla Vongole (Linguine in Clam Sauce)

(adapted from Mark Bittman)

2 dozen littlenecks or other hard-shell clams*

1/3 cup olive oil

3 cloves garlic, peeled and crushed

1/2 teaspoon dried pepper flakes

1/2 cup dry white wine

1/2 cup minced fresh parsley

1 teaspoon minced garlic

Salt to taste

2 tablespoons unsalted butter

1 lbs linguine

If you are a bit clam crazy like me, feel free to add more! I like to buy a bag of 50 count and use it all: there's never too many clams in my universe!

Bring 4 quarts of water to a boil. Place the clams in a colander and rinse with cold water. Heat the olive oil in a 10-inch skillet over medium-high heat. Add the crushed garlic and hot pepper flakes and cook, stirring, until the garlic is fragrant, about 30 seconds. Add the clams, stir briefly and cover.

Put the pasta in the boiling water and cook.

Check the clams after 2 minutes. Most should be popping open about now. Remove the lid and add the wine. Continue to cook over medium-high heat for another minute. Shake the pan, like the Food Network pros! Add the parsley, minced garlic, and salt.

Remove from heat and add the butter.

Drain the pasta when it is cooked to your liking, and serve in a deep bowl topped with lots of clams and sauce.

Some people think if clams don't open while cooking, they are bad and need to be thrown out. Hold on! Some clams are just shy and don't open as much or open at all. Use a knife to pry those open. The way to tell a good clam from a bad one is by its smell. Believe me, you'll know. Needless to say, always buy your clams from the very best source possible!

Serves 2-4

Una Princesita Yanqui: Cachapa Con Queso

He looked at me with distrustful eyes: I looked like a *gringa*, after all, and Venezuela, a once open and accepting country, now lived in a climate of great anti-American sentiment. And still, his look locked with mine in a curious way. I stuck out like a sore thumb, I'll admit, with my fair skin, blonde hair, and light eyes, out in a dusty pit stop between the cities of Caracas and Valencia, in a sea of dark-skinned, dark-haired people. Husband and I had stopped for the prerequisite *cafecito*, a doll-sized cup of rich caffeine that would course through our veins until the next pit stop allowed a refill.

I sat in the parked car, watching the men and women saunter towards the goods beckoning at the counter: a box of cigarettes, a CD, a *batido*, or fresh fruit juice. Husband waited by the glistening chrome *Gaggia* coffee machine and I chuckled out loud thinking, this is what is so lovely about this contradictory country: parked in the middle of nowhere sits a luxuriously expensive espresso maker brewing out perfect cup after cup after cup.

And that's when I saw him, each drawn to the other by our eyes: mine a clear blue, as blue as the sky allows on a perfectly pristine day and his, dark and murky like fresh mud. His clothes were dirty and ragged, his flip-flops had a huge hole at the heel and I sat in my air-conditioned Land Cruiser with pedicured feet resting comfortably on the dashboard. He walked slowly in front of my car, carrying two plastic yellow buckets filled with something, never once taking his eyes off mine. Two worlds collided in one stare. I wondered what he thought of me, *una princesita yanqui,* (a Yankee princess) most likely, and immediately I lowered my feet but kept my stare. No, he was up to something, I realized. His gaze was now locked on mine and I detected the tiniest smile. I watched and waited, stealing a quick glance at Husband way over there sipping and purchasing more coffee. He was out of my range. It was just me and this man, whose stare was so hypnotic, I couldn't help but fall under its spell. He came closer and closer to my closed window and just when I didn't know whether to be flattered or frightened he bellowed out:

"¡LA CACHAPA CACHAPA CACHAPA, VENDO LA CACHAPA CACHAPA CACHAPA, CON QUESO DE MANO, TELITA, LA CACHAPA CACHAPA, CACHAPA!"

And I knew I was safe. And I knew I was doomed. I had fallen for this scruffy man...and he sold *cachapas*. Next to *arepas*, *cachapas*, golden corn pancakes served with a chunk of fresh white cheese are one of Venezuela's most popular dishes. Immediately I lowered my window and was greeted by the warm sweet smell of toasted corn wafting from his yellow bucket. I bought five. The fresh white cheeses he offered (*telita*, *de mano*, and *guayanes*) were so outrageously delicious, I bought them all. I would have taken the man home but Husband had returned by then and, with a shocked look on his face and two cups of coffee, took notice of the mountains of sweet corn pancakes and cheese precariously balanced on my lap and gasped:

"Alona, are you all right?"

And I was all right. I was downright great. Because when you park your car in the middle of nowhere, only to get the best cup of coffee in the universe, and you have the good fortune of finding the *cachapa* man, life, my friends, is good. Life is great.

I celebrated this goodness all in one go, making sandwich upon sandwich of my steaming *cachapas* and their accompanying fresh cheeses. The cheese would give in to the heat of the *cachapa* and melt, making for a delirious experience, and, as the Land Cruiser kicked into drive leaving a trail of dust in its wake, my eyes looked for those of the *cachapa* man only to find he had already locked gaze with another woman sitting prey in a shiny red Mazda. *This is a man of many talents*, I thought to myself, as I took another bite of rich sweetness and let everything else go.

Cachapa Con Queso / Cachapa with Cheese

Cachapas are a staple of Venezuelan life and usually sold as roadside fast food. They are always served with a slice of local, fresh, white cheese such as *queso telita*, *guyanase* or *queso de mano*. Here in the States, a slice of premium *Mozarrella di Bufala* works as a wonderful stand in!

Venezuelan *Cachapas*

- 3 cups corn kernels (if you don't have fresh corn, use frozen)
- 1 teaspoon salt
- ¼ cup sugar

1 egg

4 tablespoons coarse corn meal

6 tablespoons unsalted butter, for frying

Combine all the ingredients (except the butter) in a blender and blend. Make sure not to over-blend! You don't want this completely smooth - part of an authentic *cachapa* experience is biting into small pieces of corn kernels.

Heat a skillet over medium-low heat and melt 2 tablespoons of butter. Pour ¼ cup batter for each *cachapa*, cooking until brown on each side, 4 to 5 minutes.

Repeat, adding 2 tablespoons of butter to the skillet each time. Serve with a slice of fresh white cheese on top, or you can place your cheese off to one side and fold the *cachapa* over it like an omelet.

Makes approximately 10 *cachapas*

Fish Dreams: Dolphin with Bajan Seasoning

What she didn't know is that I dream of being a fish, a dolphin, a whale; anything slick and fast that navigates easily through salty waters, pushing all worries away. Night after night after night I'd become this aquatic creature and slip through miles upon miles of sea with only speed serving as my guide. Occasionally I stir things up a bit and jump to the surface, sporadically breaking the wall of water for a moment of bright blue sky, hot sun, and prowling birds. But that is gone in an instant, because once again I dive low and deep and swim, swim, swim, fast and furiously.

"You're here practically every day, honey" she noted, slightly amused. She was an older woman from one of the islands and she'd been working at this supermarket for years, parked between produce and meats, serving sterile-looking bits of salmon and tilapia to shoppers weary of pork and beef. It seemed I did make a daily stop to visit her and her fish.

Seeing her brought me back to my childhood trips to Barbados, a sunny island with warm salty air, turquoise beaches, and beautiful people. Food was simple and direct in Barbados: every Tuesday and Thursday morning the local fish market, which consisted of a decaying wooden table and three stumps of wood painted in faded reds and yellows, would come to life with whatever the local fishermen brought in.

I loved coming to the market. It would always be hot and crowded and very chaotic, with a smell of dirt and fish guts that inevitably brought lots of flies. There'd be the occasional dog or cat scamming for scraps and plenty of Bajan women dressed in bright colored dresses haggling over the fresh catch still squirming in the buckets. It was hot and teeming with people but it was alive, and I relished being the little blonde kid in the middle of it all. It didn't take long; by noon the market was closed, all the fish was gone and the only remnant of any activity would be that happy stray cat licking a paw or two.

Some days it would be baskets upon baskets of flying fish—a sardine-sized, meaty fish with unusually large pectoral fins that enable it to take flight with each jump. This is the national fish of Barbados and it is a title that is not taken lightly. Flying fish abound, on t-shirts, store signs, and even coins. In kitchens, they are served up slathered in Bajan spice (a mixture of nutmeg, cloves, and mace) and fried to a crisp alongside wedges of juicy limes. If they didn't end up on your plate you could see them jumping carelessly about through the water.

On other days the catch was bigger and the fishermen carried orange plastic buckets flapping with snapper or dolphin. The first time my father told me he had bought dolphin my eyes welled up with tears and the images of the kind and good man who was raising me was instantly replaced by new visions of a cruel and heartless Flipper killer. A ten-year old's mind works fast.

"Dolphin?" was all I managed to mutter in my dismay. My mother's intuition salvaged the moment preventing further trauma with a casual chuckle and a quick clarification:

"No, honey, not *Flipper* dolphin, a fish called dolphin. It's also called Mahi-Mahi."

I liked the lyrical sound of Mahi-Mahi, but of course, now that I knew the truth, I preferred the shock value of telling folks I ate dolphin. With that thought, my eyes dried up and I was suddenly very hungry. I soon learned it to be a delicious fish: white and meaty with a firm texture, it was also prepared in the classic Bajan manner, slathered in herbs and pan-fried, enjoyed with a cold Coca-Cola (or a frothy Banks beer for the adults) and bare, sandy feet.

Today I see my fish lady has a fresh batch of dolphin and I am inevitably drawn to it. I am under neon lights in a large warehouse space, not under the warm and comforting Caribbean skies where I want to be. *This dolphin should be coming off the rickety fisherman's boat in Barbados*, I think to myself. And, even though I don't share the thought with her, I watch my fish lady with her graying hair, her sun-kissed smile, and her gold tooth, and I know that she might be thinking the same thing too.

DOLPHIN WITH BAJAN SEASONING

Variations of this seasoning is found all over the island of Barbados. Everyone's mother seems to have their own secret recipe as well. Level of spiciness is key! Bajan's use the scotch bonnet pepper, also known as scotch bonneys. It is a popular pepper in the Caribbean and exceptionally hot. My recipe only uses a teensy bit, as I feel too much can overwhelm the other flavors. So, if you like your mouth to really burn, just add more scotch bonnet to your sauce.

Bajan Seasoning:

1 cup onion, chopped

2 green onions, chopped

3 garlic cloves, peeled

½ a scotch bonnet pepper, stem and seeds removed (use gloves when handling, add more if you want the dish spicier, less if it's not your thing!)

2 sprigs of fresh thyme, stems removed (holding the stem, run your fingers against the leaves and they will all fall off)

2 tablespoons fresh basil

2 tablespoons flat-leaf parsley

1 ½ teaspoons dried marjoram

¼ teaspoon ground cloves

¼ teaspoon nutmeg

1 ½ teaspoon salt

¼ teaspoon black pepper

¼ cup red wine vinegar

3 tablespoons olive oil

In a food processor or blender, combine all the ingredients except for the olive oil and process to a coarse paste. Don't stick your nose in there to take a sniff - the hot pepper fumes will get ya!

Slowly drizzle in the olive oil until the mixture becomes a paste, a bit like pesto.

Transfer to a jar and refrigerate. The seasoning will keep in the refrigerator for at least 6 months.

Grill the Mahi-Mahi:

4 (6- to 8-oz) pieces mahi-mahi fillet

4 tablespoons Bajan Seasoning

Pat the fish dry, then spread 1 tablespoon of Bajan Seasoning on each fillet. Grill the fish on a grill pan over medium high heat, or on your grill, until the fillets are cooked through, about 3-4 minutes on each side. The fish can be served with additional Bajan Seasoning. Goes great with a cold beer: try a Banks!

Serves 4

WAKING UP THE DAREDEVIL: SLOW-COOKED BRISKET

Years ago I was a daredevil. Today I am chic. I am poised upon the fresh powder (that's Colorado snow, for those of you not in the know), garbed up in my razor sharp ski outfit (Spyder jacket ice white with aqua and midnight trim, white gloves, sexy black pants) helmet, goggles, boots, skis. Ready for the slopes. On top of the world.

I had somehow gotten through the ride on the lift, a contraption I gave no thought to mounting as a child, but now, as an adult, approached apprehensively. All right, approached in a panic. I haven't lived in Manhattan for years but it's as if Woody Allen and all his neurosis had infiltrated me steadily anyhow:

"Get on this thing? It's not safe? A dangling chair in subzero weather climbing precariously up a cliff with lunatics zooming down (hey wait a second, am I going to have to go down THAT?)

Husband was faithfully at my side, coaxing the daredevil back. Or at least trying.

"You're fine. You've done this a thousand times, remember? Scoot up. Sit. Bar down. Enjoy the ride. Simple. Follow my lead."

We had crept along in the crowded line, closer and closer to the ominous ride. I recounted the zillions of times I've turned down rides of any kind: roller coasters, Ferris wheels, spinning teacups. Something about my feet not being on the ground and in control just doesn't jive with this control freak. Yet here I was, my feet already not in control, straddled in clunky alien boots and slippery skis, trying to keep up with Husband (outfitted in an even jazzier outfit given to him by the number one Slovenian ski champion, Jure Kosir). In my moment of panic, I could at least appreciate how good we look.

I heard a loud sigh and turned around. The six-year old behind me was getting frustrated with my hesitation. This little bugger would zoom down the mountain three times before I even started down the slope. What is it about aging that makes some of us more cautious? Why couldn't I just have fun?

The lift came and, indeed, as riding a bicycle, every movement clicked and I sat down. As we swung through the frigid air I begged Husband to talk to me, distract me from the perilous death I was envisioning. I clung to the thin bar and cursed myself for agreeing to ride this endless and steep ride. But as the ride continued, my grip eased and I actually began enjoying myself. It was hard not to. The trees looked so beautiful and pristine, their evergreen branches comfortably hugged by mounds of fresh snow. Agile skiers flew through them with natural precision (I learned with relief that was the black diamond slope, not the beginner's green allotted to me). So, you see, the slopes looked fabulous and chic again.

Hey, maybe I can do this, I began to hope. Maybe those years and years and years of zooming down the benign Vermont bunny slope on Pico Peak with my family back in the seventies will kick in and I'll be able to pull this off as a middle-aged Suzy Chaffee.

I turned to my Slovenian ski champion and smiled. I could definitely do this. I looked at him: tall, dark and handsome, but nevertheless a tropical Venezuelan who had never set foot on skis until his mid-thirties. Husband had come a long way, now hitting the black diamonds and coming out alive. If I could only look at him long enough, maybe his fearlessness would rub off on me. I pictured our two children, off with some ski pro in their class at this moment. No doubt our wild son, who already sported a black eye that would make Rocky Balboa jealous, would find the thrill of this sport intoxicating. If he could zoom, then so would I, dammit.

So there I was, poised atop of the main summit, at 11 thousand plus feet of altitude. The air was thin and icy and lovely. I was surrounded by skiers and snowboarders and mountains. I was in the moment and taking it all in. And then, I saw the photographers. Yes! There were photographers. I snag one immediately. Husband scoffs. He thinks I am absurd. Why are we taking a picture now? Let's ski, he urges. But I know why. I must capture this moment. This moment now. When I am full of the mountain, when I don't fear it because I haven't quite met it. Where I feel free and possibilities are endless and I don't know about the pain my quads will feel as they burn their way down Jack Rabbit Hole or Red Bull Run in a stubborn snowplow that I will not let go into the risk of parallel skiing, because I must slow down, slow down, slow down and not hit that tree or that one or that one. Husband will patiently ski behind me shouting out all sorts of Zen commands: "feel the mountain, you control it, don't let it control you, put your weight into it, you know how to do this, you've DONE this before, enjoy the moment, look forward, don't look down, be one with nature." It is all going to get me and I will grow more and more impatient with him as my legs beg for a break and my mind fills with anxiety, I will manage to turn around (and ski) and shout that he please shut up and question over and over and over again, "Is this really a green slope? Is this a green?!" because there is ice (wasn't it illegal for ice to exist on a Colorado slope?) and skiers and snowboarders, the same ones that added to the ambience of excellence I needed photographed up on the summit but now just felt like intrusions on my moment of panic as they all zoom past me without a care in this world:

"On your left!"

"On your right!"

They'd shout on the way down, throwing me further and further off balance and spiraling into blackness.

And then, there we were. We'd somehow made it to the bottom and good God my two legs were shaking but they were intact, and, even though I felt like sending Husband to an ashram in India for all his philosophical spewing, he had guided me patiently down the mountain, gently prodding my sense of adventure back to life, which was slow to wake but definitely stirring, buried under years of motherhood vigilance, weighed down by moments of 'eat your peas, tie your shoelaces, look both ways before you cross the road, don't talk to strangers, hold my hand, no come back here and hold my hand.'

How could this persona be expected to fly down a mountain without a care in the world? But somehow I had. Okay, not fly, but crawl: Snowplow, zigzag. Stop. Reassess, and continue. Slowly sawing my way down Beaver Creek but here I was, still chic, victorious, and still married. Maybe I'll go up the mountain again.

Tomorrow. First, I need a glass of wine and a good hearty mountain meal.

Slow-Cooked Brisket

So simple, it's embarrassing.

- 4 to 5 pound brisket
- ½ cup ketchup
- 1 (1-ounce) envelope dehydrated onion soup and dip mix
- 8 ounces Coca-Cola

For the Gravy:

- ½ cup white wine
- 2 tablespoons corn starch
- 2 tablespoons water
- salt, to taste

Place the brisket, fat side down, inside a slow cooker. Pat the top with ketchup, add the onion soup mix and pat into the ketchup. Pour Coca-Cola around the sides. Place a lid on the slow-cooker and cook on the lowest setting of your slow cooker, usually for 8-10 hours.

Note: The cooking gods will not throw lightning bolts at you (wait, isn't that Zeus?) if you set your slow cooker on faster settings. The meat will be just fine too. It's just a wee bit more buttery-melt-in-your-mouth delicious when you cook it on the slowest setting!

Make Gravy:

Remove the brisket from the slow cooker. Scrape the ketchup off the brisket and add to the sauce. Pour the liquid from the slow cooker into a small saucepan, add the wine and bring it to a boil on high heat. Reduce the heat to medium. Mix the cornstarch and water together and whisk it into the simmering liquid. Cook for five minutes, until thickened. Add the salt.

Slice the brisket against the grain into one-inch slices and serve with the gravy.

Serves 6

Felucca Sunset: *Shakshouka*

It was a battle of the palette: hues of pinks with splatters of violet and the unrelenting but struggling yellow of the sun refusing to fade away after a long, bright day. Proclaiming its lasts rites, the defeated swollen orange began to sink into the Nile. The air was heavy with the scents of the streets, which, on a late afternoon in Luxor, meant an intoxicating mix of spices, roasted pistachios, and *Ful Mudammas*, an Egyptian fava bean stew set simmering for hours in tall aluminum pots to be scooped out and served with olive oil, lime juice, and pita bread.

We boarded our *felucca,* a traditional Egyptian sailboat, with high hopes for a memorable sunset journey on the Nile. Our captain was Ahmed (we learned his name through the jovial cheering of his fellow *felucca* skippers) and though his wavy black hair and thick eyelashes obstructed my view, I knew he was glaring at my boyfriend and I suspiciously. We were young college students and we weren't married, and he just seemed to know that. Still, times were tough, he had the boat, and we were tourists paying American dollars, so he would comply with our request for a ride. It didn't mean he had to like it. We sat in his rickety boat and began our Nile adventure.

"Please to sit apart," he ordered, interrupting my boyfriend's suave attempt to wrap his arm around my shoulder and bring me closer to him. Ahmed's request was followed by two blank stares trying to figure out why we weren't granted our postcard moment in Egypt.

"PLEASE TO SIT APART," he mustered in his most forceful English, the sweat starting to trickle down the side of his forehead. There was no negotiating with this man, and, given that we had long left the river bank and lay floating at the mercy of our very conservative captain, we had no choice but to comply. And so, the sun sunk below the mysteries of Egypt and my beloved and I sat apart.

We drifted aimlessly down the Nile and our tour guide (who was much more relaxed now that no sin was in motion) began to spew out an array of historical facts about the murky waters we were traveling on and the great sites of Luxor where grand kings and queens were laid to rest in the majestic backdrop of ancient Egypt. His English flowed a bit smoother now that he was repeating his usual lexicon of facts, but the accent was still quite thick so I closed my eyes to better focus on what he was saying. My sense of smell was assaulted by culinary aromas brewing in the desert sun. Coriander. Cumin. *Za'atar*. They were all there, intertwined with the memory of King Tut's reign and the chaos of the streets that awaited us beyond our *felucca*. When our ride was over, our guide gave us a forced smile and extended a hand to help me out.

"Thank you for your visiting to Egypt," he mustered, his gaze locking on mine, distrustful of my light blue eyes, an anomaly in Egypt. My boyfriend and I disembarked and defiantly held hands, dry land giving permission to our life of sin. I felt like turning to Ahmed and assuring him, "I will marry this man, and we will have beautiful children and be very, very happy," but I took more pleasure in leaving that question unanswered for him. Instead, I turned towards the smell of chaos and food and hand-in-hand with my partner in crime proclaimed, "Let's eat!"

The air was still warm as night arrived and we found our way up to the rooftop of a cramped building where a humble restaurant was housed. There, as the day cried its last goodbye and the awe-inspiring show of stars began, we ate a wonderful meal of *Shakshouka*, eggs poached in a spicy tomato sauce served alongside freshly-baked pita for scooping.

We held hands, and even kissed under a low and heavy, almost golden, full moon.

SHAKSHOUKA

3 tablespoons olive oil

½ cup onion, chopped

2 garlic cloves, minced

4 tablespoons *Harissa* (more if you like it extra spicy!)*

1 (28-ounce) can whole plum tomatoes with juices, coarsely chopped

¼ cup water (optional)

6 eggs

½ cup fresh parsley, chopped

Salt and pepper

Harissa is a spicy and aromatic chile paste that's a staple in North African and Middle Eastern cooking. You can find it in Middle Eastern markets, gourmet and natural food stores. Of course, you can always give it a go at making your own! Here's a quick and easy rendition:

Homemade Harissa

1 garlic clove

Kosher salt

2 tablespoons tomato paste

2 tablespoons fresh lime juice

1 tablespoon *chile* powder (such as ancho)

2 teaspoons smoked paprika

½ teaspoon cayenne pepper powder (add more if you like it super-hot!)

1 teaspoon ground cumin

½ cup extra-virgin olive oil

½ teaspoon salt

Mash your garlic clove.

No, you don't need any fancy gadget to do this, only

a knife with a nice blade and a cutting board. Here's how: place your garlic clove on a cutting board, cut the garlic clove in half, turn the cloves flat side down and smash them using the side of a chef's knife. You're going to use the heel of your hand to press down on the side of the knife. Sprinkle with salt.

Your clove should be mashed. If you need to, you can chop up whatever pieces didn't become pulp. Scrape the garlic paste into a small bowl and stir in all the ingredients except the olive oil and salt.

Gradually drizzle the olive oil into the paste, stirring as you do so. Add the salt.

Store in fridge.

Now to the Shakshouka:

Heat the oil in a large skillet over medium heat. Add the onions and sauté until translucent, 3 minutes. Add the garlic and stir for another minute. Add the *Harissa* and cook until combined and fragrant, 30 seconds. Add the tomatoes, bring to a simmer, reduce the heat to medium-low and cook, stirring frequently, for 20 minutes. If the sauce looks too dry, you can add ¼ cup water. Season with salt and pepper.

Crack the eggs open on top, cover the skillet, and cook,

6-8 minutes more, until the eggs are set. Sprinkle with the freshly chopped parsley and drizzle with additional olive oil.

Serve hot with pita bread.

Serves 3

Fish Delirium

I can't take my mind off the fish. It is with me day and night. I shower. *The fish.* I drive the minivan. *The fish.* I pretend to acclimate to reality. *The fish.* There was so much fish. Three stories-worth, to be exact. It appears the fish have left their mark.

The place was Madrid, more specifically, *El Mercado de Ventas*, just a short walk from the metro stop of the same name. The Metro, it turns out, is the best venue of travel around this majestic city, if you don't have a Vespa that is (I vow to move to Europe just so I can have my bright red retro Vespa to romantically zoom around in).

My brother-in-law, Mario, a true *Madrileño*, took a sabbatical from his bustling metropolis and headed for American suburbia, where he was horrified to discover, amongst other things, that no one walks on the streets in the 'burbs. No one at all. In his two-year stint of trying to mold into American life, what kept him grounded was a constant fixation on finding the proper '*pescadería*,' or fish shop. You'd think, living in South Florida, that would be a no-brainer, but it proved difficult, in fact, impossible.

Over late-night *cafecitos*, he'd recount to me his failed attempts at finding the proper fish store: this one was too small, that one too dirty, only frozen fillets, smelled funny. And then he'd launch into stories of Spanish fish and markets, and most specifically, this one near his home in Madrid, *El Mercado de Ventas*, housing three floors of sustainable, fresh seafood. Time and time again he'd serve up his signature *paella* with a sigh that said this version of the vibrant and memorable dish would never live up to a Spaniard's standard. I found no fault in the numerous helpings I'd treat myself to, quite the contrary, I enjoyed the meal ravenously, always complimenting and savoring each bite. But his look was slightly deflated and resigned and he'd always answer me the same way:

"*En España es diferente.*" In Spain it is different.

And, although I knew vaguely what he meant, (I had, after all, spent five weeks discovering the culinary gems of this incredibly rich country years ago,) I had chosen to forget, or not know, or play the safe ignorance-is-bliss card, because, sometimes, choosing not to know is easier than dealing with the reality of knowing. Especially, it seems, when it comes to fish.

Until I landed in Madrid on a recent visit and knew, amongst the overscheduled events lining my crowded calendar, I needed to include a trip to the famed fish market, *Mercado de Ventas*, the one my brother-in-law wouldn't, couldn't, stop talking about.

When I arrived, late, from various inviting distractions encountered on the way, visitors were leaving and fishmongers were dousing down their stations and cleaning up shop, shutting operations for the three-hour lunch break, only to open up later in the day for evening shoppers

They must have seen the look of delight and desperation in my American eyes as my neon orange crocs crossed the threshold to fish. They must have known. *This poor tourist, we can change her with this. We can alter her concept of fish if we let her in here. Even for a peek. Even for a peek of one stall.* For I can't tell you how many stalls there were, but I can tell you there were three stories' worth of stalls, and each stall as full and resplendent as the next, beaming and glistening with mounds of the ocean's best catch. So they were generous and let me in, even though everything was closing down.

And there I was, a sole visitor in a happily crowded world of seafood, taking a momentary break, just me, the fish, and fishmongers cleaning up the muck. And I was happy, oh so happy to be there. Men who were wrapping up their morning shift couldn't help themselves but stare as I walked from stall to stall in awe, carefully lifting up plastic sheets that had already been placed over the resting seafood. Keenly aware that what lay underneath would forever taunt me, they offered to remove the plastic sheeting for me to better see, to better understand this culture of seafood of theirs unlike any other.

And that is how I came to appreciate my brother-in-law's incessant and futile quest for fish in South Florida. With a glimpse of this market I had become transformed and changed to understand the need for fish. The few shops still open were apologetic: "*Come back in three hours, Señora,*" they begged, "*when we will be open, and you will see more, so sorry to be cleaning up, Señora, so sorry not to have it all out.*"

But there was much, so much more than I'd ever seen before, anywhere, anyplace, and I've been to so many places, but none like this. The fish was reclining on snowy beds of ice, and all seemed to wink at me, as if to promise they'd just, moments ago, been swimming in crisp clear waters, and I believed them all. There was no hiding or lying in this fish market. They sang freshness and the smell in the air was not dank, but sweet and strong and clear and I wanted to never leave this place, to tour its three stories' worth of salt and sand and sea and stay amongst these fishmongers forever. Even though they chuckled at my child-like zeal, I knew they appreciated it. I knew they knew the role they had in shaping me. In my change. In the way I'd never look at fish the same way again. Never would a measly single display case be enough. All fish stores would now be compared to this. I knew it was unfair. I knew it was like comparing a dingy to an ocean liner. I knew everywhere else would pale, particularly in my South Florida suburb. I had been altered, it seemed, by the *Mercado de Ventas*. I finally understood my brother-in-law's restlessness, his need, his constant search, because now it would become mine.

Mario's *Paella*

4 plum tomatoes, minced

1 red pepper, cut in julienne

1 green pepper, chopped

1 8-oz. can tomato sauce

1 15-oz. can green lima beans

1 15-oz. can sweet peas

1 lbs. short-grain rice (Bomba rice, if you can find, to be a true Spaniard, if not, Arborio works great!)

¼ cup olive oil

4 cups seafood broth*

1 cup white wine

2 1.6 oz. packages of *Latin Sazón Mix with Saffron*

1 lbs. Corvina, cut into strips (Corvina is a white fish, similar to sea bass; you can substitute any firm, white fish, such as grouper or striped bass.)

1 16-oz. bag frozen assorted seafood mix, thawed

1 lbs. whole shrimp, unpeeled

1 lbs. mussels

*If you are going to make the seafood stock:

2 fish heads (ask your fishmonger, they keep them in the back!)

shells from your peeled shrimp

2 tablespoons kosher salt

2 tablespoons vegetable oil

1 cup diced yellow onion (about 1/2 large onion)

½ cup diced celery

2 medium cloves garlic, crushed

½ cup dry white wine

5 cups water

1 bunch flat-leaf parsley

1 bay leaf

Place all the ingredients in a stock pot, bring to a boil, then reduce to medium and allow to simmer 20-25 minutes. Let cool, then strain.

My brother-in-law has the real deal *paella* maker, called a *paellera*, which is shallow and wide and has splayed sides. It does not have a lid. The idea is to keep the rice in a thin layer, so that it gathers all the flavor evenly. Of course, he makes his *paella* over a charcoal grill, because that is the only place a *paellera* will fit, and because it gives the dish a special smoky flavor. Don't fret though. You can still make a delicious *paella* straight out of your American kitchen. Just use your largest skillet over your stovetop and your dish will come out spectacular.

*Mario tip: Whatever you are sautéing goes in the center of your pan. Once you are done with that, scooch it over to the perimeters to make space for the next item.

Heat the olive oil over medium heat. Add the red and green peppers and sauté 4-5 minutes.

Move the peppers to the sides and sauté the fresh tomatoes in the center, until very soft, 10 minutes.

Add the fish and seafood mix and sauté 5 minutes, stirring.

Add the shrimp, tomato sauce and 2 cups of fish stock and mix everything together.

Raise the heat to high until the *paella* simmers, then reduce to medium and allow to simmer another minute.

Add the wine and *Latin Sazón Mix with Saffron*.

Add the rice (not rinsed) and the remaining fish stock.

Bring to a boil, reduce heat to low and simmer for 30 minutes.

Add the peas and lima beans.

Add the mussels along the perimeter of pan.

Cover the pan with a lid or aluminum foil and let simmer another 5-10 minutes, until the mussels are cooked through.

Remove from the heat and let rest, covered.

*Mario tip: It is tradition in Spain to cover the paellera with newspaper.

Also, paella is normally a communal project! Everyone participates in the creation of this dish, everyone also has an opinion on this dish: what makes it a "true" paella, what ingredients are used, methods applied, etc. etc. In other words, no two paellas are alike, so, if there is something you'd like to add to yours, go for it, you'll be acting in true Spanish style!

Serves 4

Mercado Rapture

Close your eyes and imagine this with me. Smoky *chiles* and crisp, spicy radishes in glistening pyramids on a wool blanket for all to see and buy. The air, rich and exotic, redolent of *comida* being made on the spot: sizzling tacos of mouthwatering meats and sausages, corn tortillas toasting on a cast iron griddle seasoned by time and history, and the citrus freshness of plump limes whose juice is a constant: drizzled over everything. This is the *Mercado in Valle de Bravo* in Mexico: a Sunday market housed in a cramped labyrinth of makeshift stalls connected by a roof made of blue plastic feigning the sky. It is an infinitely raw and vibrant world nestled within *Valle de Bravo*, a scenic vacation town of picturesque cobblestone roads and a spectacular lake where tourists enjoy mountain fresh air, feast on *trucha fresca*, fresh trout, and escape the pollution and population of Mexico City.

Steps away from such manicured tourism lives this world of the *mercado*, its blue lit alley beckoning those who dare enter it, and of course, taking that sharp left and following the locals and stray dogs is the obvious choice for Husband and I.

It is crowded and sweaty and lively and wondrous. Men carry sacks filled with blender parts, indigenous women kneel on the dirt floor selling woven baskets, bright green *nopale* (cactus) leaves, and action figure dolls that saw their heyday in the early eighties. It's all here.

The local butcher chops yellow chickens that peer at me with eyes still open. I know they haven't lived a life in a windowless, cramped coop but rather roamed a field picking worms most likely hours ago. And then, the famous *taquerías*, or taco stands are everywhere, lacing together this maze of shopping. The sound of meat sizzles throughout the market like an orchestra: *carnitas, tacos de carne, de barbacoa*.

Huge, battered aluminum vessels, the size of small bathtubs, simmer with *Sopa de Tortilla*, a hearty, spicy soup that is ladled in tin bowls, sprinkled with golden tortilla crisps, silky slivers of ripe avocado, and a rainfall of salty grated *cotija* cheese.

Freshly grilled meat is chopped on a *tronco*, a big slab of wood resembling a tree trunk and in the air floats a thick smoke of flavor that stubbornly lands on your clothing and refuses to leave, so even if you don't stop at one of the plastic tables for a quick bite, the food travels with you.

Speckled throughout the market are the fruit carts. Glorious cups loaded with colorful chunks of freshly chopped tropical delights: pineapple, watermelon, *sapote*, and of course, mango. Mango is a celebrated fruit in Mexico and rightly so: every mango I've ever eaten there is a memorable exchange between my palate and my memory: smooth, juicy and bursting with flavor, there isn't one fiber to be found, just fleshy fruit generous with juice. And here, Mexicans have defied all logic and introduced this sweetness with a spicy bite: adding their homemade assortments of *chile* sauces and powders, they take cups of the chopped chunks of golden mango and drizzle and sprinkle and drizzle and sprinkle and drizzle some more.

My Culinary Compulsion   279

I am intoxicated by this market. I am in love. Camera in hand, I cannot get enough of this place. I want to see, smell, and eat everything. The locals all stare at me curiously. I am a *guera*, a slang term for someone blonde, blue-eyed and fair-skinned- unheard of in this wave of Aztec rich complexion and dark eyes.

We are drawn together by our differences, the local market folk and I. I long to be a part of them, and they generously take me in, accepting me into this underworld of theirs, this weekly ritual they will forget today but I will carry with me forever.

The mango girl smiles at me and my camera. "*Como lo quieres?*" she asks. *How do you want it?* And then she dares me, "*Con todo?*" *With everything?*

And of course, because I know no other answer when it comes to food, I reply, "*Si, todo,*" and she begins the procession with my fabulous cup of diced mango (which she has rinsed in a dirty red bucket filled with suspiciously grey water). She drizzles and sprinkles and drizzles again. This *chile* powder and that *chile* sauce. I ask her several times what it is and she tells me. But I cannot catch the names. I am a fluent Spanish speaker but this simply isn't enough: there is the cadence of the speech, soft, courteous, and rhythmic and then the many Aztec names woven into Mexican Spanish. They slip away from my memory with their foreign sounds. I do understand that the last cayenne-colored sprinkle comes from some region in Mexico, whose name, again, evades me, but by the shine in her eye I know, this is the good stuff.

I take the cup from her and offer up a big *gracias* and then, as if by intuition, I close my eyes. I am circled by life. I smell the street, the dogs, hear the sounds of bartering, the clang of pots, and I hold a cold cup of succulent fruit laden with Mexican secrets for my taking. It is a moment I want to freeze in time. But instead, I take a bite and allow my tongue to dance with the sweet and spice.

TROPICAL SCALLOPS WITH CHILE AND MANGO

4 tablespoons olive oil

¼ cup minced shallot

¼ - ½ teaspoon chipotle *chile* powder (depending on your spice tolerance!)

¼ cup minced red pepper

½ cup minced mango (if in season, use fresh, but you can also use frozen mango cubes)

3 tablespoons minced cilantro

juice of ½ lemon

1 pound sea scallops

¼ cup balsamic vinegar

salt and pepper, to taste

In a small skillet, over medium heat, heat 2 tablespoons of olive oil and sauté the shallots, *chile* powder, and red pepper until translucent, about 3 minutes. Reduce heat to low.

Meanwhile, prepare the scallops: Use either a cast iron pan or a grill pan: both give great sear! Heat the pan over high heat. Add the remaining oil and sear the scallops, 2 minutes on each side. While they are cooking, salt and pepper them. Place the scallops on a plate and set aside.

Finish making your sauce in the small skillet: raise the heat to high, and add the balsamic vinegar. Boil and reduce to medium-low heat and cook, stirring often, for 3 minutes, until the sauce is syrupy. Add the lemon juice, ¼ cup mango, cilantro, and combine. You can also add any extra juice from the scallops on the plate. Simmer on medium-low another 5 minutes. Adjust the seasoning. Remove from heat and stir in remaining ¼ cup mango.

Plating this dish is entirely up to you and how much Food Network chef you are channeling that day.

You can add a thin layer of sauce and place the scallops on top, adding a few cilantro leaves as garnish (big brownie points from the judges if you do it this way), place your scallops on a plate and spoon some sauce over them (for a more rustic, homey feel) or just plate your scallops and have a spoonful of sauce on the side (for those control freaks who like to decide how much sauce and scallops should mix!).

Serves 2

Silence Is Golden, Or at Least Silky Green: Chilled *Sopa de Aguacate*

I came to Mexico to cook but all I do is eat. An angel has appeared in my life, a woman by the name of Angelica whom I hired as my maid. Everyone in Mexico has one, or two, or three; and when I first arrived, that was what everyone insisted I do:

"What? No maid yet? You must get someone to help you out!"

I confess my Spartan feathers bristled at first, after all, I was used to doing everything myself, even darn proud of it. I was supposed to hand over the household reins to someone else?

I was supposed to hand over the household reins to someone else.

I was supposed to hand over the household reins to someone else!

The good thing about feathers is that they smooth quickly.

Angelica has arrived. She is sweet and frail and oh so quiet.

Oh so quiet.

She is, as it turns out, a chef. A chef willing and dying to please. Me. Her *Señora*, as she calls me.

I am in luck.

I am in awe.

I am totally beside myself.

Out from the pristine kitchen (she keeps it this way) come fabulous combinations of her native Mexico: *chiles en nogada, fideos secos* (served with ripe avocado and a drizzling of crema), *sopes*, and *tinga*. I ecstatically eat it all and she quietly awaits my response, my reaction, my amazement, which always feels understated in the enormity of flavors I dance in.

The other day she produced a soup of green silk.

"What is this?" I asked, mystified and excited.

"*Sopa de aguacate*," she muttered, altering my crusted vision of avocado being only a salad item or something to be scooped up with tortilla chips. "*Espero le guste, mi Señora*" she continued, thirsty for my approval.

This bowl of elegance, creaminess, and intoxicating delight, was licked clean in a matter of minutes. I asked for more and got some, all the while cursing my self-discipline for going AWOL under the culinary spell of the woman. This will definitely cost me in the jean-tightness department. The soup was divine, delicious, memorable, enjoyed in the peace and quiet and cleanliness that realms in my Mexico home these days. Angelica and I are both pleased. My enemy remains a pair of stubborn jeans.

CHILLED CREAM OF AVOCADO SOUP

Serve in shot glasses at your next get-together and watch it become an instant hit!

3 tablespoons olive oil

½ cup onion, chopped fine

3 ripe, Hass avocadoes, seed removed and peeled and chopped into 1" cubes

3 cups chicken stock

1 cup heavy whipping cream

1 ½ teaspoons salt

3 tablespoons fresh lime juice

1 tablespoon chopped cilantro (for garnish)

jalapeño powder or chipotle *chile* powder (for garnish)

Heat up the olive oil over medium heat and sauté the onions until translucent, about 5 minutes.

In a blender or food processor blend the sautéed onions, avocado, and broth. Add the cream and salt and blend until smooth. Taste and adjust the seasoning, if necessary.

Transfer to a bowl and add the lime juice. Cover and refrigerate until well chilled.

Ladle the soup into bowls and sprinkle with jalapeño or chipotle *chile* powder and chopped cilantro.

Serves 6

Learning to Love...Maybe?   Mary de Pedro Cookies

"*Oooh, you have a Mabe,*" all the upper-class Mexican housewives crooned when I first moved here and showed off my kitchen and apartment. "*Absolutely the best: Mabe,*" they continued, alerting me to my ignorance on the subject of Mexican kitchen appliances. I've heard of General Electric, KitchenAid, Viking and Dacor but *Mabe*, whose name suggested my biggest fear; "maybe?" Never.

Mabe and I weren't friends from the get go. She was too small. Too simplistic. Too foreign. Fahrenheit was out the window, Mexico being a Celsius land, I had to contend with the concept of baking in unknown numbers. I felt like a lonely American. Luckily, there are all sorts of apps for lonely Americans and *Kitchen Converter* is a very popular one.

Next, there was turning the darn thing on! In the States, with my roomy Dacor oven, all I had to do was push a button and *voila*! Dacor beeped at the designated Fahrenheit temperature. With Mabe I encountered a whole other beast: the gas beast. I had to have the building's maintenance man, Javier, come show me how it's done. Mabe wouldn't come to life for me and I was positive she was broken.

Javier dutifully arrived in his navy blue jumpsuit and friendly smile and didn't even give me the courtesy of tinkering with my accomplice. Mabe just turned on straight away.

"How'd you do that?" I demanded, slightly hurt and fully shocked.

My Culinary Compulsion   287

"Just like this," he patiently showed me, turning Mabe on again.

I felt frustrated that the oven responded to him and not to me.

"Just leave the door ajar for five minutes before you close it. That way it will be sure not to go off," Javier instructed, making me realize the trick to the gas oven.

"Ahhhh, the door has to be open for the oven to ignite," I declared unintelligently.

Javier stared. I think it was polite pity that cast over his face.

"*Si, señora,*" he answered dryly.

So Mabe and I were off to a bumpy start but I didn't lose faith either way. I was an avid baker in Florida and I'd continue to do so in Mexico City, Mabe by my side. We were going to have a beautiful relationship, whatever the price.

The price was several burnt cakes, several flattened cakes, and several undercooked cakes. I can't particularly pin the blame solely on Mabe; after all, Mexico City boasts an altitude of 7,349 feet. Baking gets wacky and frazzled way up here. During my most frustrating days in my high-altitude kitchen I'd find solace in a family favorite: Mary de Pedro cookies, a delicate, nutty treat that did not require rising. Named after a close friend of my mother's, these cookies defy temperamental ovens, bakers, and elevation. You may know them by their more mainstream name, "Mexican Wedding Cookies."

These sweet, melt-in-your-mouth cookies are quick and a cinch to make. In Mexico, they are a very popular everyday sweet found in neighborhood *panaderías* (bakeries). But don't ask for them by their mainstream American name, "Mexican Wedding Cookie" or you'll get blank stares. In Mexico they are known as *polvorones*, which comes from the word *polvo*, or dust, because of how light and crumbly they get with just one bite.

With a little bit of time and a lot of patience, I perfected my *polvorón* with Mabe and even though I no longer need Javier's help turning on the oven, he'll show up anyways, these days with a grin and a question: "Any *polvorones* today, *señora?*"

Mary de Pedro Cookies

Preheat the oven to 400°F.

1 cup unsalted butter, softened

½ cup confectioner's sugar

1 teaspoon vanilla extract

2 cups flour

¼ teaspoon salt

1 cup chopped walnuts, toasted *(see page xxv)*

Cream the butter and sugar until light and fluffy. Add the vanilla. Blend the salt with the flour, and add this to butter/sugar mixture. Add the nuts, and shape into 1" balls.

Place the cookie balls on an ungreased cookie sheet and bake for 10-12 minutes.

While still hot, roll the cookies in powdered sugar. Cool, and roll again.

Makes 48 cookies.

Lured by A Fragrant Flower: *Agua de Jamaica*

If the sip of a crimson drink will take me there, I will go. I will go freely and happily, as this tart, crisp flower that stained my water to a delicious and refreshing memory lures me to. I will go willingly. Because even though the traffic is horrendous, like Bangkok's gridlocks and Cairo's chaos, and the news of crime and kidnap and danger ricochets from its warm embrace terrorizing those outside its magic and charm, I will go, gladly: I will go back to Mexico.

I gravitate towards the most crowded spot in the city, the *Mercado de la Merced*, the Saturday market, a tangle of dank alleys and passageways leaking with cow guts and blood from pigs' feet, where chickens dangle upside down in skinned nudity, waiting to be snatched and boiled into some tasty broth or *mole* or *taco*.

The spaces are small and dank and festering with people, some toting their goods precariously stacked on wheelbarrows which they deftly navigate through the city that is this market. Whistling serves as their horn to warn others of their passage. And many would feel claustrophobic in this dimly lit anarchy, nauseous perhaps: the smell of life and death are pungent; inescapable. But I, I am invigorated here, shoved along this wave of food and people. I feel embraced by the millions of stands overflowing with produce and meat, and even though I am the only fair-skinned, blue-eyed woman in the entire market, a *guera*, I am embraced by the Mexican's characteristic courteousness:

"*Bonita, guera, aquí, bonita, aquí.*" 'Here pretty blondie, here', the vendors coax, offering up free samples of fresh cheese, a slice of a mango, a piece of tripe. They are curious of me, each peering out from behind their stalls loaded with their life's work, becoming bashful and hiding safely behind a bag of *tortillas* or a mountain of fresh *nopales* when I turn to shoot their image. But still they all call after me, wanting me, and we share a moment of laughter, a smile, and a taste; always there's a taste. I apologize that I can't buy their goods: I have no kitchen of my own here in Mexico and it aches to leave empty-handed. I am weak with temptation.

An aged lady at a corner stand senses my eyes softening and draws me in, offering up dried flowers the color of rubies, placing a bunch delicately in my hand:

"*Bueno para el corazón, bueno para la mente: un pedazo de México,*" she promises and I reflect on her wisdom as it echoes my whole experience of this country:

"Good for the heart, good for the mind, a piece of Mexico."

And so I buy a bagful of these beautiful flowers, called *Flor de Jamaica*. They are dried hibiscus. I will cradle their delicacy amongst my lingerie, brushing away the image of a U.S. Customs dog attacking my suitcase to confiscate my goods. I risk it all because they are lovely and when boiled with water and chilled they make the unmistakably Mexican drink of *Agua de Jamaica*, a small part of my experience I refuse to let go.

I take the bag from my Mexican muse and hug it close to me. I hear the bustle of life. Something cold drips on my toe and I dare not look down. I am in Mexico. I am in the market. The waves of passer-byers behind me feel like a mammoth embrace. A man carrying several sacks of jalapeños on his head brushes by. A woman slices a lime and it explodes with juice, leaving a trail of citrus oil within smelling range.

A row of pig feet salutes me in the next stall. I breathe in the flower's fragrance and feel myself irrevocably drawn into this country. In this culinary bedlam I am home.

Agua de Jamaica: Dried Hibiscus Punch

2 cups dried hibiscus flowers*

2 quarts water

½ cup sugar**

1 cup orange juice

2 tablespoons fresh lime juice

*found in specialty Latin stores

**½ cup is tart, a cup is sweet: add, taste, and sweeten to your liking...

Bring the water, hibiscus flowers, and sugar to a boil in a 4 quart pot. Reduce the heat to medium and simmer for five minutes. Turn the heat off and allow to cool completely. Strain. Add the orange juice and lime juice. Chill.

Makes 6 cups

FISH GUTS AND LOVE: COCAZO DE CAMARON

When I want to fall in love I go to *Mercado de la Nueva Viga*. Because there are fish guts on the floor and the sweet scent of questionable oil penetrates, infiltrates, becomes you, I fall in love. It's not the quantity of fish that gets my heart *rat tat tatting*, no, I am a market veteran and I've seen plenty more. I've visited *Mercado de la Venta* in Madrid, Spain, where three floors-worth of fish and seafood beckons you. This can't hold a candle to that kind of seafood seriousness. *Mercado de la Nueva Viga* in Mexico City is only eight or ten aisles at most. Its selling point is the small, makeshift restaurants, four or five wobbly tables accompanied by neon plastic chairs, that line the outskirts of the vender's stalls.

The ladies and gentlemen of these establishments stand vigilant, peering through the aisles luring you with their song:

"¡*Empanadas empanadas empanadas de cazón, de pulpo, de pescado, los camarones camarones, sopa de marisco fresco fresco fresco vengan señores vengan!*"

I hear their call and I am in a trance. I don't even want to buy fish. I want to eat.

Husband is a willing partner-in-crime and together we pick the perfect spot to sit, closest to the blackboard announcing the specials of the day. Mind you, there is dirt. Flies. Questionable open containers on the table. I could get violently ill. There's no joking around when it comes to seafood. But I see the lady frying my empanadas right in front of me. I see the family of four enchanted by their piping hot soups ("*Oh my! What soup is that? I must have it!*", I demand of Husband). And everyone looks so happy. And safe. And content. And though I am clearly not a native I am one of them, I know I am one of them and nothing will happen but good things, nothing but good. So the waiter senses my longing to fit in and willingly complies.

'*Sopa de mariscos*,' he proclaims, when I ask about the family dish: Seafood soup.

'*Empanada de pulpo*,' he promises me when I point at the lady frying with a smile: octopus empanada.

'*Tostada de ceviche de pescado*,' he repeats, when I order on impulse a favorite: tostada with fish ceviche.

Husband smiles and meekly nods his head. He is enamored by this seafood-madwoman. He digs me like this.

And we wait together eagerly.

The *empanada* arrives first. The one stuffed with octopus. It's like no other *empanada* I've had before. The Mexicans have managed to Mexicanize it and raise my expectations of this stuffed fried patty to a whole new level. Now I am doomed. Every other *empanada* I have will never live up to this one. I know it. They have just ruined me.

It is sliced. Sliced! An *empanada* (my first traditional thought of course being, *how dare they slice an empanada*)!

But no. These guys are pros. They know what they are doing.

They have sliced it, allowed the rich broth of octopus and tomatoes to steam and they have placed thick slices of velvety avocado, spicy pickled onion and aromatic cilantro inside. Then a hefty dollop of mayonnaise seals the deal. They have done this brilliantly so that these flavors have molded into a rich, creamy, crunchy, fresh delight. Thoughts of E. coli and health code violations evaporate instantly with the first bite. In fact, I must close my eyes to fully experience and I am glad to be snug in my chair lest I lose my composure under this dish's powerful spell. I can splash some spicy sauce on if I care to, and I do, now feeling newfound appreciation for those questionable bottles. They are now my pals. The prerequisite bowl filled with juicy limes, a Mexican staple at any eating establishment, sits on my table. As does a bowl with additional chopped onion.

Thousands of conversations happen around us, but we are not speaking, savoring easily taking priority to sharing coherent thoughts. The *empanada* disappears quickly, the *tostada de ceviche* wolfed down too. And then the soup arrives- teeming with the seafood we spotted in the stands moments before. It is sublime, a heap of clams, mussels, and prawns bathed in a spicy broth the color of liquid gold. We are stuffed beyond recognition and then I see a miniscule, dented cardboard sign swinging in the wind. What does it say?

Husband looks worried and excited. *There she goes again*, he thinks to himself, falling in love with me all over again.

"*Cocazo de Camaron?*" I read out loud, claiming it mine. You can't turn down deep fried coconut shrimp, I don't care how full you are.

When the *Cocazo de Camaron* arrives, a large plate filled with tender supersized shrimp, coated in freshly grated sweet coconut, we somehow find space to devour the entire dish. It will become the highlight of the day. The essence of this seafood extraordinaire moment. We will take back friends and family and business associates to this grimy spot, we will relish in their look of horror and doubt, and then, we will sit them down and order this coconut shrimp, and they, too, will be forever changed. These are no ordinary shrimps. They are delicious on so many different levels I feel dizzy as my teeth sink into that first, crisp, nutty bite. Fresh ocean, sweet water, crunchy coconut. I am in love.

The family of four looks at us and smiles. We share this moment of plastic chairs, dirty floor and exquisite unsurpassed seafood. I pull off the head of my last shrimp and lingeringly place its sweet body in my mouth.

CRUNCHY COCONUT SHRIMP

1 lbs. jumbo shrimp

2 tablespoons fresh lime juice

¾ teaspoon salt

¼ teaspoon black pepper

½ cup all-purpose flour

3 eggs, beaten

1 ½ cups unsweetened coconut flakes   *Note: If you are lucky to live in a place where you can get fresh coconut, grated, use that instead.*

1 cup panko crumbs

6 tablespoons butter

6 tablespoons canola oil

Peel and devein the shrimp. Of course, you can buy the shrimp already peeled and deveined, it'll just cost you a bit more. To devein (removing the thin blue line that runs down the underside) run a paring knife alongside it and gently pulling it up.

Put the shrimp in a mixing bowl and toss with the lime juice, salt and pepper. Let marinate for 5 minutes.

Place the flour in a shallow bowl, the eggs in another shallow bowl, and the coconut and panko breadcrumbs in a third.

Melt the butter and oil in a large heavy skillet over medium/high heat.

Now get ready to triple dip your shrimp: first in the flour (make sure to coat it well), then in the egg, and finally in the coconut/panko.

Sauté the shrimp until golden brown, about 1 minute per side.

Drain the shrimp on paper towels.

Goes great with apricot jam (see page 228 for homemade version.)

Serves 4

Saturday Prayer: *Chilaquiles*

Because I've had so much *pollo a la plancha* and *ensalada* and have bypassed bread and cookies and, *gasp*, even wine.

Because I've been so good, forcing myself onto the treadmill, elliptical, and stationary bicycle. (*Ouch!* On a poorly designed seat!) And still I ride, run, and walk.

Because I am one that adores food, builds altars for it (usually involving lots of sugar, vanilla, and cinnamon) and now my well has gone dry, turned off, chastised and set on zero, all in the name of losing a few pounds. Okay, maybe more than a few.

Because of all this and more it builds: that pining, destitute, fervent yearning.

It builds *unnoticed* while I do my sit-ups.

It builds while I bake double-fudge brownies for the kids (and don't even sample the batter, *I don't*!)

And there it is, on the brink of my sanity, I feel that urge, that desire, that longing, and I know it will burst because there is nowhere left for it to go and Saturday, *oh glorious Saturday*, Saturday comes along, the day I have allotted to put down my culinary flogging and eat!

I wake, this beautiful sunny Saturday, even the birds seem happier, their chirps welcome me and I rise with an extra *oomph* in my step, no longer worried by scales and their rising digits or pants and tight waistlines, no, no worries on this Saturday of that sort. I dart into the kitchen on this glorious of all glorious days and announce, as loud and clear as a bell:

"*¡Yo quiero chilaquiles!*" (Translation: I want *chilaquiles*.)

And there it is. For when you are blessed with the angel of Saturday that is *Angelica,* my live-in Mexican cook, you make such pronouncements and they aren't left for your dreams, they do become true. She makes them so.

So begins the slow simmer of a spicy *tomatillo* sauce, the careful layering of fried, crunchy *totopos* (think tortilla chips from heaven) and the quick drizzle of warm sauce topped with generous shredding of *cotija* cheese, a Mexican staple hard, white cheese with a salty edge. And just to top off the decadence, (*why not, it is Saturday?*) there's the drizzle of the richest of all riches, *la crema,* the cream, another Mexican favorite, a type of *crème fraiche* that gets spooned and poured on practically every dish.

Chilaquiles is a favorite breakfast food in Mexico, usually served with fried eggs and/or shredded chicken, and always with a side of *frijoles* (beans) but today I want, I *need* this luscious, addictive indulgence straight up. Angelica places a steaming plate in front of my *still-not-thin-enough* face. I forget all numbers, all calories, all counting, all exercising, and live in the moment: a moment where *totopos, salsa de tomatillo,* and cheese blend into crunchy, tangy, zip, and ooze all smothered in the decadence of the richest cream. Caloric concerns are not invited. Happiness, on this Saturday, reigns.

Chilaquiles en Salsa Verde

For the Sauce:

    1 pound fresh tomatillos

    6 tablespoons corn oil

    ½ cup chopped onion

    2 garlic cloves

    2 fresh serrano *chile* peppers, chopped*

    ½ cup cilantro, chopped

    ½ cup chicken stock

*A few words on serrano chile peppers:

Please use caution when chopping, making sure you wash your hands immediately afterwards to remove all traces of spiciness from your hands, or better yet, use gloves! And another useful tip: if you like to turn up the heat on your dish, include the seeds. If spicy isn't that much your thing, remove the seeds!

    For the Chilaquiles**:

    Homemade:

    ½ cup corn oil

    10 tortillas, cut into triangles

    Store bought:

4 cups worth

*For help deciding whether to make or buy the tortilla chips, see below!

For topping:

1/2 cup Mexican *crema* or crème fraîche

1 cup shredded Mexican Oaxacan cheese or mozzarella

¼ cup cilantro, chopped

½ cup onion, cut in thick rings

Make the sauce:

Remove the husks from the tomatillos and rinse under cold water. Place in a bowl and add 2 tablespoons olive oil plus the salt and pepper, to taste. Mix well, then pour out onto a baking sheet and roast until the tomatillos are slightly charred, 10 minutes.

Remove the roasted tomatillos from the oven and allow to cool for ten minutes.

Reduce oven to 350°F.

In a skillet, heat 4 tablespoons of corn oil over medium heat. Sauté the onion, garlic, and *chile* peppers, until fragrant, about one minute.

In a blender or food processer, puree all the ingredients, along with the fresh cilantro.

Make the totopos (tortilla chips):

The true die-hard will make their own. I'm obliged to write this: I stand in a long line of faithful cooks (including my beloved Angelica) that make anything and everything from scratch. I want to tell you that I do too. Always. Everything. But, well, sometimes, I'm too rushed, or just plain lazy, or, heck, want the dish RIGHT NOW. So, for those of us that slip up and take a short cut, for those in need of a cheater's guide, here you go, I give you permission: you can just buy the chips and not make them from scratch. Make sure to buy the best quality tortilla chips out there - there are some good ones - preferably the ones that call themselves by their true name: *totopos* - which tend to be slightly thicker, with a heartier flavor and crunch.

I offer the recipe for homemade *totopos*, which, really, isn't such a big deal at all:

Pour the oil into a large skillet over medium heat. When the oil is hot, add the tortillas, working in 2 or 3 batches, and cook until lightly browned and nearly crisp. Drain the tortillas on paper towels and discard the remaining oil. Wipe the pan with a paper towel and use the same skillet to heat up your sauce. Bring to a boil and reduce to a gentle simmer. Simmer for five minutes.

Add the tortillas and stir.

Sprinkle with cheese and drizzle crema, cover, and simmer another five minutes.

Remove from heat, add cilantro, and onion and serve.

Serves 4

Chicken Mole and Life

Mysterious bags of dark powders now line my cobalt kitchen counter. They are next to my boundless row of specialty salts giving the space its own market feeling.

I could put them in glass jars.

Tupperware.

Away.

But I choose not to.

I've left them on the counter, not only because their quasi-drug look proudly reminds me how they all slipped by rigorously-trained airport beagles, but also because they represent the constant, intoxicating chaos of the Mexican market I recently left behind and still long for.

It's all good here, of course.

Suburbia is nice.

The grass is mowed.

The kids are clean.

The DIRECTV guy came when he said he would. Even fifteen minutes early.

But chaos?

What is it about chaos I long for? Miss? Crave.

Is it the packed pedestrian streets of *Sabana Grande* in Caracas where I grew up? The ones my best friend and I use to own when we were sixteen? We'd plop our lanky bodies smack down in the center of the crowded promenade and engage in a made-up Krishna chant that would draw curious crowds around us. Man I loved that.

Or the cramped Tel-Aviv roads, the ones where I learned how to parallel park my 1964 Volkswagen Beetle when I was a college student? If you didn't know how to squeeze into the miniscule space in the first five seconds you'd have a group of nosy passersby tapping on your window telling you to turn more to the left, and then another group ordering you to turn to the right. Then a heated discussion would follow. Man I loved that.

Perhaps it's the classic feel of New York City, where I finished my studies and experienced early adulthood? I was one with the patchwork of cultures, customs, and cuisines there. The Dominican Republic doorman eating his snack of *tostones*. The Turk dining a dizzying array of appetizers at a miniscule yet rowdy restaurant, wrapping it up with an aromatic *keskur* (coconut pudding). And most definitely the gregarious Frenchman rollerblading through Central Park with a cigarette dangling out of his mouth and a cold beer in his hand. I was all of them and they were a part of me.

It was glorious. Invigorating. Challenging. Man I loved that.

So those dusty plastic bags of earth-colored mole I bought in the Mexican market are worth more than gold to me, it appears. I almost thought I'd never use them. But then I did. I had some leftover chicken, a casualty from my chicken soup. It sat in a Tupperware awaiting its next destination, which was unknown. Until I realized one day while I watched the city workers in orange shirts, the only folks wandering about the neighborhood (save for the occasional dog walker) diligently watering the magnolia tree they had planted on my swale (city property: city watering), I realized then and there that tonight I must open the bag. Use the chicken. Make mole. Make magic.

And so I did. It was easy and ravenously delicious. The chicken shred itself willingly and danced happily in the blessing of chocolate, *chile* powder, and other mysterious elements. It was quick. A dash of broth, a squeeze of lime, a hot tortilla, and I was back. One bite and I was back. To crowds. To cities. To people. To life. Man I love that.

Chicken Mole

1 chicken, boiled in chicken soup, cooled and shredded*

1 cup onion, diced

2 tablespoons olive oil

5 tablespoons mole powder or 1 cup homemade (*see below*)

1 cup chicken broth (only when using mole powder)

cilantro to sprinkle on top

If you are rushed for time, a supermarket-bought roasted chicken works too!

A few words on mole…

In Mexico, mole is a religion. There are countless varieties of mole and infinite amounts of ingredients, depending on the region and history. Normally, the making of mole is a family secret, guarded fervently by members who graciously offer their final product in clear plastic bags they sell at local street markets. Of course, there are the commercialized versions of mole, sold in supermarkets, which, while they aren't nearly as transformative as the mole sold by *Doña Manuelita*, sitting on her plastic chair every Sunday from 7am to noon on the corner of *Avenida Guadalupe* and *Calle La Resistencia*, aren't bad at all.

Mole comes in wet and dry versions, dry being a concoction of spices that need only be mixed with stock to turn into magic. The wet version is almost clay-like, the utmost concentration of the up-to 75 ingredients it can be comprised of, and also requires stock to thin it out.

In the U.S. you can find premade mole in most local supermarkets, but if you are feeling bold and wanna give it a go, I say, *fantastico*! Mole usually take hours to make, but here's a *guerita* (an endearing Mexican term for a blond hair-blue eyed gal) version that's fast and fun:

Guerita's Mole

    4 tablespoons vegetable oil

    ¼ cup toasted pumpkin seeds

¼ cup toasted sliced almonds

1 teaspoon New Mexico *chile* powder

1/2 teaspoon pepper

1/2 teaspoon kosher salt

1/2 cup chopped onion

1 medium garlic clove, chopped

½ teaspoon cayenne

1 teaspoon ground cinnamon

½ cup tomato sauce

½ cup chicken broth

¼ cup dark chocolate morsels

2 tablespoons peanut butter

¼ cup water

In a small skillet over medium-high flame, heat 2 tablespoons of oil and add the pumpkin seeds, almond slices, *chile* powder, salt, and pepper. Cook until fragrant, about 30 seconds. Add the remaining ingredients, bring to a boil, and reduce heat to low. Cook, stirring frequently, for 15 minutes. Blend in ¼ cup water. Adjust salt, if necessary.

Makes approximately 1 cup, which will last up to two weeks in the refrigerator.

Now let's get cooking!

In a skillet over medium flame, heat the oil and add the onion. Sauté for five minutes, until translucent.

Add the shredded chicken and the mole. If you are using mole powder, add the chicken broth. Simmer for 5 minutes to heat through.

Serve with warm tortillas.

Serves 4

Tea Stop, Moroccan Style

Aziz must have been all of seventeen, a mere five years older than my daughter, but in his presence I felt safe, comforted, and loved.

Was it his sly smile, tweaked by honey-colored eyes with rich long lashes the color of coal? I couldn't stop gazing into those eyes, they seemed perfectly made up, a subtle tease of light and dark, the epitome of contrasts that defines Aziz's hometown of Marrakech. Perhaps it was the gregariousness that poured out of him with each vigorous wave, hug, and pat on the back he graced my family and I with (and there were many). It was infectious. Here was a stranger we'd stopped to ask directions from (*'L'Mellach synagogue, s'il vous plaît?'*) and somehow, willingly, ended up visiting in his closet-sized shop crowded with smells, powders, and crystals.

"You look. You no buy. I show. You no buy. No buy nothing. I teach you. Only teach you." He dangled that promise over Husband and proceeded to slather me in creams and powders, (*"this one for smooth, young skin, this one for the cooking, this one to open sinus."*) I had heard about the Moroccan *herboristerie*, or natural remedy shop, in my travel guide, but could have never imagined this delight to the senses to be such a friendly and available experience.

Whatever ailment, in whatever language, we threw Aziz's way, he had a remedy and a smile.

"Your son not breathe good? Here. Sniff. Good, yeah?"

My son was a willing volunteer, gently inhaling tar-colored

pebbles packed into a burlap sack and shoved up against his nostril. Within seconds his face lit up and his congestion improved.

"Y tu...bella," Aziz motioned to my teenage daughter in a smooth mixture of Spanish and Italian, "You use this on the skin, yeah?" He tossed a small amber block towards her with one hand while rubbing a second block over his own shirt. "*Jasmin, para perfumar el cuerpo.*" Jasmine, perfume for the body, he promised and delivered.

With each trick he produced I grew happier, announcing loudly:

"We'll take two of those, half a kilo of that, a bottle of this!"

Husband watched me nervously as he added the mounting *durhams* in his head, quickly translating them into euros. He stayed quiet to appease my new-found bond with my herb son.

"And you, *madame?*" Aziz asked, confident he'd soon cure all my troubles.

"Stomach." I offered, cursing my tragic predicament of food lover and stomach wimp. "Something for the stomach."

Aziz's eyes sparkled extra bright for this one and he added an extra jump to his step, startling all of us (for the store was miniscule and any extra jumping threatened to rattle a shelf or two).

"Well of course, I have the perfect remedy just for you! Tea!"

Tea is a familiar pastime in Morocco. Every stop in one's day is measured by a glass loaded with fresh mint leaves, hot water, and a generous spike of sweetness. But Aziz promised us a new experience:

"This isn't mint tea: different tea."

And with that he ran wildly around his shop, producing powders from jars, dried leaves from bags, and an unidentifiable petrified object or two. He popped these all into his battered metal kettle, set out the prerequisite glasses always used for tea, and waited with the same excitement a child waits to open Christmas presents on Christmas day. His energy was infectious and I noticed my entire family sat on the edge of our seats for this miraculous elixir to be ready to drink.

When the brewing time was up, Aziz gave the honors of tea pouring (a Moroccan art and tradition that places emphasis on the kettle being as far away from the glass as possible) to my eight-year old son, who mastered the job like a native. We all clapped and grabbed a glass. I wasn't sure what was in the tea but that didn't seem to matter. A quick compliant glance at Husband and a silent prayer we'd not get deathly ill ingesting this and then, down the hatch it went! The tea was smooth, with slight spice overtones and not sweet at all.

When we were done we said our goodbyes like old friends departing after a long visit. More hugs and picture-taking followed as we piled out of his magical little shop holding our bags of powders and potions we would forget how to use by the time we got home. As we headed down the crowded streets, slightly enchanted, fully disoriented, and not minding one bit, I heard Husband's familiar chuckle.

"Here we are," he proclaimed. "The synagogue."

Sure enough, we stood in front of the ancient structure, closed on that particular day.

We laughed together and agreed it had been a most expensive visit to a closed synagogue. Then we quickly conceded it was well worth every penny.

Mint Tea

It's hard to come by the unnamed herbs and spices that Aziz used to make tea in his shop, so I'll offer you the next best thing (and oh is it good!): mint tea! Only the freshest mint leaves will do. Use a ton. Use even more sugar. Serve in a small heatproof glass. (Moroccan tea glasses are a bit larger than a shot glass and come with beautiful designs!) Enjoy with a travel book in hand.

- 1 cup fresh mint leaves
- 5 to 6 tablespoons sugar, or to taste
- 2 cups boiling water

Add all ingredients into teapot and steep 4-5 minutes.

Serve in small glasses.

Serves 4

Not Made in America (And How to Cope with It)

There are many perks to having a world-traveling husband whose focus lately has been China. Girlfriends will notice my new array of alleged designer handbags, a different one for each day of the week it would seem, but I don't pay them much mind, I'm stuck on the culinary props that are introduced regularly to my home.

I've gotten all sorts of classics: woks, steamers, long chopsticks, and frying spoons setting me up for variations on *chow mein* for the next 365 days. I've gotten obscure, corroded contraptions he's picked up in dingy, crowded alleyways of clustered markets filled with friendly locals entertained by the arrival of this 6"2' Western man. *This is to peel pineapple. This one takes the kernels off the corn. This mashes the garlic.*

But then there was the knife. Handed to me in a primitive wooden box with rusted hinges, a box you'd inevitably be apprehensive about, secretly calculate when you had your last tetanus shot while making sure there are no small children around, making sure you are not *too* upset at your older children.

As I held the box I could have sworn I heard one of those country singers, with names as comforting as a warm slice of peach pie: Blake or Hank or Garth crooning a song about how great America is. I don't even listen to country music but there it was, playing in my ear, as I'd picture an oversized pickup truck following a pack of rugged cowboys herding cattle, and in that second I'd be overridden with guilt, I'd admonish myself for even holding this contraband, scary knife box and will myself to put it down, give it back. I should accept knives made in America, good solid workmanship from Massachusetts or South Carolina or upstate New York.

But that lasts seconds, because I am weak.

I'm sorry.

I open it and I am in love, or at least, in a trance, as if you were dangling a gold medallion in front of me and asking me to count to ten. Maybe I'd get to three.

The knife is beautiful. It is a cleaver that is large with a gleaming blade and an exquisite wooden handle.

And sharp. So sharp I could splice an eyelash with it.

So I spend my days conjuring up recipes where I can use it.

Orange Roughy fits tonight's bill.

I bought the fish because it had such a complicated and unattractive name.

I had already passed over it and focused on names that were easier to pronounce, names I've grown to love: salmon, red snapper, trout.

Here was *Orange Roughy* staring me in the face.

"What is that?" I asked my fishmonger.

"That's *Orange Roughy*," he stated, looking at me like I was an idiot.

My Culinary Compulsion   317

"What's it taste like?" I ventured, now intrigued by his incredulous glare.

"Delicious. Like grouper meets crab." he said, pleased with his analogy.

Grouper meets crab? Two of my favorites dancing in one fish flavor?

I had to try it.

I bought several fillets and rushed home to my new Chinese knife.

The fillet I'll leave intact, of course. You don't want to mess with crab-meets-grouper, you just want to heighten it, and my Chinese knife and I know how.

We'll take loads of fresh flat-leaf parsley and *chop, chop chop*!

Seriously, try this at home, if you have an unforgettable blade.

Buy loads of parsley and chop it fine.

You'll feel so much better after you've done that, no matter how lousy the day.

Of course, be careful of the fingers. Keep them away. Losing a finger would really spoil the day.

To that I add some fresh spinach. The cutting board is covered in dark green. The knife works seamlessly and I have found bliss. I don't even remember what knockoff purse I'm carrying these days, is it the Prada, the Michael Kors, the Gucci?

I am done and I throw these ingredients into a bowl, drizzle it with some olive oil, grate some fresh *Parmigiano-Reggiano*, add a sprinkling of sea salt and black pepper over it all, and top it off with some lemon zest to freshen the whole thing up.

Wait!

I've forgotten garlic! Something else to chop! A clove or two, depending on your love of the stuff, who you'll be kissing tonight. Husband is already off to some other distant country, so I can go nuts on the garlic, mince a bunch up real fine. This will take seconds now, you are a pro.

The minced garlic is staring us in the face. Add that to the bowl and mix it all up real good. You've got what looks like green mush. Fragrant green mush. Take a spoonful or two and coat it on your fish fillet. You can top it with some *panko* bread crumbs if you want it crusty (I'd mix those with a bit of melted butter for extra yum.) Or you can throw some *panko* straight into your green mix. Or opt to go *panko-less* if you are on a carb witch hunt, that's fine too.

Ten minutes in a preheated 350°F oven and you're done! Crab-meets-grouper is a perfect description. Sweet and meaty flavors meld wonderfully with the citric zest and earthy, peppery bite of parsley and spinach.

I think even the cowboys would forgive the Chinese transgression, if I sat them down to this meal. So long as I play some country music in the background.

Orange Roughy with Citrus Herbs

I can't take credit for this recipe. It was given to me by my dear friend, Ana Paula, whom I met in an over air-conditioned corporate office years ago under the guise of becoming executive hotshots. The allure of fluorescent lighting and confining cubicles wore off quickly and we both left our positions respectively, but the friendship remained strong, most notably because of our love for our families and our passion for food. I'm always picking up great tips from this pal. This is one of many.

2 fillets of Orange Roughy (any soft white fish works)

Citrus Herb mixture:

½ cup flat-leaf parsley, chopped very fine

¾ cup fresh spinach, chopped very fine

2-4 cloves of garlic, depending on you, minced

2 tablespoons mayonnaise

zest of 1 lemon

1/3 cup freshly grated *Parmigiano-Reggiano* cheese

salt and pepper, to taste

Panko mixture:

4 tablespoons panko crumbs

1 teaspoon melted unsalted butter

Mix and add into greens or on top for extra crunch!

Preheat the oven to 350°F.

Combine all the citrus herb ingredients and slather onto fish fillets. Top with panko mixture.

Place the fillets in a baking pan, lined with aluminum foil (makes it mess-free!)

Bake 10-12 -minutes.

The fish should come apart easily with a fork when done.

Makes 2 fillets

322   Alona Abbady Martinez

CHAPTER SIX

EXTRA HOLIDAY POUNDS

Feliz Navidad: Venezuelan Pan de Jamón

Growing up in a tropical country during the winter holiday season had its apparent disadvantages for a young child. Snowfall, for one, was a glamorous occurrence reserved for the obscure North where Santa and many flush-faced giddy elves allegedly worked under a flurry of longed for snowflakes. The foliage didn't help set the mood either: not a pine tree in sight, in fact, my family's backyard alone was cluttered with trees adorned with sun-drenched fruits like limes, mangoes, and bananas.

Then you had to fight your way through the hummingbirds, lizards, parrots, *guacamayas*: macaws, most notable known for their bright red and blue plumage, and, of course, Murtle the Turtle, our tenured pet who inconveniently preferred strategically treacherous spots, such as the walkway, to sunbathe its crusty head. None of this was shouting *ho-ho-ho*, if you know what I mean.

Still, the benefits of a December spent eight degrees north of the equator seemed to far outweigh the desperate longings for a Nordic Christmas. Top on the list was the annual holiday television commercial, a much-anticipated event where all the local soap opera celebrities crooned about peace and love and the Holy Spirit in a 7-minute spot played incessantly on television during the month of December. Hanukkah never quite made it to the predominantly Catholic airwaves. Anticipation for this would commence as early as October, when viewers would begin to wonder what spin the holiday commercial would have. When December would arrive, everyone (and I mean everyone) gathered and watched as the *telenovela* icons (who enjoy Supreme Being status in Venezuela) would shed their nightly bouts of runny mascara, lost fortunes and forlorn love and gather in one big happy circle of love and holiday spirit singing about the joys of Baby Jesus and the prosperity promised for the coming New Year. An impressive imported tree that would make Rockefeller's look like a key chain ornament, sparkled in the background and big chunky pieces of foam rained down on the celeb fest in attempts to transform the humid climate into one of winter.

I admit I was a *telenovela* junkie from the early age of about seven. While my American contemporaries basked in the morally correct episodes of *The Brady Bunch* and *Little House on the Prairie*, I nourished my distorted sense of reality with scandalous classics such as *Crystal* and *Topacio*. I followed all the trials and tribulations of each and every character, knew who was the real sister, who stole whose fortune, and what the hospitalized mummy with the lustrous blonde hair was muttering through her gauze when no one else could understand. So, to say I was obsessed with these Christmas commercials is putting it mildly.

Food was often tied in to these lovefests. After the camera tired of trying to make Eduardo Serrano appear tall or hide Hilda Carrero's double chin, it would pan out to a glorious table loaded with Venezuelan Christmas goodies. Each dish looked more delicious than the next, from the pineapple-glazed Christmas ham to the steaming *hallaca*, a traditional tamale-like specialty wrapped in plantain leaves and stuffed with a stew made from pork, chicken, beef, olives, capers and raisins. Displayed up front would be a golden *pan de jamón*, ham bread, another indispensable item for a

Venezuelan Christmas. I could never eat just one piece of *pan de jamón*. The combination of warm sweet dough filled, jelly-roll style, with salty ham, smoked bacon, briny olives and plump, juicy raisins almost forced me to keep eating, always leaving me a little too full. And as much as I adored my soap opera idols, I remember feeling envious of them; not particularly for the honorary role of shedding good cheer to all the Channel 4 viewers, but because of the amazing spread that I believed awaited them after each performance. I imagined them finishing their carol, brushing off the fake snowflakes and devouring all the delights on the table, while I'd be trapped watching The Flintstones, awaiting their return.

Venezuelan Ham Bread

For the bread:

- 2 cups milk
- ¾ cup unsalted butter
- ½ cup granulated sugar
- 2 packages active dry yeast
- 4 eggs
- 2 teaspoons salt
- 6 cups bread flour
- 1/3 cup cornmeal
- 1 tablespoon cold water

For the filling:

6 tablespoons unsalted butter, softened

1 pound best-quality ham (Black Forest, Virginia, or Tavern-style), sliced regular

4-6 slices of raw bacon

1 cup pitted green olives

1 cup dark raisins, soaked in 1 cup Port wine*

*Allow raisins to soak for at least 30 minutes.

Preheat the oven to 200°F. When it reaches this temperature, turn it off. You have now created a warm space for your dough to rise.

Bring the milk, 6 tablespoons butter, and the sugar to a boil together in a medium-size saucepan. Remove from heat; pour into a large mixing bowl and let cool to lukewarm (105 – 115°F). Stir the yeast into the milk mixture and let stand for 10 minutes.

Beat 3 of the eggs in a small bowl, add salt and combine with the milk/yeast mixture. Pour the egg/milk/yeast mixture in the bowl of your standing mixer, and using the paddle attachment, stir in 5 cups of the flour on medium speed, 1 cup at a time, until you achieve a sticky dough.

Change to the hook attachment and mix on high for 6

minutes, until the dough becomes elastic, forms a ball, and pulls away from the sides of the bowl. *(Note, you can also knead dough by hand on a floured surface.)* Take the dough out, and wash and dry bowl. Smear the reserved 2 tablespoons butter around the inside of the bowl and place the ball of dough into the bowl, turning to coat it lightly with butter. Cover the bowl with a towel and set in your pre-warmed oven to rise until tripled in bulk, approximately 2-3 hours. Turn dough out onto a lightly floured work surface, lightly punching dough down, and cut into half.

Wash and dry bowl. Put each half into separate, buttered bowls, using the remaining 4 tablespoons of butter, cover and let rise another hour. On a floured surface, roll out the first ball to about ¼ inch thickness in a rectangular shape. I make one bread at a time, simply because I don't have the counter space to do both. If you are blessed with an expansive kitchen, go ahead and make both breads in tandem! You'll have two beautiful and delicious loaves- one of which makes a memorable gift to the hostess of your next holiday party!

Smear 3 tablespoons of butter all over each rectangle. On the top part of the dough, begin placing the ham, slightly overlapping, working your way to the bottom of the dough, leaving about one inch of dough at the end. Add four slices of bacon with about a three-inch gap.

Add olives and raisins - BUT WAIT! Here's how you do it, and I have my good friend Sebastian Martinez to thank for this tip:

Add the olives and raisins in straight lines along the dough. Don't just sprinkle them about haphazardly. Why, you ask? Because if you do it the Sebastian way, you'll be guaranteed to have a piece of olive and a raisin in every slice! *Gracias, Seba*! Gently roll dough towards you to form a log. Pinch tightly on ends to seal and fold ends underneath.

Repeat with other ball of dough.

Sprinkle a large baking sheet with cornmeal and transfer the loaves to the sheet. Leave room between the loaves for them to rise. Cover loaves with the towel and let rise another hour (this time outside of the oven).

Preheat the oven to 350°F.

Prepare sweet wash for bread:

¼ cup *papelón**, grated

½ cup warm water

*Papelón, also known as *panela* or *piloncillo* is raw, hardened sugar cane juice typical of Central and South

America. It is sold in blocks or cylinders in Latin specialty stores and many mainstream supermarkets as well.

Mix grated *papelón* with warm water until fully dissolved.

Prepare egg wash:

Beat the remaining egg and 1 tablespoon cold water together in a small bowl.

Pierce loaves on top with a fork.

Brush the sweet wash evenly onto loaf and then follow it with the egg wash.

Set the baking sheet on the middle rack of the oven. Bake for 30-35 minutes, or until loaves are golden brown. Cool on rack.

Makes 2 large loaves

Namaste, New Year: Low-fat Lemon Cheesecake

He whispered the words slowly into my right ear seconds before he snapped my neck.

"Sugar is evil. Flour too."

There was a loud crack.

"No bread."

Crack.

"And no bagels."

Crack, crack.

I looked at my chiropractor, a diminutive but strong man, in disbelief. This was his response to my inquiry on his never-aging appearance.

"You should be feeling better now. No more headaches. Your TMJ was completely out of place."

It's true.

The migraine that had welcomed me into the new year and overstayed its visit began diluting in strength.

But no bread, no bagels?

"What the hell do you eat then?" I asked, knowing the answer.

"Grains. Veggies. Protein."

I've heard this mantra before.

From people who look amazing.

Take my chiropractor, for example: in his mid-fifties and could easily pass as 35. Or my sister-in-law: excommunicated wheat several years back and lost about 100 pounds. Or my best friend's sister. I don't know what the hell *she* does but every time she appears smiling on Facebook she is a younger and trimmer version of the Susan I used to know.

All these people's faces glow.

Their energy level is up.

I know January is the month of aspirations and promises. Resolutions are brand new and ready to go on their test drive.

And I am so tempted to get on board with that! I am! But I am weary of the whole ideology. You see, it's not even a week into it and I've already stumbled.

Wasn't I supposed to pick up exercising regularly?

And didn't I already miss one day, no, sorry, two?

Not a good track record when it's only January 4th.

I know myself better than to openly announce exile from carbohydrates and sugar. It's what I love, it's what I do.

I wonder if my chiropractor sampled my challah, the one where the butter gives in to the warm, fluffy dough, or bit into my pineapple upside-down cake when it's fresh out of the oven and dripping with caramelized dark brown sugar, would he feel the same way?

Dr. Larry prods my back with expert hands. There are a series of unresolved issues along my spine and he finds them all, jabbing at discomfort I had grown used to.

"Ouch!" I scream as he pushes on a particularly tender area.

"Yeah, that C4, that one's real bad," he concurs, twisting and snapping something back to where it belongs.

The pain is gone.

In fact, as he pulls and pushes me into place, patient, ever so patient with my bickering, I start to feel better.

Way better.

When we're done I stand up and stretch. I feel taller. Renewed. Lightheaded, in a good way. Oxygen is reaching spots it hadn't before.

My energy level is up!

My skin glows, I bet.

Perhaps the adjustment even sliced a couple of years off my appearance.

Perhaps.

Quick! Take a picture and post it on Facebook!

"I can't," I tell Dr. Larry resolutely.

"You did great, you trusted me, and let me adjust you," he

responded, remembering the phobia I used to have with cracking bones and chiropractic work. I have come a long way in the years I have known him.

"No. I can't do *no bread*. No sugar!" I shout, slouching a bit, tempting C4 to misbehave.

Dr. Larry smiles. He is a forgiving man.

"I'm happy you came in," he offers quietly. "Don't wait so long before coming back."

I leave his office thinking about the new year and the promises we tend to load up on at this time.

I'm glad I've made no commitments for self-improvement.

Which doesn't mean I'll be guzzling melted butter or gorging on *Panettone* all year long.

Privately, I decide to make minor adjustments, now and again, like the overdue visit to my chiropractor, snapping some things into place.

So I skipped a day or two of exercise. I have the whole year to catch up.

My head is clear and my back pain gone.

I'm feeling a bit of a cheesecake craving coming on.

I remember Dr. Larry's warm smile, how he whispered *Namaste* on my way out, almost as if he didn't think I'd heard him.

I heard him.

Light Lime Cheesecake

(Adapted from The New Basics Cookbook, Julee Rosso & Sheila Lukins)

Not your traditional cheesecake loaded with sugar and fat. Go ahead and serve yourself a second piece of this one!

- 1 cup graham crackers, pulverized
- 2 tablespoons dark brown sugar
- 1 tablespoon grated lime zest
- 2 tablespoons butter
- ¾ cup low fat key lime pie Greek yogurt
- ¾ cup ricotta cheese
- ½ cup cream cheese, softened
- 2 teaspoons cornstarch
- 1 teaspoon vanilla extract
- 3 eggs
- ½ cup sugar

Preheat the oven to 350°F.

Combine the graham crackers, brown sugar, and 1 teaspoon of the lime zest in a food processor and process until fine. Add the butter and process until the mixture begins to come together.

Press the mixture into the bottom and sides of a 9-inch pan and bake for 10 minutes. Remove from the oven and let cool. Leave the oven on.

Puree the yogurt, cheeses, cornstarch, and vanilla extract in a food processor. Add the eggs, sugar, and remaining lime zest. Process until smooth.

Gently ladle the filling into the prepared crust and place the pan on a baking sheet.

Bake until set, 30 minutes.

Cool on a wire rack, then refrigerate until chilled.

Makes 8-10 portions

Goy Toffee

When I sent my best friend, Beth, my family holiday card this year (complete with the image of a Menorah proudly lit and a gothic font announcing "Happy Holidays") she told me, not only was I becoming too American, but extremely goy as well. Her tone conveyed part shock, part disappointment, and part victory. Shock, most likely because I had always put up such a good argument during my years living in this country that I would never succumb to the cheesy Sears-like family portraits I deemed beneath me; disappointment because I did succumb to the cheesy Sears-like family portraits I deemed beneath me; and victory because I succumbed to the cheesy Sears-like family portrait I deemed beneath me. Beth knows me better than I know myself, so, none of this came as much of a surprise to her, and in truth, she was actually happy that I had finally grown up enough to accept this American tradition of sending a family portrait picture out for the holidays – whether Christmas or Hanukah.

Having a family has helped curb some of my rebellion against such traditions. I guess I have rebelled against them all these years because:

a) accepting them and partaking in them would actually make me a grown-up (something I have a hard time processing even as a well-seasoned adult)

b) having grown up in Venezuela within a patchwork of cultures and customs can leave a person with a pretty confused identity, and...

c) before you have a family and lose all couth to an uncontrollable urge to share your adorable offspring with anyone with a functioning eyeball, you do know those Sears-like portraits really ARE somewhat cheesy.

But things are all different now. I look forward to those portraits (yes, Beth, I do) and I have adopted another American goy tradition as my own as well: the giving of holiday cookies.

During this time of giving and goodwill and hohoho and all the rest, millions upon millions of tins filled with thousands upon thousands of holiday treats are being swapped. I can smell it in the air and hear it in the buzz of conversations, but none ever come my way. It is a Christmas Club I have not been invited to, so, like any good Jew will do, I invite myself.

In this melting pot of cultures and beliefs, food trumps it all, so I am sure no one will mind. I simply cannot resist the urge to bake, and no one can resist this particular treat: sharing something uberdelicious is a tradition we can all claim!

Easy Goy Toffee

A show-stopper and oh-so-easy!

1 cup unsalted butter

1 cup brown sugar

1 4-ounce package saltine crackers

1 cup semisweet chocolate morsels

½ cup chopped walnuts

Preheat the oven to 400°F.

In a small saucepan over medium-high heat, melt the butter with the brown sugar. Bring to a boil and cook for 5 minutes without stirring. Remove from the heat. Meanwhile arrange the crackers (salt side up) on a jelly roll pan. Pour the butter mixture over the crackers.

Bake for 5 minutes. Turn the oven off.

Remove from the oven and sprinkle the chocolate morsels and nuts over the crackers.

Place in the still warm oven for 2 minutes.

Remove and let cool. Slice up into squares.

Makes 35 pieces

Latkes with a Side of Love

These are the things I knew about my Uncle Joe: he was the tallest man I'd ever seen (soaring above all the adults at about 6'5"), he emigrated from Poland to Israel during WWII with a broken, unspoken past, and he idolized Charles Bronson, his iconic tough-guy American role model. He also made the most memorably delicious latkes I'd ever tasted.

Uncle Joe wasn't really Uncle Joe. His real name was Eliasaf. But when my family traveled half way around the world to visit my father's sister and him, he'd insist in his limited English that we call him that. We'd arrive, *en famille*, for our annual visits to Israel late at night and wearily traipse up the stairs towards his miniscule Jerusalem apartment on *Rehov Rashba* where we'd find him, towering above the doorframe, waiting to greet us. He'd break out in a dazzling smile and give my sisters and I fierce bear hugs and pinches on our cheeks, his trademark signs of affection.

Uncle Joe adored us, but he was particularly enchanted by my mother, the beautiful blue-eyed, Vassar graduate whom my father had somehow managed to marry. Uncle Joe always seemed very impressed by this feat of my father, who was a good fifteen years younger than him, and every time we'd arrive at the door, he'd greet my dad first, offering up a big slap on the back and belt out proudly in Hebrew, a congratulation: "*Kol HaKavod!*" - literally, "all the honor," - as if still stunned that my father, the scruffy Israeli boy he used to place in a headlock, had managed to pull off this whole *snag-an-American-Ivy-League-bombshell* thing so successfully.

My mother would enter, followed by all three girls: all blue-eyed, all American like her. We'd plop onto the only couch in the apartment and instantly be showered with coloring books, lavish slices of chocolate mousse cake, and whatever accessories the hottest Barbie doll was wearing while the adults caught up over steaming cups of café Turkí, whose spicy cardamom always made me sneeze.

My aunt's domain was in the kitchen, and she tenaciously claimed her dominion by filling our bellies with her legendary repertoire: lemon cream pie, spice cake, and hearty *Cholent* stew. But there were a few exceptions left to Uncle Joe, which included his unrivaled potato latkes. Latkes are deep fried potato pancakes traditionally served during Hanukah, an eight-day holiday when Jewish people eat fried food to commemorate the oil in the menorah that miraculously lasted for eight nights after the victorious Jewish rebel Maccabees vanquished King Antiochus's troops many, years ago.

I don't remember having many conversations with Uncle Joe, but the sparkle in his eyes never faded from my memory – or the image of him clad in a raggedy undershirt and faded shorts, bent over the stove, frying up a batch of golden, crispy latkes. He'd grate the potatoes and onions by hand, gently stir in the eggs, and somehow make magic, delivering us a plate full of golden, crispy love, that didn't even require the customary sour cream or applesauce accompaniments. Something tender, even a tough man like Charles Bronson would have swooned over.

Uncle Joe's Fabulous Latkes

Although I never got his original recipe, these come pretty close.

- 2 pounds (about 6) Idaho potatoes
- ½ cup chopped scallions (including green part)
- 1 cup onion, grated
- 2 eggs, lightly beaten
- ½ cup unbleached all-purpose flour
- ½ teaspoon baking powder
- 1 teaspoon salt
- ¼ teaspoon freshly ground pepper
- ¾ cup canola oil

Peel the potatoes and place in a bowl with cold water.

Using a hand grater, grate the potatoes.

Place the grated potatoes in a colander and rinse with cold water. Let sit for five minutes, then rinse again, making sure the water rinses all of the shredded potato: this helps eliminate the starch, which turns the potato a reddish color.

Squeeze the water out of the potatoes and let sit in the colander while you prepare the remaining ingredients.

Grate the onion.

Mix the onion, scallions, eggs, flour, baking powder, and salt and pepper in a bowl.

Add the grated potatoes and mix well. I find tossing mixture with your bare hands works best.

Heat the oil in a 12-inch nonstick skillet on medium-high heat. When the oil is hot, using a large spoon, scoop up ¼ cup of the latkes mixture and press it into spoon with your hand. Gently drop the spoonful into the skillet.

Fry until the latkes are golden on each side, approximately 2 to 3 minutes each side. Drain on paper towel.

Place in oven on low heat to keep warm.

Makes 18 3-inch latkes

Racing for Forgiveness, or at least, A Good Meal: Sephardic Meatballs

I have vivid memories of my family's cameo synagogue appearance during Yom Kippur services when I was a child. Even growing up in South America, where it is assumed you would come to any event late, we would be extra late. After fighting three daughters over the injustices of having to wear a dress, my mother and father would quickly shuffle us out the front door and we'd make the quiet drive to the synagogue. Once there, we'd be marched up the front steps by my father, who, with the zest and zeal of an army officer, always walked much faster than any of us. Our religious experience was all haste: mumbled hellos to important-looking men waiting by the door, a hand quickly slipping a heavy and worn prayer book into our hands, half in Hebrew, half in Spanish, and up the stairs we'd go to the main part of the sanctuary, which looked more like a reception hall than anything else. And as slowly and softly as my father would try to open the big wooden door to enter, it always creaked and my face inevitably turned beet red with embarrassment at our continual failure to arrive unnoticed for services. And just as quickly and clumsily as we had arrived, we'd leave, a mere half an hour later, trying to keep up with my dad who was racing down the stairs, hastily returning the prayer books, muttering goodbyes with an occasional handshake, and back into the car for the drive home where something much more familiar and comforting awaited us: a fragrant dinner prepared earlier that day.

I never understood the fuss about, what would in the end, be a big hurry to go and come back. I knew it was inescapable: we'd go to synagogue, no matter how many times my sisters and I whined about it. Eventually, I let my fighting go, considering it a duty to appease my dad, to race after him as we dipped ourselves in one night of strange song and prayer that he somehow felt connected to and I knew nothing about. The only thing I could grasp was the blast of the Shofar, the ancient ram's horn trumpet sounded during the High Holy Days; its plaintive cry signaled the end of services, and year after year I anticipated its long, loud call, wondering what meal would be waiting at home.

Sephardic Meatballs

This isn't the Italian meatball you've met on top of spaghetti. Popular amongst Syrian Jews, these are easy and fast and can be prepared the day before. Fifi Bakal, a beloved family friend, was the inspiration for this dish.

- 1 cup onion, thinly sliced
- 6 tablespoons vegetable oil
- 1 cup jellied cranberry sauce
- ¼ cup red wine
- ½ cup water
- 1 lbs. ground beef

1 egg

2 tablespoons matzo meal

1 teaspoon salt

¼ teaspoon white pepper

½ teaspoon cumin

¼ teaspoon allspice

1 cup tomato sauce

2 tablespoons brown sugar

In a bowl, combine the ground beef, egg, matzo meal, salt, pepper, cumin, and allspice. Roll into small meatballs, about 2" in diameter.

In a large skillet over medium/high heat, add 3 tablespoons of the oil and sauté the meatballs until golden, 5-7 minutes.

Remove the meatballs from the skillet and add the remaining oil. Sauté the onions until translucent, 3-5 minutes.

Add the jelly, tomato sauce, wine, and brown sugar; raise the heat to high and bring the sauce to a boil. Lower the heat to medium and stir for 5 minutes. Add the meatballs and reduce heat to low. Cook another 10 minutes.

Makes 2 dozen meatballs

To Life! Chocolate Matzo Cake

Passover begins this Saturday, and now, bottle upon bottle of the Jewish version of fine wine (also known a Kosher Sweet Concord Grape Wine) is flooding stores promising to add unquestionable delight to the celebration. It's true, as a people we are not really known for our consumption of alcohol. We tend to gravitate more toward food items: a tender brisket, an unbeatable chopped liver, homemade *kugel*, and, of course, the famous cure-all chicken soup. Still, holidays are created to forge exceptions, and Passover, one of the most festive and culinary-charged celebrations, paves the way in placing alcohol on the same pedestal as food.

Wine is introduced as an all-inclusive package: with cup after cup after cup, carefully paced throughout the reading of the *Haggadah* (the book that recounts the tale of the Jews' escape from slavery in Egypt), we toast, drink, toast, drink, splatter drops of wine on plates and drink some more. It is a night of jovial lunacy that would make even the Irish proud.

Growing up in primarily Catholic Venezuela, I was pretty much the only Jew around. I could always count on my parents' ingenuity in somehow finding Kosher sweet wine, so we could, as all good Jews should, enjoy one night (or two, if you are lucky) of total, dizzying celebration. My mother found clever ways to include the intoxicatingly sweet wine throughout the meal, beginning with a Tropical Passover Sangria and finalizing with the show-stopper of the evening: Matzo Chocolate Cake (the secret is in the soaking the matzo in the wine before assembling the cake). Bottoms up and *l'chaim*!

Tropical Passover Sangria

1 (750 ml) bottle Kosher Sweet Concord Grape Wine

64 ounces fresh tropical juice blend (orange/strawberry/banana)

2 Granny Smith apples, peeled and cut in 1-inch cubes

2 peaches, peeled and cut into 1-inch cubes

4 bananas, peeled and cut into 1-inch cubes

1 mango, peeled and cut into 1-inch cubes

1 cup seedless red grapes

1 cup seedless green grapes

2 kiwis, peeled and cut in 1-inch cubes

thin orange slices for garnish

ice, if desired

Combine all the ingredients except the orange slices in a large pitcher. Add ice, if desired, and garnish with the orange slices. Stir well. When serving, garnish each glass with an orange slice, scoop out some of the fruit into the glass and pour the sangria over the fruit.

Makes 12-15 8 ounce servings.

Drunk Matzo Chocolate Cake

Another reason I knew Husband was the man for me was that he had his own amazing version of this cake. Ever the mediator, he adapted his rendition with my mother's, making a spectacular cake even better!

6 ounces semisweet chocolate

2 ounces unsweetened chocolate

1 cup milk

1 (14-ounce) can sweetened condensed milk

2 tablespoons cornstarch

2 tablespoons vanilla extract

1/2 cup Kosher Sweet Concord Grape Wine

1 1/2 boxes regular matzo

2 cups walnuts, ground finely in a food processor

Over medium-low heat, melt both chocolates with 1 cup milk. Add the condensed milk and cornstarch and mix over the heat, cooking for 2 minutes or until slightly thickened. Mixture will thicken more as it cools. Remove from heat and add the vanilla extract. Pour the wine in a shallow dish. Dip the matzo pieces in the wine, making sure they become fully moist. Then build a layer of the soaked matzo in a 9 x 13-inch pan. You may have to break some of the matzo to make it fit. Drizzle with 1/4 cup of chocolate and sprinkle with 1/4 cup nuts. Continue to layer like a lasagna until you have 4 layers. End with a layer of the chocolate mixture, then sprinkle with the remaining nuts. Refrigerate for at least 4 hours.

Serve 16

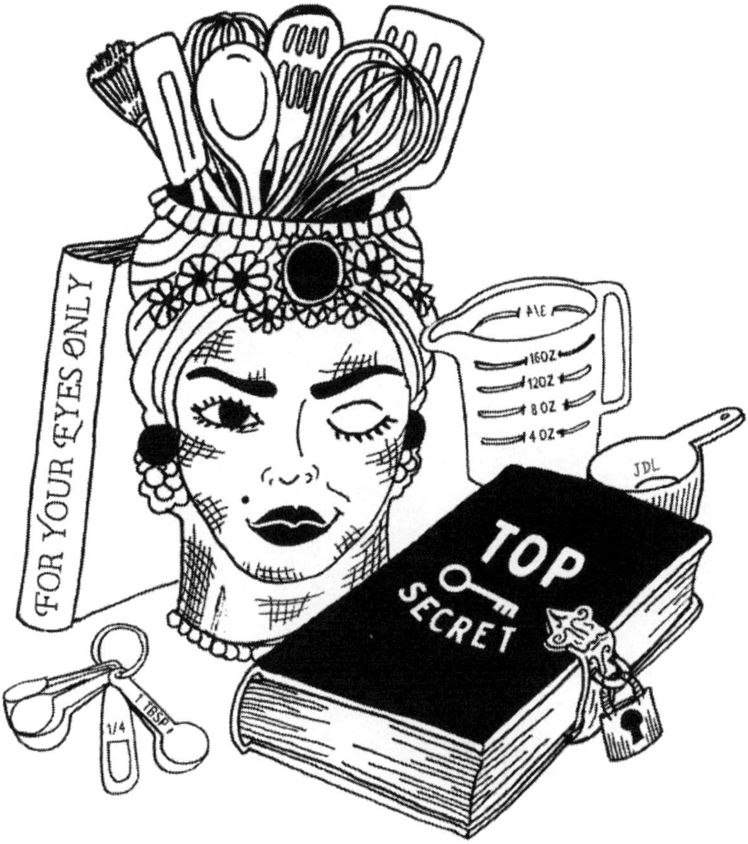
FOR YOUR EYES ONLY
16OZ
12OZ
8 OZ
4 OZ
JDL
TOP SECRET
1 TBSP
1/4

CHAPTER SEVEN

DELICIOUS ADDICTIONS AND SECRETS

The Vice of Mayonnaise:
Huevitos de Codorniz en Salsa Rosada

In the abyss of a quiet night, when children have succumbed to their struggle of sleep and Husband snores lazily on the stained blue sofa, I eat mayonnaise from the jar. We're not talking a light lick of the knife to cleanse it of its miniscule residue of spread, but rather a flat out, flagrant finger-scooping of the delightfully forbidden stuff.

I readily swallow in big gulps of happiness. It's the same giddiness with which children gobble their chocolate pudding and in these moments of silence, with the glow of the refrigerator lighting my way, my joy is complete, my crime only witnessed by Goldie, the obese hyperactive goldfish that would join in the fun if she could figure a way out of her cloudy fish tank and into the white delicacy of my family-size jar of mayonnaise.

I know this is a horrible thing, to eat mayonnaise out of a jar. Particularly from someone so versed in the nuances of artisanal butters, *Iberico* ham, Himalayan salts, and other fine culinary things. I know that when I am horrified at folks who dare house plastic bottles of minced garlic, instead of using fresh, or who sport blank looks at the thought of making homemade icing (i.e., not from a can) with fresh strawberries (i.e., not dehydrated, frozen ones), that I am nurturing my own dirty little secret with the big bottle of Hellmann's tucked away behind my homemade yogurt (white on white, who will know?) Which is why I do it only when no one is watching me. Like the clueless, bland husband played by Richard Bowens in the "The Big Chill", I find a quict solace in the secret midnight ritual of eating mayonnaise.

There shouldn't be any shame to such a ritual, really. My life is anything but bland. It brims with passion, lust and good food, which is why it wouldn't feel complete without an unbashful celebration of mayonnaise. And not the homemade stuff whipped with fresh garlic, olive oil, and organic eggs but the proudly processed jugs of soybean oil, water, whole eggs and egg yolks, vinegar, salt, sugar, lemon juice, natural flavors, calcium disodium and EDTA, respectfully.

On a Freudian approach, I could blame this all on my childhood. In Venezuela, 5-gallon jugs of Kraft Mayonnaise seemed a prerequisite, where they sat alongside the 2-gallon tubs of margarine. Savoring the salty creamy spread was a daily excursion. Breakfast beautifully began with a basketful of *arepas*, the Venezuelan solution to all life's evils. These delicious round cornmeal cakes made a cameo appearance in every meal, but come morning time, they were deliciously available with wavy layers of mayonnaise and thick slices of smoked Virginia ham. For lunch, as kids in the U.S. turned their noses up horrified at the prospect of ingesting a vegetable, eager Venezuelan children lined up for seconds simply because their produce arrived slathered in mayonnaise. Some days it was boiled beets with thin slices of red onion, a squeeze of fresh lime juice, and immeasurable amounts of creamy whiteness, leaving the final dish in a pink glaze of sweet, salty and sour delight. Cucumbers also made their debut swimming in a river of mayonnaise, tickled by finely minced parsley and scallions. *Ensalada Rusa* embraced boiled carrots, potatoes, and whatever other abandoned vegetable wanted to join in the fun into a disco party of mayonnaise. Pretty much anything that was cuddled by the stuff won my heart over and in such fashion I grew up nourished and blessed by mayonnaise.

As an adult desperate to break free and create my own culinary identity, I temporarily moved away from the soybean oil and calcium disodium and took a radically different approach. Suddenly my evenings were filled with lentils, curry and tofu, all of which I concocted into strange and wonderful dishes my palate avidly consumed. But still, something was missing and I couldn't help imagine how perfectly a dollop of mayonnaise would nourish my crispy zucchini pancake. Eventually, I came around.

Mayonnaise has once again been invited into my fridge. It does not play the manic role it did in my youth, where it danced in nearly everything I ate, but its presence is carefully felt, whether it be alongside a tender chunk of herb-infused chicken schnitzel (yes, organic), or comforting a lonely crab cake (add lime zest, lime juice, shallots, and basil for a party), or simply blended with ketchup and hot sauce to be dipped into by another Venezuelan favorite: hardboiled *huevitos de Codorniz* (quail eggs), a creamier version of their more commonplace cousin, the egg.

And on those late nights with only Goldie as my witness, when it is quiet and there are no distractions and I find myself in a moment of delirious weakness it takes center stage for me, my memories and my palate in a delicious, finger-scooping swallow.

Huevitos de Codorniz con Salsa Rosada
(Cornish Hen Eggs in Pink Sauce)

Salsa Rosada is one of those condiments once readily available in Venezuela. It goes on everything and anything, from hot dogs to chips, to Cornish hen eggs. Pop these into a freshly grilled *arepa* for a favorite Venezuelan snack!

Salsa Rosada:

½ cup mayonnaise

¼ cup ketchup

2 tablespoons hot sauce, preferably made from scotch bonnet peppers

squeeze of 1 lime

2 dozen Cornish Hen eggs

Place the eggs in 4 cups of cold water and bring to a boil. Boil for 4 minutes. Turn off the heat and allow the eggs to sit in the hot water for ten minutes.

Peel as you would a regular hard-boiled egg, only with lots more patience. To help the time pass, I recommend a hands-free phone call, a cheesy show, or downloading the Rosetta Stone App for a quick lesson (any language will do).

These little eggs are very delicate and tear easily.

Dunk in sauce and enjoy.

Serves 4-6

Vanilla Anonymous: Tipsy French Toast

I am addicted to vanilla.

There are many things that feed my addiction. To begin with, there is the packaging which offers a dizzying array of sizes, from mega-sized containers of pure vanilla extract gloating proudly from the aisles at suburban superstores to the dainty apothecary-looking glass bottles whose subtle clinking sound as it taps against my mixing bowl brings me back to a bygone era where people were not in such a rush. Then, of course, there is the revered source of this delectable liquid: the orchid, whose perfect beauty, elegance, and sensuality merits such culinary exquisiteness that would have anyone completely and forever infatuated.

Still, my true obsession is rooted beyond these things. As a child in Venezuela, pure vanilla extract was unheard of. My mother, an avid list maker and meticulous planner, made note to stock up on this culinary treasure during our semi-annual trips to the United States. Little black bottles would be carefully packed amongst our new socks and underwear, where, nestled in 100% pure cotton, they would find their way safely into the tropics and then be carefully lined up in our bright blue pantry closet.

Getting clearance for the vanilla seemed harder than entering the Pentagon. Mom, as loving and nurturing as she was, was unreasonably strict on the usage of this coveted elixir (making it all the more tempting and necessary for my sisters and I to have.) Still, Yolanda always had a soft spot for our big, blue eyes and would regularly sneak in an extra drizzle of deliciousness into our milkshakes just for the satisfaction of receiving our overzealous hugs.

Today, living in the United States where vanilla bottles are bountiful and available at any time of the day, I still buy four or five bottles at a go and neatly stack them in my cupboard with the same revered respect and adoration. Clearance is a bit more lax at my house than at my mother's, still, every drop, every memory, and every recipe, is worth gold.

Tipsy French Toast

4 slices Challah bread

1 egg, beaten

1/3 cup milk

1 tablespoon pure vanilla extract

1 tablespoon Port wine

½ teaspoon ground cinnamon

Heat the skillet on medium-high heat. Combine the egg, milk, vanilla, wine, and ground cinnamon in a shallow mixing bowl. Dunk the bread until moist; flip and repeat. Cook over medium heat, 4 minutes on each side. Serve with seasonal berries and warm maple syrup.

Serves 2

Spellbound by Butterscotch:
Butterscotch Sauce with Sea Salt

I made this sauce to drizzle over ice cream.

To dip fruit in.

To fill a pie.

But this sauce has plotted against me.

This sauce has other plans.

This sauce sits (oh so discretely) in the back of my refrigerator. The very back. Behind leftover pasta, to the left of my son's favorite veal *piccata*, way below my daughter's indispensable slab of duck liver pate and several levels away from the imported French butter.

It sits in the forgotten guts of the refrigerator. The third class to everyone else's first.

And still, it reigns.

It does so much more than reign, really.

It mocks.

It laughs.

It controls.

Yes! From the very back and bottom of the refrigerator! Can you believe this?

Because all day long I am thinking of it.

When I should be parenting.

Or paying bills.

Or…gasp…even writing.

It's got me.

I am thinking of its velvety texture.

I am thinking of its rich, oh so rich, taste.

I am thinking of that luscious dance of sweet and salty.

How perfect a tango it is!

I am reprimanding myself for ever buying a butterscotch sauce before.

Ever.

Buying.

Before.

I am certainly not parenting.

Or paying bills.

Or…gasp…writing.

See how this sauce has got me?

There's big talk about how computers will take over and rule the day. It made the cover of The Atlantic and I heard them discussing it on NPR. We've created these sophisticated machines to think for us and before we know it, we'll pretty much be screwed.

But who's to say that can't happen with butterscotch sauce?

Because one batch of this stuff will bring you to your knees.

Shut your logic off.

Have you thinking of nothing else.

And you'll cave, like I have.

Regardless of how deep in your fridge you hide the stuff, or how busy your day is.

It will inevitably get to you, I promise.

You will find yourself with spoon in hand and sticky lips and not a clue how it happened.

You've been warned.

(Now run off and make it.)

Because the folks at The Atlantic and NPR forgot to mention one thing:

There are only a few things worth giving a wee bit of yourself up for:

True love.

The perfect croissant.

And this mind-controlling sea salt butterscotch sauce.

Note: I have the momentous blog, Smitten Kitchen, to thank for this recipe. If you don't know this blog, good golly, get over there now! Well, first make this wickedly simple and bewitching sauce.

BUTTERSCOTCH SAUCE

(Adapted from Smittenkitchen.com)

- ¼ cup unsalted butter
- ½ cup packed dark sugar
- ½ cup heavy cream
- 1 teaspoon flaky sea salt
- 1 ½ teaspoons vanilla extract

Melt the butter in a medium saucepan over medium heat. Add the sugar, cream, and salt and whisk until well blended. Bring to a gentle boil and cook, untouched, for 4-5 minutes. Remove from heat and add the vanilla, stirring to combine.

Take a spoon, dip into the sauce and remove. Your spoon should be nicely coated with sauce. Note: Your sauce will harden as it cools, this is the way to test it and make sure it is thick enough!

Put the sauce in a glass jar and allow to cool. This can

be served cold or hot, over ice cream, cake, fruit, or just plain out of the jar at any given time of the day.

This sauce will last up to 2 weeks, refrigerated.

Makes about ¾ cup

Leek Freak: Potato Leek Soup

I was in the supermarket's produce section buying some leeks. An older woman approached me and very cautiously asked, "What is that?" referring to the two robust bulbs I held in my hand. The question caught me off guard. For a second, I couldn't tell if she was joking or not.

"These are leeks," I replied, very matter-of-fact.

"Leeks?" she said, the word clearly rolling off her tongue for the first time. "And what do you do with those?"

These are the moments where I dive into my own personal world of self-pity, revisiting my self-appointed tragedy as the urbanite trapped in a suburban universe where leek cluelessness reigns. There are so many positive reasons to live in the 'burbs, of course: the great schools, pretty parks, and safe and quiet environment, and, I happily enjoy all of these perks. Still, dark and gloomy moments such as my encounter with leek illiteracy seem to hit hard, leaving me wanting to surrender all that comfort and run for a crowded, expensive city fast!

"Yes, what do you do with those?" the woman asked again, this time more forcefully, snapping me out of my self-inflicted haze. She clearly wanted to know. Clearly *needed* to know. It was a small glimmer of hope that promised to rattle me out of my spiraling loss of faith in the suburban culinary capabilities. Here, amongst pristine and newly waxed rows of brightly colored everything, this woman held out her hand in hopes for some epicurean enlightenment that *I* was supposed to give to her. It was a second that made perfect sense to me, and, there, among the under-ripe bananas and two-for-one specials, I blushed with an overriding sense of purpose and jumped at the chance.

"Leeks are wonderful, actually," I began, waving my leek about as if it were a baton and I the conductor. "They are related to the onion, but have a subtler, sweeter flavor. Although the leek originally comes from Central Asia, it was revered by the ancient Greeks and Romans for its beneficial effects on the throat. In Wales, leeks serve as the country's national emblem! And why not? Legend claims it's because the Welsh soldiers placed leeks in their hats to differentiate themselves from their enemy and thus won some huge battle, but I think their flavor merits an emblem. After all, they make the most divine soup, and then there are leek tarts, leek omelets, leek fritters, and even leek pie." I stopped to breathe and realized I had scared the daylights out of my potential disciple. She seemed paler then when we first met and her face was frozen on mine, almost as if she wasn't sure how to move. Quickly she maneuvered past the other shopping carts leaving a forced "thank you" in her trail and, having cleared the aisle, proceeded to dash for her life, never looking back.

I've been a lot of things, but this can truly be the first time I had turned into a leek freak. I was still clutching the leek I had been waving around during my short, frenzied lecture on its historical value. It looked a bit limp from so much manipulation, but, as I chuckled to myself on my newly discovered zealousness, I knew it would do just fine. After all, leeks are resistant to all sorts of craziness, even mine, and they truly do make the most divine soup.

Potato-Leek Soup

4 leeks

6 tablespoons unsalted butter

1 potato, peeled and cut into 1" cubes

3 cups chicken stock

salt, to taste

Clean the leeks: cut off the dark green portion and discard. Cut off the ends and slice the leek in half lengthwise. Open up the leek slightly (like fanning a deck of cards) and run under cold water. There is a lot of dirt trapped inside the layers so keep fanning your leek to get all that out! Once clean, slice the leeks into fine pieces. Melt the butter over medium-high heat. Add the leeks and sauté, stirring frequently, for 5 minutes. Add the potato and stock. Raise the temperature to bring to a boil. Once the soup boils, reduce the heat to medium-low and simmer gently for 30 minutes. Season to taste. Blend the soup up in a blender or with an immersion blender. Enjoy!

Serves 4

OUT OF THE (CULINARY) CLOSET:
CHILI CON CARNE CON CUBITO

It is with great secrecy that I pull the tiny foil cube out of its box. I admit to being temporarily riddled by a wave of guilt, hordes of culinary experts would immediately disregard me as a cook not worthy of gastronomic attention if they knew I housed these in my closet, let alone *used* them.

The conspirators are my bright yellow boxes of bouillon cubes. I have every flavor on the market: "*cubito de pollo,*" "*cubito de carne*" and "*cubito de pescado,*" with a haphazard scribble of a chicken, cow and fish to clarify. I always buy the box in Spanish. It tastes exactly as salty and processed as its English counterpart, but I believe most things sound and feel better in Spanish: *deja de jurungear* (stop messing around), *dando y dando, pajarito volando* (scratch my back and I'll scratch yours) *la guayabera es vino tinto* (the shirt is maroon). So I stick to the lyrical and comforting bounce of "*cubitos*" instead of a formal, more somber bouillon cube and already I feel better.

When I was growing up in Venezuela, our assortment of *cubitos* was proudly displayed amongst the bottles of imported dried rosemary, thyme, and cardamom my mother would smuggle back from our annual trips to the States. There was no shame to them back then. *Cubitos* were just a part of the daily meals Yoli made, adding an extra boost of flavor to each bite.

I remember watching her plop the little squares into vats of boiling soups, simmering shredded beef and pots of bubbling black beans as her final measure in bringing the dish to its appropriate end. She was never one to mess with seasonings. The cylindrical spice stand of imported goodies remained untouched, as much as my mother tried to encourage her to use them, explaining endlessly about the virtues of dried basil, curry powder, and allspice. Yolanda pegged them as unfamiliar, from their elegant glass bottles to their curly English labels she couldn't understand, and left them alone, only occasionally wiping down the dust that settled on their tops. She stuck to the basics: salt, pepper, garlic, and *cubitos*.

And sticking to this simple formula would produce, time after time after time, incredible meals. It was an uncomplicated procedure really. She'd toss in the *cubito*, grab the same worn, nicked wooden spoon she used for everything (a large one carved out of Amazon wood with a burnt mark on the tip) and give the dish in question a quick stir or two, then proclaim:

"*Ahora si esta*", (now it is done), as if the *cubito* was what sealed the deal.

Then she'd guide the huge spoon towards my mouth, poised and ready to taste during each meal-making session and allow me to sample the final product, which was always amazing. The dish was most likely remarkable prior to the bullion's arrival, but in my young mind, the little dark cubed paste was the magical ingredient that instantly transformed a meal into an experience.

Somewhere along the way my bouillon line got blurred and I began hiding mine and only slipping them into my cooking in the privacy of my kitchen when no one was looking. I don't have a wooden swiveling stand with ten basic spices like my mother. I have two entire drawers filled with enough spice to run my own successful trade route and I used them brazenly. But I still find the need to have my neon cubes nearby, for the soup that needed an extra kick, the chicken fricassee that lacked a briny depth, or the *muqueca de camaron* that begged for the ocean flavors to shine.

Cooking is as much about feeling as form and even though the venerable food institutions would look down upon my casual affairs with mass-produced, dehydrated stock, I confess to continue using them even after I've spent hours boiling chicken bones and necks to make a perfect homemade broth. There's just something about the occasional plop of neon that makes it all taste better.

My spoon isn't as big as Yolanda's but it is from the same weathered Amazon wood. I stir my dish with it and pull out my yellow box for the final touch. Today I am making *chili con carne*, a dish I perfected under my mother's guidance. It became a household favorite and quickly was the barometer for spice tolerance in the house. My father and I were off the charts with our need for heat, brandishing our sweaty temples as victorious badges. Yoli, on the other hand, was on the opposite end of the spectrum, skittish around black pepper, let alone jalapeños. I always made sure to have some *chile* set aside without spiciness, but invariably, in my mischievousness, managed to trick her into trying the spicy batch. Yoli fell for it every time, or, looking back on it now, took the fall for me every time: it seems listening to my giggling was worth the heat for her.

As if on cue, my daughter races up to the stove.

"Now Mom, now?" she asks excitedly.

I haven't taught her this, but she knows adding the *cubito* will seal the deal.

I carefully unwrap the foil and let it dissolve amongst the meat, beans, corn, and spice. Two big stirs follow and as the revised aroma reaches me I inevitably find myself taking a deep breath and muttering,

"Ahora si esta."

Chili Con Carne con Cubito

4 tablespoons olive oil

½ cup onion, chopped

2 garlic cloves, minced

1 jalapeño, seeded and deveined, minced*

1 lbs. beef chuck, ground

2 tablespoons tomato paste

1 teaspoon ground cumin

3 tablespoons chili powder

1 tablespoon oregano

2 tablespoons grain mustard

2 teaspoons salt

½ cup red wine

1 16-oz. can of whole, peeled tomatoes

1 beef bouillon (*cubito*)

1 16-oz. can of red kidney beans

½ cup corn kernels (canned is okay)

¼ cup sliced green olives

*less for more mild *chile*, leave in seeds/vein for spicier!

For *garnish*:

1/4 cup tortilla chips

½ cup sour cream or Mexican *crema*

½ cup chopped scallion

½ cup shredded sharp cheddar cheese

Heat the olive oil in large skillet over medium/high heat, add the onion and garlic and sauté until tender, 3 minutes.

Add the jalapeño and cook until fragrant, 30 seconds.

Add the meat and cook until brown.

Stir in the tomato paste, cumin, oregano, chili powder,

mustard, and salt and cook another 3 minutes.

Add the wine, canned tomatoes, and *cubito*, bring to a boil, then reduce heat to medium.

Add the remaining ingredients, correct seasoning, and simmer gently for 15 minutes.

Adjust for seasoning.

Scoop into bowls and add the toppings to each bowl.

Serves 4-6

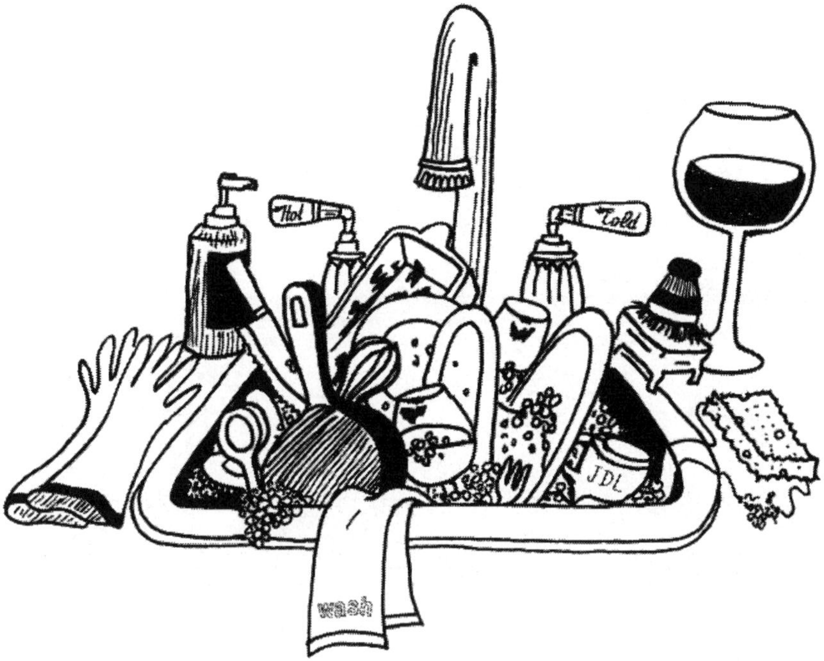
Hot
Cold
JDL
wash

EPILOGUE

It seems appropriate that I should write this epilogue as hurricane force winds whip through my South Florida neighborhood. I've been putting off the ending of this book for so long, with the words of a trusted screenwriter resonating in the back of my mind when he read the draft of the book: "You need an epilogue, Alona: every good book needs to tell the reader how the story ends."

How the story ends?

That idea never crossed my mind.

I know how a great dessert ends (oohs and ahhs of pleased and pleasantly full friends) or the warmth of an aged spirit (better neat than on the rocks). I know how a child's tantrum ends (with some sort of freshly baked cookie, because if grandma had been around, she'd have just pulled them out of the oven). I know how a lovers' tryst dissolves (that smile that you gave each other years ago during that "through sickness and through health" part). I know these things almost as reliably as the back of my hand, although, I do, in my defense, have a very bad memory. But I know. I know.

But how this book ends? Well, it's a bit like the hurricane tearing through South Florida now, the one that has so far taken down four of my trees (even my beloved mango tree, yes, that one!) and yet, mysteriously, left my house with electricity and television. I've been able to produce some killer meals in the time newscasters forecasted to be Armageddon. There's been cumin-marinated lime chicken and garlic grilled ribeye steaks, chicken and Oaxacan cheese quesadillas, with tortillas brought back from Husband's last trip to Mexico. I've made roasted thyme asparagus and dilled deviled eggs, and even *Abuela* Margarita's dish made an appearance, with extra shredded sharp cheddar. The staple vats of pasta have been made and with it, a variety of sauces: pesto, Bolognese, pink sauce, and garden herbs. Because, why not? I know how these all end: with happiness and a "more, please." My family ate, behind the protection of our hurricane-proof windows, and watched our papaya tree succumb to the wind.

Hurricanes are stress-inducing and I baked a lot to combat that: peanut butter cookies (thanks to Beth for supplying the best recipe ever), classic chocolate chip, bananas in rum sauce served with a generous amount of ice cream, because, you know, any minute now, the power could go, and it would melt away.

The hurricane is clearly, thankfully, not an ending, but rather, another story to be told. A story where family gathers, gets cabin fever together, play a heck of a lot of games (how did my daughter get so good at Scrabble???) and eat to their, our, hearts' content. We'll deal with the aftermath of Mother Nature's wrath when these angry winds calm. We'll have lots of leftovers. For now, we'll be together right this moment, live it for the good and the bad it holds, and share the memory forever. I can't think of a better ending than that.

Alona Abbady Martinez

ABOUT THE AUTHOR

Alona Abbady Martinez is a food, travel, and lifestyle writer in South Florida with over fifteen years of writing experience. She freelances for *The Miami New Times, International Opulence Magazine,* and *Lifestyle* Magazines. Previous work has appeared on *Alimentum Journal, Brain, Child Magazine, Humor.org, Every Day With Rachael Ray Magazine, The Dallas Morning News, The Miami Herald,* and *The Sun Sentinel.* Her global food memoir, *My Culinary Compulsion,* is inspired by her blog, Culinary Compulsion, based on her adventures with food, family and travel. You can reach her at alonamartinez.com.

Mercury HeartLink
www.heartlink.com

Made in the USA
Lexington, KY
28 March 2018